ETHICAL CHOICES IN BUSINESS

विमृश्यैतदशेषेण यथेच्छसि तथा कुरु

Reflecting on it fully, act as you will.

Bhagavad Gita
Chapter XVIII, Sloka 63

About the Author

R.C. Sekhar is Professor Emeritus at the T.A. Pai Management Institute, Manipal. Beginning his career as a member of the Indian Audit and Accounts Service, he later worked as Finance Director of Coal India, as Financial Advisor to the National Mineral Development Corporation, and as the National Manager of the Gramophone Company of India. He was also the Bank of Baroda Chair Professor at the Institute of Rural Management, Anand.

Professor Sekhar served as a member of the Advisory Committee for Handlooms, Department of Textiles, Government of India; is presently a member of the Expert Advisory Committee, Department of Science and Technology, Government of India; and is an Associate of the Institute of Cost and Works Accountants of India. Professor Sekhar has a wide variety of interests including textiles, energy economics and rural science, and has written extensively on diverse subjects ranging from finance and controls to culture and ethics. Known for his innovative methods of teaching ethics in management, he has been the keynote speaker at several conferences on the subject.

ETHICAL CHOICES IN BUSINESS

R.C. SEKHAR

Response Books
A division of Sage Publications
New Delhi/Thousand Oaks/London

First published in 1997 by

Response Books
A division of Sage Publications India Pvt Ltd
M–32, Greater Kailash Market–I
New Delhi 110 048

Sage Publications Inc
2455 Teller Road
Thousand Oaks, California 91320

Sage Publications Ltd
6 Bonhill Street
London EC2A 4PU

Published by Tejeshwar Singh for Response Books, lasertypeset by Anvi Composers, New Delhi, and printed at Chaman Enterprises, Delhi.

Library of Congress Cataloging-in-Publication Data

Sekhar, R. C., 1933–
    Ethical Choices in Business/R.C. Sekhar
      p. cm.   (cloth : alk. paper)   (pbk. : alk. paper)
    Includes bibliographical references and index.
    1. Business ethics. I. Title.
    HF5387.S435   1997   174' .4—dc21   97–14485

ISBN: 0-8039-9371-4   (US-HB)   81-7036-619-4   (India-HB)
         0-8039-9372-2   (US-PB)   81-7036-620-8   (India-PB)

Production Team: **Anita Misra, Richard Brown** and **Santosh Rawat**

Dedicated to the memory of
Appa
who wore his ethics lightly
and led by example and not by precept

CONTENTS

FOREWORD

With liberalisation and globalisation bringing sweeping changes in the concept of doing business in the closing years of the 20th century, there has been a spurt of activity towards evaluation and validation of goals, concepts and practices both in government and in business. While transparency and accountability are insisted upon from governments, what is asked for from business seems to be efficiency, competitiveness and quality. There is very little debate either in business circles or in society about the ethics of doing business and what it demands from the business people, government and the consumers. Because of widespread illiteracy, poverty and the culture of a protected economy operating in a seller's market, the system either had very few occasions to seriously handle ethical questions or had trusted the government to handle them through law and administration. Either way, the issue is not yet in the priority agenda of the business community and is not receiving the attention it deserves from policy planners in government and industry.

The problem with ethics is not that there is lack of knowledge about it or the acceptance of principles of behaviour underlying such knowledge. The problem is to make ethics form part of human behaviour naturally and, in the present context, part of making business decisions individually and collectively. It is paradoxical that many individual businessmen are extremely 'religious' in their private lives while in their business they hardly take account of the extent of human suffering that their actions might cause in society. It is in this context that Professor Sekhar's book makes a valuable contribution both through the material it has assembled and the method it has employed to present it.

To a discerning observer of the contemporary scene, what is important is to reflect on the key areas of human relations where nothing but moral and ethical conduct alone could resolve the problems in society. Thus, if corruption is difficult to be tackled by law alone, an intelligent manager or policy-maker will look for better ethical alternatives in addition to the law. Similarly, if legal regulation by itself cannot accomplish environmental goals which concern the producer and the consumer alike, the management approach will evolve new strategies and techniques which can influence behaviour in the right direction. Similar would be the approach in gender justice, child labour, consumer grievances, etc. Professor Sekhar has addressed each of these issues with clarity and vision using a style that is at once persuasive and readable. There are treatises written on all these, and standards have been evolved and adopted in meetings and conferences of the business community. The beauty of the book lies in relating principles to practices with examples and experiences which are native and real. If training can inculcate values and if choice of materials can determine the quality of training, what is contained in this book is excellent stuff to enthuse, inspire and influence. One may not agree with all the conclusions the author wants the reader to draw from his samples; nevertheless one is persuaded to read and to seek arguments to refute his assumptions and messages. That makes it a useful tool as a teaching aid in management schools and other institutions which are training decision-makers for the arduous task of managing situations involving diverse pulls and pressures.

It is common knowledge that the basis of business decisions is profit. However, in deciding how much of it and in what manner, there are options available where the businessman is likely to seek support from law, public interest and organisational goals. This is what makes management a profession, an activity based on the higher principles of life. The book provides a rich variety of sources from which the decision-maker, if so inclined, can seek support for an informed decision. A manager with personal integrity is more likely to make ethical decisions for the organisation. He tends to become a true professional and an asset to the organisation.

Reading through the various chapters, I felt that it is much more than a textbook. It does project a persuasive framework for ethical management and, as such, is a useful professional aid. Read with relevant laws on the subject, one can draw the *lakshman rekha* in business ethics, whatever be the nature and range of business. Law, after all, is the minimum of ethical conduct expected of persons in society. However, one cannot necessarily claim to be ethical if one is on the right side of the law. Ethics has a wider circumference than law and sometimes it is a source of law itself. As such, except for technical details, an ethical decision more often than not will be legal as well. That is why many business persons, without actually knowing the law, remain well within it.

A good business manager aware of public (consumer) interest, professional interest and organisational interest cannot but act in accordance with law and ethics. Personal interests, even if not conducive to the above, are invariably moderated in the case of a professional because of his awareness of the competing interests and the need to take credible decisions to fulfil his professional obligations while supporting organisational goals.

The subject is analysed by Professor Sekhar in the context of Indian culture and ethos and this is a unique characteristic of this book. 'Issues to Ponder Over' and the selectively organised case studies, again from Indian experience, at the end of the chapters make an excellent teaching aid to an otherwise difficult subject matter. Professor Sekhar has subtly and with a great deal of success introduced current themes such as environment, corruption and gender justice into the mainstream of business concerns with a view to explore the emerging challenges of economic management.

I have read the book with great interest and intellectual satisfaction, and would recommend it not only to students and academics but to everyone concerned with organisational efficiency and social accountability. I congratulate the author for his painstaking efforts in organising the material in an intellectually stimulating style and addressing it to the professional managers and young hopefuls in Indian business.

Dr N.R. Madhava Menon
Director
National Law School of India University
Bangalore

PREFACE

The increased interest in business ethics in India is no doubt related to the sordid events of the past few years in the public affairs of the country. The nexus between business, crime and politics has led many to believe that the country is close to destruction unless it reforms its business ethics. There has been, therefore, a felt need for writings on ethics which could help in seeking better ways of handling this situation. This book attempts to provide a measured response to the need without necessarily subscribing to such panic reactions.

Essentially, the book draws upon my exciting and, in the Indian context, rare experience of teaching ethics to postgraduate students in business management at the T.A. Pai Institute of Management, Manipal. The material also owes much to several workshops on business ethics held in India which were attended by practising managers and management educators. One of these organised by the T.A. Pai Institute of Management in December 1995 was particularly designed to bridge the gap between the traditionalist and modern schools of thought in regard to business ethics. Similar efforts have been made elsewhere in the world—the Rockefeller Foundation saw the wisdom of trying to get the traditionalists to understand the practical utility of the pragmatic approach advocated by the modernists. At the same time they have attempted to persuade the modernists to desist from sneering at the 'mushy emotionalism' of ancient traditions and instead benefit from their tremendous insights (Ryan and Scott 1995).

Business ethics is extensively taught in business schools in the USA. It is done with great fanfare at Harvard. This followed serious concern when it became apparent that there was a management graduate at the root of many of the worst scams in the USA (Piper *et al.* 1993)!

The young Indian management graduate has fortunately not acquired such notoriety. But there is cause for concern. Young people in India, as much as anywhere else in the world, are eager participants in ethical discussions. This is contrary to the views of the harbingers of doom, those who cry hoarse at the rapidly falling ethical standards of the young—as if the old were any better! Young people are however less tolerant of shams. Quick-fix ethicists, religious demagogues and evangelists may dazzle for some time, but they could soon become a source of boredom for the young. Their impression on young minds tends to vanish rapidly. Precisely for this reason and to counter this failing, American business schools frame their courses and therefore their textbooks with greater rigour but with less self-righteousness. They have adopted the paradigms of management education of objectivity and sharp analysis.

This book, while adopting this trend, goes far beyond. The parting of ways has come primarily because American writings in business ethics, being generally analytical, allow little room to appreciate the great traditions of ethical thinking of the past. There has also been far too little attempt in American books to get the sense of sociology, culture and history into ethics. They have often missed the important issues of today owing to a very myopic and fragmented empiricism. As Mcdonald (1993) puts it, 'They avoid many contentious connections with broader political systems and the world characterised by an unjust division between the poor and the rich and where fragile ecosystems are being torn asunder.' The book has studiously avoided being critical of managers from India or elsewhere in the world. Such slanted descriptions of reality coming either from the West (MacIntyre 1981, Jackal 1988) or India (Chakraborty 1995a: 110–11, Garg and Parikh 1995) are neither reliable nor useful in the long run, but their polemical positions can serve as pointers. In this book I have reiterated that moral and ethical values are embedded in the ethos of civilisations. The art of living uses them much more effectively than ethical Cassandras, some management educators or reductionist moral philosophers are willing to grant (Nash 1995, Anthony 1995).

In this book I have tried to judiciously combine reverence and irreverence with serious arguments and earthy examples to sustain the reader's interest. At the same time, I have desisted from taking the easy and comforting path of merely reaffirming what is already known or accepted. The reader may also be somewhat surprised by my deliberate attempt to steer clear of the intricacies and niceties of philosophy. Hare (1986) observes that in a multi-ethnic and multicultural world a debate on moral philosophy may not be the best way to start on the ethical path. Attempts to act can bring people together better. As Chaturvedi (1995) says, 'No sophistry or analysis of philosophic implications is required . . . there is a convergence on the social and operational significance of the matter . . . ethics is like electricity . . . felt immediately when the power is switched on.'

The first two chapters of the book outline the basic sources of ethics and the processes of ethical decision-making. They are self-contained and taken together give the essence of all that the book covers. Chapters 3 to 7 expand the ideas contained in the first two chapters into an exposition of the role of the basic institutions to generate and administer ethics, i.e., the market systems, the legal framework, psychological processes in institutions such as the family for socialising, professional intermediary councils, the new type of organisations of the later phases of capitalism and the ever vital and pervasive culture. This presentation of the dynamics of applied ethics represents a more comprehensive framework than offered earlier, typically by Novak (1982) and Ostas (1995), who attempted to show how business ethics as an outcome of the cultural system fits in with other economic and political systems. The mind-stilling exercises described in Chapter 5 are useful but they are not offered in the book as unique pathways to ethical development. Chapters 8 to 14 have more varied and detailed examples, cases and theoretical discussions than the earlier chapters, but with a narrower functional or topical focus. Chapter 15 sums up simply and briefly some broad considerations that emerge from the reading of the previous chapters.

At the end of every chapter, I have provided a set of issues to ponder over and to test the reader's critical understanding. I have also included several examples and cases in the book, positioned under different chapters as appropriate. If the book is used for teaching, the instructor may find it more useful to position the issues elsewhere, depending on the style of teaching. Most of the cases and examples are based on my experience of about 40 years and are largely based on real situations, although some are fictional. Three cases emerge from a specific study I did of three organisations well known in India for ethical clarity. The material has been presented in the book in a focussed-case format rather than an extended and full-blown case-study format of a publicly identifiable organisation. Pedagogically this seemed useful (Sagar et al. 1971). The anonymity in two of the cases also ensures that any self-righteous or hostile response from the respective organisations in a public discussion will not vitiate the very essence of ethical discussions, namely, that of dispassionate understanding. Two cases are from published material on the company (Case 3.1 The Bhopal Gas Tragedy in Chapter 3 and Case 11.1 The Tomco–HLL Merger in Chapter 11). Some well-known American cases have also been used as examples. The analyses of these cases have however been developed in the context of Indian ethical thinking to show their universal applicability to modern Indian and foreign ethical situations.

Readers of the book can follow any sequence of the chapters. They can read only the cases and examples in the first reading and the theory thereafter, or vice versa, depending on their inclination. Policy-makers would find something new in Chapter 3 on market systems, Chapter 4 on law and Chapter 6 on professionalism, as also in Chapter 9 on whistle-blowing, Chapter 11 on finance, Chapter 12 on corruption and Chapter 13 on environment. Right through the book, I have highlighted the importance of resolving conflicts and working towards solutions to situations, problems and issues aided by freer communication.

Ethics is no longer a 'rhetoric'. Ethical education can be and is designed to produce balanced, pleasant, flexible and effective managers with the power of insight and the courage to create and use ethically desirable means to sustain organisations in an ambience of liberalism and democratic choice. They must learn to see people as they are—mostly good but sometimes vicious. Management education and training must consciously try to prevent a manager from having a chip on the shoulder about the virtues of a dog-eat-dog attitude or get into a frenzy of the fanatical self-righteousness of a fundamentalist who has a maniacal desire to 'reform the world' (Sekhar 1995).

One last word. For convenience and to avoid awkwardness, I have used the pronoun 'he'. However, no gender bias is intended or implied.

R.C. Sekhar

ACKNOWLEDGEMENTS

I gratefully acknowledge the kind permission of two well-known Indian companies with a strong commitment to ethics, to allow me to use information gathered from them for constructing two of the cases in the book, Case 8.2 Excellent Pesticides (Chapter 8) and Case 7.2 Satyakam Foundations (Chapter 7). The identity of the companies have been kept confidential to avoid any bias in discussions. The facts are being used in the cases with the following disclaimer:

> While some of the facts of the study have been drawn from a real organisation, the context in which these are presented and the evaluations made therefrom are purely the indulgence of the author to suit pedagogic needs. They have not necessarily been endorsed by the organisation.

The first idea of Case 6.1 The Computer Whiz-Kid (Chapter 6 on professionals) came from the faculty of the computer department of the T.A. Pai Management Institute. The drafting in the present from, after trial teaching on two occasions, was done by me. Several ideas and incidents given by many, too numerous to be listed here, triggered off many cases. I acknowledge the permission to reproduce material from B.R. Nanda's book on Gandhi in Case 14.2 My Shame and Sorrow (Chapter 14 on gender ethics) and the literature provided by the single-minded environmental activists of the Indian National Trust for Art and Architecture for Case 13.1The East Coast Road (Chapter 13 on environmental ethics). Vikas very kindly permitted reproduction from D.D. Kosambi's book. I also thank the National Academy, Musoorie, for The Uncouth Assistant (Example 14.4). I owe a great debt to successive batches of students at the T.A. Pai Management Institute who responded most warmly and critically to the material contained in the book. The classroom discussions with them have been memorable occasions. Chapters 3 and 12 on market systems and corruption were seen by Mrs Bhavani Sekhar. The section on medical ethics (Chapter 5 on professional ethics) was similarly vetted by one of India's leading cardio-surgeons, Dr M.S. Valliathan. Case 14.1 on the ultrasonograph (Chapter 14 on gender ethics) was critically examined by Dr Vani Ramkumar, a leading gynaecologist. Prof. D. Nagabrahmam, Director of the T.A. Pai Management Institute, was the first to suggest the book. Without his continuous encouragement, the book could not have been completed. His interest in developing a network of ethically sensitive managers and management educationists in India and abroad was undoubtedly a source of inspiration. Early encouragement from Dr N.R. Madhava Menon, Director of the National Law School of India University, Bangalore, sustained confidence in the book. I am also grateful to him for his Foreword. The book has gained immensely from the criticism of an anonymous referee and the extremely frank but supportive advice from Mr Ranjan Kaul of Response Books. I would also like to acknowledge the contribution of Ms Anita Misra, who edited the manuscript and made it more readable.

The preparation of the manuscript took a heavy toll on the time, energy and patience of Mrs Shantha Nayak, Ms Anasuya Bhat, Mrs Meera and Ms U.G. Chitra; they did it with a smile. Mr K. Hariprasad prepared all the figures. Mrs Bharati Bhaktha helped in the computer processing of field data reported in the book. It goes without saying that any errors, omissions and other imperfections are entirely due to my own shortcomings.

R.C. Sekhar

1

SATYAM SHIVAM SUNDARAM
Evolving Ethical Values

Values Plus Knowledge Equals Ethics

The simplest way of defining ethics and moral values would be to not distinguish between the two and say that they describe what is 'right' and what is 'wrong' in human behaviour, and what 'ought to be'. Business ethics are the desired norms of behaviour exclusively dealing with commercial transactions. However, such approaches limit one's understanding of the rich variety of issues and situations we propose to deal with in this book. At the same time, it would be pointless to get into a sophisticated, hair-splitting and often contradictory wordplay on the subtle differences between the different words used in the subject: morality and ethics, moral philosophy, meta-ethics, ethics and applied ethics, and so on. Many have written at great length defining these words, though Michalos (1995: 8) and White (1993: 2) have consciously and deliberately avoided it, as has this book.

The scope of ethics as seen in this book covers a description as well as the rules and norms of human behaviour relating to each other as well as to nature and animals. The actual 'is' could be vastly different from the normative 'ought to be', both of which can be measured objectively. Sociologists like Durkheim (1957) and Jackal (1988: 4–5) have in fact adopted this pragmatic approach of giving adequate importance to the 'is' to understand ethics, as it has greater scope for observation and measurement.

Moral values, on the other hand, are deep-seated ideas and feelings that manifest themselves as behaviour or conduct. These values are not so easy to measure or express in words. In this regard, Chakraborty (1991, 1993a, 1995a) has made useful efforts to establish a relationship between Vedic and Buddhist values and ethics. He says: 'As the consciousness in the individual—in his/her equation with Nature, with the Infinite, with the Adorable Energy, with Brahman—begins to ascend holistic heights, a major outcome becomes evident in the sphere of his/her relationship with others' (Chakraborty 1995a: 43).

For our purpose, tentatively, we can say that if we know the consequences of our actions, we can convert values into rules of behaviour that can then be described as ethics. To convert this statement into a formula—values plus knowledge equals ethics. Ethics in business includes values governing commercial transactions not only among persons and among organisations, but also among persons within organisations and political processes that regulate such transactions. We will see later in the book that such a holistic approach leaves very little of ethics or values which are not also relevant to business.

Before we discuss these concepts further let us for a moment move from the world of science and rationality to the realm of emotions—the stuff of life itself. Would you, for instance, relate the elation one feels when admiring the beauty of the Himalayas or seeing a gurgling baby to business ethics? Indian thinking has always attempted such a holistic grasp of values, where their interconnection is well established.

Some recent writers in the West who describe themselves as belonging to 'the school of post-modernism in business ethics' recognise the need for such an approach (MacIntyre 1981, Johnson 1993, Mangham 1995). Typically, they would say that a book of great fiction is far more potent an ethical sensitiser than a tome on moral philosophy (Johnson 1993). Literature may never explicitly and logically clarify an ethical position, but would comprehensively and in more real terms put across both 'what is' and 'what ought to be'. Informed aesthetics would undoubt-

The Triumvirate of Indian Values		
Satyam	Shivam	Sundaram
Truth	Welfare	Beauty
(Ethics)	(Economics)	(Aesthetics).

—Sanskrit meanings follow usage by Kalidasa (Apte 1965)

edly lead to a better understanding of ethics. If we do not perceive, feel and value beauty, it would ultimately reflect in 'wrong' behaviour. Logic and beauty are incomplete without one another and cannot be independent ends in themselves. Let us now try to illustrate the connection between moral values and ethics.

For Whom the Bell Tolls

Economists of the Chicago school (Becker 1964) imply that ethical administration should view human beings entirely as animals who can be subjected to psychological manipulations through the legal systems of rewards and penalties. But people are not like pets whose conduct can be fully conditioned by rewards and penalties for good and bad behaviour. There are two main reasons why such a simplistic understanding is not true to life. First, the chain of cause and effect between behaviour and consequences is often long and not always visible. Second, we humans are far more complex in our thinking and reflection than animals.

An initiator of action begins with an inventory of moral values. These get converted to intentions for action, which then get articulated as actual behaviour. All such behaviour results in consequences to oneself as well as to others; they either damage or enhance the values of the affected person. However, this may not always correspond to one's intentions.

This causal chain is fraught with uncertainty at every link, which can result in varying consequences emerging from the same set of moral values. Conversely, similar consequences can also result from varied moral values (Michalos 1995: 10). To illustrate this, let us take the example of the dairy industry. We will discuss five causal chains of ethics that can and do prevail in this industry. The first four start from the moral value preached by the *Kural*, the classic on ethics, that increasing the productivity of the farmer is of prime value.

> **Causal Chain in Ethics**
>
> Value → Intention →
> Behaviour → Consequence

> **The Ethical Duty towards Farmers**
>
> The state which will foster agricultural productivity will enjoy pre-eminence.
>
> —*Kural, 1st century BC, Verse 1034*

This value can be converted into an intention of either getting better procurement prices for the milk or that of just building better-informed farmer institutions. The first act—of increasing prices—can lead to three alternative causal chains, all of which can result in setting up farmer cooperatives. While this can ensure better prices, there can be three different consequences. If the act results in improving the productivity, it can provide better nourishment to the nation as a whole, as well as to the farmers themselves.

A second consequence can be better nourishment for the nation but it may deprive the farmers' families of milk, leading to a decline in the nutrition standards of their children. A third consequence can be that to enhance farmers' revenues, the cooperative produces baby milk powder and sells it at a higher price than ordinary milk, using misleading advertisements. Hundreds of babies may consequently suffer because of infected feeding bottles and the loss of the natural protection of breast-feeding. The fourth causal chain avoids the exclusive route of better prices. Institutions can also choose to co-opt women to ensure sustainable moral consequences arising from institutional values that are not obsessed with prices and profits.

However, planning a higher price for farmers can just be a strategy for the fulfilment of the greed of the corporate sector for profit with reasonable social and legal restraint, a value with which several modern ethical writers sympathise. The route then is via the private sector and not through cooperatives. This fifth of the causal chain also begins with the *Kural* but could end in killing babies due to reasons already described earlier. This was the case of Nestle, the Swiss multinational (Beuchamp 1983: 221–33).

In all these examples of causal chains, the ethical dimensions cannot stop at the choice of either values or intentions or behaviour. The consequences have to be considered too. An understanding of the likely consequences falls in the realm of knowledge and not of values. Since ethics is deeply concerned with consequences, these demonstrate the formula we described earlier in the chapter: values plus knowledge equals ethics.

> The bell doth toll for him that thinks it doth . . . Any man's death diminishes me . . . Never send to know for whom the bell tolls . . . It tolls for thee.
>
> —*John Donne, 1987, Devotion Upon Emergent Occasions.*

It would also show that an ivory-tower idealist is no ethicist. John Donne (1987), the English poet of the 17th century, and Ernest Hemingway (1948) reflect on this ethical obligation of the intellectual to keep track of the consequences of action or inaction.

Why the Wise Often Look Foolish

The wise sometimes end up looking foolish when it comes to business ethics. This assertion may appear as scandalous anti-intellectualism. According to Anthony (1995), practising managers are ahead of management educators in grasping the essentials of the subject. To go along with this view would perhaps be going too far. But it is a good counterpoise to an implicit and somewhat misplaced belief in magical solutions and tools of analyses offered by moral philosophers and teachers of business ethics. Poets and writers who have lived close to the common people have often felt that native wisdom born out of experience can guide equally well. Maxim Gorky (1923) found that he seldom came across ideas in philosophy which he had not already encountered in common conversation. Subramanya Bharati (1957) says that the wisdom of Saraswati, the goddess of learning and the arts, could be in the minds of great sages but no more than in the people's common speech.

However, more than common intuition, conceptual training creates an awareness of the interplay of conflicting views and the manner in which they fit into the fabric of ethics. It can adapt them to varying contexts. There has to be this uncommon way of integrating commonsense (Beteille 1996).

Ethical Theory Mimics Life

Ethical theory as it has evolved over time can hardly be credited with having determined action. Society has often found ways to cope with emerging situations, and theory has evolved as a process of legitimising practice. It was therefore inevitable that there be strong situational overtones in ethical theory. So was it in India.

Ethics can never destroy the operational logic of any society. Such a logic would recognise the situational aspect of ethics. Indian theory and practices, ignoring its several inequities, often faced this issue squarely, even brutally, through caste-based ethics. Thus ethics in ancient India was relativistic and pluralistic in its imitation of life. Aswatthama's remark is a reflection on the characteristic twist to ethics when applied realistically to business situations. This is how it is likely to remain till we become more noble and better integrated.

> No Duryodhana. No one from the warrior caste should use the game of dice to win his kingdom that is cheating. Only the trader's caste can cheat as that is their profession.
>
> —*Aswatthama in Mahabharata, 1000 BC (Subramaniam 1993a)*

The Delightful Drama of Contradictions

The first lesson in ethics is to learn to see life as it is, without bitterness or expectations. Once we recognise that it is a delightful drama of contradictions we can go about moulding it to what it 'ought to be'. It is increasingly being recognised by the post-modernist schools of business ethics that to see life as it is needs studied practice and self-discipline. In some respects, the Buddhist way of looking at ethics attempts to do precisely that.

> If man sees things as they really are, he will cease to pursue shadows and will cleave to the great reality of goodness.
>
> —*Gautama Buddha, 4th century BC (S. Radhakrishnan 1993)*

That Which Holds Together

Recognising the situational aspect of ethics is not reason enough for going berserk in permissiveness. The Indian tradition has a subtle understanding that whatever be the dialectics of ethical arguments, it has to be able to hold society together. As Kane (1969) notes, the word *dharma*, which also covers ethics, is derived from the Sanskrit root *dhr*, i.e., that which holds together. To apply this test of consequence of behaviour is tricky, for that which holds together should certainly not destroy the individual in the process. We will see in the later part of the book how these conflicting objectives can be achieved by society.

The 'DNA' Concept in Ethics

Goodpaster (1995) speaks of the 'DNA' feature of ethical values, representing the descriptive, normative, and analytical nature of ethical discussions. This can also be described as the 'is', 'ought to be' and 'why' of ethics.

Therefore, when we describe the values that civilisation has evolved, we must be able to discern the differences between the values falling under the three 'DNA' categories. Values can also be classified as 'primary and terminal values' or 'instrumental values' as a means to an end (Schwarz and Belinsky 1987).

We do not intend at this stage to follow any of these distinctions and instead propose to classify values into four aspects:

1. Criteria for accepting values
2. Values which are required to be optimised
3. Values in the nature of rights where the stress is on minimising societal interference
4. Means of institutionalising ethical implementation of values

Since ethical theory is by and large a legitimisation of the actual processes adopted in society, the emphasis is on action and insights. The instruments for implementation also become as important as the core ethical theory.

Several recent writers have attempted a listing of values. Chakraborty (1991: 19–21) has abstracted 13 Indian values. Hosmer (1995: 396–99) traversing Western thought from Aristotle to the present day has provided 11 values. Hass (1994: 506–9) has reduced the principles to a bare six which are down to earth and pragmatic, and not derived from any core principle. All of them have ignored the rational classification cited above.

Several recent writers of business ethics consider it less important to academically rationalise the categorisation of values in a neat scheme, and emphasise instead the importance of getting a feel of the complexity of reality as an aid to action (Habermas 1987: 449–51).

The 29 values identified roughly are as follows:

Criteria for acceptance of values:

1. Test of universalisability
2. Test of the greatest good for the greatest number

Values which would be required to be optimised:

1. Controlled greed
2. Pursuit of pleasure
3. Efficiency and work ethics
4. Truth
5. Transparency and honesty
6. Compassion and charity
7. Piety
8. Sacrifice
9. Stoic dignity
10. Righteousness in envy, pride, anger and violence
11. Camaraderie and fraternity
12. Trust and cooperation
13. Tolerance, pluralism and meliorism
14. Gratitude and respectfulness
15. Harmony with self, society and nature
16. Evolutionary destiny

Values in the nature of rights of beneficiaries (where it would be necessary to minimise societal interference with these rights):

1. Right to privacy
2. Right of individual choice
3. Right to a minimum standard of life

Norms and means for institutionalising ethical implementation (and the processes for aggregating individual ethical needs and integrating them with societal needs):

1. Distributive justice
2. Democratic dispassionate discourse
3. Market systems
4. Respect for processes of social adaptation
5. Respect for law
6. Respect for professional codes
7. Ensuring organisations are used as vehicles for ethical synergy
8. Respect for rituals and symbols

When we apply these values in relation to business ethics, we find that they overlap or often contradict each other. We can also arrange the same values on the lines of the 'DNA' or into primary and instrumental values. Finally, we need to reflect if there is a strong difference between different cultures that gives rise to concerns of ethical relativism (Donaldson 1996). We will reflect on these issues towards the end of the chapter.

Conscience and Consequences

The first two of the inventory of values are widely used criteria for screening the other more contextual values. Typical of ethical discussions, the two criteria are propounded by two warring factions. Before we conclude that these are irreconcilable, let us look at the two points of view.

1. Criterion of universalisability

The criterion of universalisability (Kant 1985) lays down that whatever be the context, and even if it involves prioritising generally accepted standard ethical principles, we should not do anything that we would not like to be done to us in similar circumstances.

Only when a code of behaviour can be universally applied should it be considered ethically correct. This is a general principle that enables us to evaluate all other values and provides a balance when there is a conflict of values. Kant was its most famous modern proponent. But this principle was propounded much earlier by Jesus Christ, Thiruvalluvar and

> If you are cruel to someone ask yourself the question if you would face similar cruelty to yourself.
>
> *—Kural, 1st century BC, Verse 250*
>
> Whatsoever ye would that man should do to you do ye to them.
>
> *—St Matthew 7.12*

the Chinese Lao Tze. This process would tend to make us choose values as 'absolute standards' by invoking 'conscience'. Universalisability would not reason on the basis of the consequences of action. It would tend to emphasise the ethics of the means and not assume that the ends justify the means. Lastly, it would focus on individuals and therefore see them not as means but as ends in themselves. Such an approach is labelled in ethical literature as deontological. In the situation of business ethics, it would typically ask an advertiser of falsehood, 'Would I have liked another advertiser of the product used by me to tell a lie?' 'No' would be the answer of conscience. The false advertisement therefore fails in the test of universalisability.

We have so far assumed that individual conscience applies and tests the criterion of universalisability. This could cause a bewildering variety of decisions by different people, each following his own conscience. Arendt (1961), the German Jewish philosopher, shows how such an unfortunate contingency need never occur in practice if 'everyone in a community exerts their imagination in disinterestedness, liberating themselves from their own private interests'. *The Bhagavad Gita* describes this as *nishkama karma*, a recurring theme in this book.

2. The greatest good for the greatest number

This ethical concept was developed by England's Jeremy Bentham and John Stuart Mill (Mill 1897, Sidgwick 1925). It attempted to make ethical evaluation precise by aggregating the happiness of everyone affected and deducting their unhappiness, both being consequences of every action or rule of behaviour. This is the guiding principle of much of modern welfare economics. Even if it could never provide a mathematically satisfactory solution, it offered options in the search for the most ethical aggregation of individual good to compute total social good. Such processes were inherent in Indian philosophic thinking even though it was constrained by the caste system. This aggregating of values can be done with greater ease if all values are subordinated to one single value. In the case of Bentham and Mill, this value was the equivalent of 'pleasure' discussed later in this chapter. They called it 'utility'. In this scheme the right and wrong are not independent of the good and bad. This approach is labelled in ethical writings as teleological. The same issue of false advertisements, which we examined earlier using Kant's concepts, can again be seen in this concept. If everybody told lies in the advertisements, no one would know the truth and everybody will be unhappy. Therefore, it is unethical and since every one will tend to tell lies unless controlled and one will be unhappy if one's greed is thwarted (see controlled greed as a value discussed later in this chapter), we must have laws against it which are collectively determined and rationally legitimised.

Unfortunately, this latter criterion would pass muster even in the case of the murder of one individual, if it were to give happiness to the rest of the community. But Kant's criterion would not countenance this.

However, ethical practice has in various ways been able to practically blend both criteria. Thus, in reality, the dichotomy between the two criteria is more in the writings of moral philosophers than in actual practice.

Neither Maximum nor Minimum but Optimum

There is a whole range of sometimes even contradictory values that business ethics has developed over time. Pragmatic understanding shows that we should seek an optimum mix of values that can function satisfactorily in real life. This can again be subject to the criteria discussed earlier.

1.   Controlled greed

There is an intuitive apprehension that human greed may destroy society. *Lobha*, the Sanskrit word for greed, is described in the Indian tradition as one of the six disturbing elements of human harmony (Patanjali's *Yoga Shastra* in Wood 1992). But ethical thinkers have grudgingly accepted the driving force of this overwhelming passion. There was feeble support for a balanced and controlled greed among Greek philosophers such as Protagoras (Hosmer 1995), a more positive support in the 19th century from Adam Smith and an overwhelming and exuberant support from the modern American Chicago school of economists (Amartya Sen 1990), who argue that if everyone worked greedily for themselves, it would miraculously turn out to be good for all. This depended on a mechanism of 'markets' which we will describe later in the chapter. Even without a very strong market system, Indian ethical philosophy also accepted greed as essential and conceived of systems that could put it to positive use.

Greed as a Positive Force

. . . The *samanyas*, the generality will do good to others provided it does not hurt them, only a few will harm others to do good for themselves.

— *Bhartrihari's* Neeti Sataka, *6th Century* AD, *Verse 64 (Rangathananda 1968)*

When prosperity comes to a good man from a good family upbringing it is like a village tank being filled with water; it helps every one.

—*Kural, Verses 215/951*

This value is by far the most critical in discussions of business ethics. This is because a business entity can best operate when its terms are simple and its operations congruent with social needs. And most people would agree that this cannot happen unless an element of greed is inbuilt into its operations. How much of it,

Self interest is the most powerful factor in the life of anyone. The entire world is pivoted only on this one factor.

—*Bhishma to Yudhishtara in Mahabharata, Shanti Parva, Chapter 11 (Subramaniam 1993a)*

is the debatable issue. Indian thinkers depended severally on 'internal controls', genetic cultivation and nurturing family culture to contain greed. Some others suggested control by 'external methods' (Kautilya 4th century BC and the *Mahabharata*).

2. Pursuit of pleasure

The pursuit of pleasure was considered an ethical value by Epicurus (1926) of ancient Greece, Charvaka of the Lokayata school of ancient India (Chattopadhyaya 1989), Bentham and Mill of 19th century England, and modern philosophers like the British Bertrand Russell (1930) and American John Dewey (1920). Importantly, they did not perpetrate lasciviousness, self-indulgence and depravity. Epicurus was the noblest of persons and Charvaka a profound humanist. Happiness and pleasure for them could not be just pleasures of the flesh but also of the mind.

Pleasure must be distinguished from greed. Altruism and absence of greed can indeed be a cause for giving pleasure, as in the case of the Alacrity Foundation of Tamil Nadu whose shareholders decided to endorse the policies of the management and accept a lower return on their investment for the satisfaction of participating in a company with high ethical values. The shareholders of Excel Industries in Gujarat similarly endorsed the social welfare programmes of the firm.

3. Efficiency and work ethics

Western ethical thinkers, strongly wedded to Aristotle and Plato and subsequently steeped in feudalism, were oblivious to the greed of the ruling classes for power and the suffering they caused to the common man. They never felt the need to produce enough goods and services to feed, clothe and shelter everyone. They

> **Work Ethics of *Kural***
>
> They only live by right who till the soil and raise their food. The rest are parasites.
>
> — *Kural, Verse 1033*

had so much disdain for manual work that it was treated as ethically trivial. The tremendous potential for doing human good by improvement of efficiency of operations was realised much later. This happened with the unshackling of the constraints of feudalism by capitalism. The core ethical value of improvement in productivity was measured by the index of profits (Adam Smith 1952). This was reflected in the Protestant movements glorifying the ethics of work (Tawney 1926, Weber 1958, Jackal 1988). Capitalists saw themselves as saviours of mankind and were convinced that their new powers were for the common good. This was 'a secular-theological concept' (Sethi *et al.* 1984). In the Western social setting of its time, work ethics also seemed to be a natural consequence of capitalism and individualism; it was presumed that they could be the only support to work ethics. Recent experiences show the possibility of a strong work ethic in a totally nonindividualistic setting. They owe their inspiration to the joy of communal activity (Kautsky 1906, Brenkert and Cambell in Simmonds 1985) or the precepts of frugality and work in Shintoism in Japan and Confucianism in China (Kao *et al.* 1994).

This should be no surprise to Indian thought. The Tamil Thiruvalluvar, unlike Aristotle and Plato of Greece, was not tainted by slavery, and held that the greatest ethics of mankind is in productive and innovative hard work on land.

The *Bhagavad Gita* extolled the virtues of work and action as an affirmative step against inaction and alienation, and also condemned the magical ritualism of the earlier societies (Chattopadhyaya 1989). The work of Deming (1980) in total quality management (TQM) has shown why and how inspiration for efficiency improvements goes beyond profit maximisation and comes from creativity and ethical impulses. It borrows much from Eastern thinking.

> TQM meshes traditional Western values of craftsmanship and Asian values drawn from Zen and Confucianism.
>
> —*Robert Grant (1995)*

4. Truthfulness

Speaking the truth is most universally accepted as a prime ethical value. While Aristotle and Plato have enunciated sophisticated reasons for this (Albert *et al.* 1987), it is a spontaneously and commonly accepted value in most tribals. It is not only accepted as right but is always followed in practice.

Indian tradition has an obsessive attachment to this value and has developed an impressive philosophic and episodal inventory to ensure that speaking the truth comes instinctively. There are however contextual situations where Indian tradition exempts one from strict adherence to truth.

Truth is ethically valued because of its universalisability and also because it makes for the greatest good of the greatest number. In business ethics it is the first step to building relationships based on trust.

5. Transparency and honesty

Transparency and honesty require total openness. Nothing is to be hidden from those who would be affected by the information. Whereas Aristotle and Plato saw this as a necessary part of nobility (Albert *et al.* 1987), modern capitalists would view this as the bedrock of an ethical market system. Thus Thomas Jefferson, to ensure transparency in trading transactions, was involved in drafting the Standard

> **Transparency in Business**
>
> Give full measure and full weight in justice ... do justice even though it may be against a kinsman.
>
> —*Quran, 13th century AD, Surah VII 153*

Weights and Measures Act even as he was drafting the Bill of Rights (Boyd 1950: 444–46). The *Quran* insists on this in its advice to the traders.

Transparency was however not always recommended in Indian ethical tradition. The *Kural* says that it is not wise to reveal everything prematurely before decisions are taken.

Indian Limits to Transparency

Avoid unnecessary trouble to yourself in (political) decisions, by revealing the thinking prematurely.

—*Kural's advice to the king, Verse 663*

The *Mahabharata* discusses the dysfunctional result of the self-imposed discipline of transparency in democratic governance. According to this thinking, transparency and democracy weaken the system (Murthy 1965). This profound difference between the business ethics of autocracy, even if it be benign and paternalistic, and democracy, even if it be tumultuous, vibrant and troublesome, is discussed later in the book.

6.   Compassion and charity

Though most religions place a high value on compassion and charity, the obsession with these concepts is more evident in Buddhism, Jainism, Taoism and Christianity. Long after Christ, Christian theologians wedded the simple and direct ethical principles of Christ to the lofty philosophies of the ancient Greeks. But charity and compassion remained the focal point of all endeavours. The compassion of the Jains extended to all living beings; the earliest animal hospitals in the world were run by them in India. Indian business ethics was strongly conditioned, at least normatively, by considerations of charity and compassion. Though these considerations are sometimes thought irrelevant for the capitalist market systems to do the greatest good for the greatest number, real-life organisations can never get rid of this underpinning from religious thought. This gives them an aura of respectability (see Chapters 7 and 8). Charity can sometimes be combined with arrogance and pride, as will be seen in Case 7.2.

7.   Piety

Piety or *bhakti*, a basic feature of all religions, need not be a necessary or sufficient step towards compassion. Chakraborty (1991) considers this to be one of the basic values and the fountainhead of good business ethics. But there are many who would contest this. Massey (1994) bemoans the fact that Christian practice all over the world including India does not always see compassion as flowing from piety. Considering the widespread thinking on this, it needs to be counted as one of the values that have a say in business ethics. There are several examples of Indian businesses which encouraged piety as a means to ethical conduct. One may pause here and wonder if modern ethical theory has been too wary of considering the reality of the 'sacred' (Gupta 1996) in the psyche of the business manager. Wishing it away is not the solution.

8. Sacrifice

An acute extension of compassion is the concept of self-sacrifice, as advocated by the Jains and Buddhists. Chakraborty (1986) sees it as absolutely different from the West. Its implications and articulation in business ethics are most felt in areas where individuals in the organisation undertake intense effort at great deprivation to themselves but yielding immense social benefits. Yellapragada Subba Rao could never have given the world Aureomycin if he had not had the willingness to sacrifice. The Indian chemist P.C. Roy lived an austere life but developed the basic pharmaceutical and chemical industry in India.

9. Stoic dignity

The ennobling dignity born out of enduring with courage, pain, adversity and failure, draws spontaneous applause universally. While philosophic support comes from the Graeco-Roman school of Epictetus (Albert *et al.* 1987), Indian mythology is full of heroes and heroines who exhibited this stoic dignity. Business ethics witnesses this quality in several situations— the failures faced by entrepreneurs who take risks all the time, those within organisations who stick to their own values in an ambience of adulation, women who bear their sufferings with stoic dignity so that their over-engrossed spouses may achieve their goals.

10.   Righteous pride, envy, anger and violence

Righteous pride, envy, anger and violence is a running theme in the literature of all nations. This has a strong presence in the *Vedas*. Nietzsche gives it philosophic clarity.

> I teach people to say Nay in the face of all values for weakness and exhaustion. I teach people to say Yea in the face of their need for strength, that pursues strength and justifies the feeling of strength.
>
> —*Nietzsche (1924)*

Its fascination for many Indian managers is through the angry writings of Ayn Rand (1968) who sees market systems of capitalism and selfishness as the most powerful stimuli to fulfilment of the ego in a positive sense. Its most current populariser as the message of the East is Ching-Ning-Chu, the author of the bestseller *Thick Face and Black Heart* (1995). Though books on business ethics do not usually deal with this as extensively as books on general ethics, real-life examples from business makes this relevant. The hardhitting and much admired styles of chief executives like Iacocca of Ford Motors and Chrysler of the USA are explicit examples of this syndrome. Young Indian executives are much taken in by this glamorous image, made larger than life through popular literature and cinema. Its great attraction enables it to qualify for the select inventory of ethical values. Case 7.2 also illustrates how this can be combined with considerable compassion.

11. Camaraderie and fraternity

The concept of camaraderie and fraternity is an emotive slogan, which was used by both the French and the Socialist revolutions. It has special significance for Indians as the caste system is in many ways a negation of this principle.

> **Why Usury is Unethical in Business**
>
> That which ye give in usury in order it may increase on (other) people's property hath no increase with Allah.
>
> —*Quran, Surah XXX 39*

The message of brotherhood comes out loud and clear in India from Islam and Sikhism. It braves the caste restrictions in India. The practical implication in business ethics is the consequent religious injunction against usury in Islam which goes against their concept of camaraderie and fraternity.

12. Trust and cooperation

Hosmer (1995: 394–99), having reviewed Western ethical writings in business, finds them lacking in the most critical of ethical principles—trust and cooperation. He notes that relationships created by market systems in a capitalist society can function only if there is an element of trust. The absence of trust would make it impossible for partners in a transaction to operate with efficiency, and could ultimately result in the collapse of the capitalist system. Many other recent writings in the West have worried themselves with the 'opportunistic behaviour' of contractual partners, be it employer–employee or supplier–purchaser.

The quality of trust and trustworthiness within nations has been found to vary at different points of time (Michalos 1995). Ancient Indian as also Islamic writings do not have the gap of trust found in the original inspirers of current Western thinking—the Greeks. Thiruvalluvar, who lived among the trading classes of the day, talked of the need to cultivate trust relationships; ancient trade practices in India also bear out the prevalence of this ethical value (Bardhan 1996). Prophet Mohammed as a trader's agent was known as Al-Amin, 'the trustworthy'.

Recent field studies in India (Sekhar 1995) have however shown a paradoxical phenomenon that most Indians are trustworthy but there is a much lowered level of trust among them. Thus, two perfectly honest people transacting business could

> Agents should consider the principal's money as their own and treat it with prudence and care. That is good business.
>
> —*Kural, Verse 120*

lose out if they failed to develop a relationship based on mutual trust. The ethical questionnaire and its analysis provided in this chapter explains the possible causes for this phenomenon. Without trust, business transactions would become tortuous, clumsy and expensive. Its implications in international business are increasingly becoming evident, whether it relates to flow of foreign investments, export transactions or strategic alliances, all of which require a high degree of trust. One Bhopal gas tragedy can destroy this trust for a long time. Difficult as it is to develop trust in relations within the country, the magnitude of the task in external transactions is truly formidable.

13.   Tolerance, pluralism and meliorism

Indian managers will soon have to face the problem of contending with multi-ethic situations. Over time and with global interconnection, they have to realise the practical utility of tolerance, pluralism and meliorism. Pluralism can be defined as a rejection of the destructive quest for some comprehensive and exclusively determining principle. It recognises that the legitimate ends of life are many, that there are wide varieties of the good and moral, and that there need be no single blueprint for heaven (Rorty 1992: 38–62). Meliorism is an aspect of pragmatic ethics (McDormitt 1986) propounded by the American philosopher John Dewey. A modest but deep pragmatic morality, meliorism is a way of life in which there are no solutions, yet we strive to improve things.

Both these concepts also have strong Indian roots. Their importance in business ethics can be seen in the need for 'working together' in organisations. If organisations do not cultivate these ethical qualities, they are bound to either work at low efficiencies or collapse.

14.   Gratitude and respectfulness

Gratitude and respectfulness are typical of cultures that have not yet been overtaken by the strong individualism of the more recent Western developments. The Asian cultures have found no reason to follow these developments and instead have honed these ethical values to great benefit. For instance, the famous Japanese company Matsushita uses these in its 'value education' with great success (Hawley 1993), while the elderly patriarch in the Indian business is the source of stability and its strength (Dutta 1997: 64–70). The importance of this value in business ethics is obvious. The tremendous success of the Japanese as against the American is evidence of its positive consequences. It is now being understood that the East has to offer this value as a desirable antidote to the ethics of greed and pleasure. It has thus to be seen not in isolation but in conjunction with other values.

15. Harmony with self, society and nature

The ethical writers of ancient Greece and China laid great emphasis on harmony. But its studied cultivation is a special feature of the Indian *Sankhya* philosophy and Patanjali. Harmony with nature is also a feature of ancient Indian traditions and its current tribal cultures.

This concern is echoed in the modern writings of Tagore and Bharati and innumerable writers in various Indian languages. With the resurgence of environmental ethics, these trends are now finding universal acceptance all over the world.

Sanctity of Forests

Now I have praised the lady who is perfumed with balm and is well-fed, Although she tills not.

—*Rig Veda, Mandala 6, Aranyani, Verse 146, 5000 BC*

Yoga and Harmony

By being friendly he discerns the power of friendliness; by feeling for joy for others he discerns the power of joy.

—*Patanjali, 2nd century BC, Yoga Shastra (Wood 1992)*

16. Evolutionary destiny of cooperation

Several ethical theorists believe that ethics is but a means to achieve the ultimate goal and purpose of the universe. Darwin and Herbert Spencer believed in the survival of the fittest. Marx believed in the inevitable

Blessed are the meek; for they shall inherit the earth.

—*St Matthew 5.5*

evolution of communism. Henri Bergson of Sweden, George Bernard Shaw of Ireland and Aurobindo Ghosh of India all believed in man evolving to a superior spirituality. All their current supporters however accept that this evolution is a process of cooperation rather than of destructive competition. Survival of the fittest means the survival of the most cooperative rather than the most fiercely competitive (Wright 1995).

The ethics of cooperation as against competition is seen as crucial for the future business ethics. It has found a place on the basic precepts of business in the Caux Principles adopted internationally (reproduced in Chapter 8). A vision for human destiny is the root of these principles. The philosophy of 'speaking ethics' expounded in this book is sustainable only if some such vision forms the background.

The Unsettling Demand for Rights

The ethical concept of rights and the three rights listed in this chapter have become more important in modern times, with the birth of individualism and capitalism. Purohit (1994) holds that India did not need this concept because being so deeply rooted in duty, rights were redundant. On the other hand, demands for rights could unsettle the cohesive forces of dharma. What is perceived by many as the greatest liberation of mankind and has been enshrined in the Indian Constitution is considered its greatest curse.

> Human rights could only possess a negatives function ... it betrays an anti-social character. The only right which anyone possesses is the right to do his duty.
>
> —*Auguste Comte (Purohit 1994)*

1.   The right to privacy

The right to privacy, a major issue in the Western business world, is likely to catch up in India too. Computers have made it easy technologically to pry into other people's business and private affairs. Paternalistic personnel managers and aggressive market researchers tend to violate this right. Issues that have been bothering business ethics are lie-detection tests, information sought by firms on their employees' health—if they are afflicted by diseases such as AIDS or epilepsy which may not affect the quality of their work, their private sexual preferences, etc.

2.   Right to individual choice

The right to individual choice has become the core of ethics after the French and American Revolutions. It had a muted existence in India except in the context of religion; the most prominent among those who asserted this right was Kabir (15th century AD). The right to individual choice could be within the structure of capitalism as propounded by Nozick (1974) or within the structure of socialism or its variants as propounded by Prince Kropotkin or Bertrand Russell (1949). Kabir's fierce dislike of 'establishments' makes him a kindred soul to these thinkers.

In business ethics, its implication is the right to choice of goods and services by the consumers and right to choose employment by the employees. The right to free speech, correct information, and free trade are necessary preconditions to the right to choose. The issues of marketing and advertising ethics are therefore derived from this basic right.

3.   Right to a minimum standard of life

This ethical value has a profound meaning for India which has a substantial population of the poor. Many ethical thinkers of the West, in particular the neo-Marxists, see this as a major ethical value of present times (Habermas 1990). This right also covers gender exploitation. Much of the ethics of industrial relations and gender justice is derived from this right. These are discussed in Chapters 8 and 14 respectively.

Means to Achieve Ethical Ends

We had mentioned earlier that the means of implementing ethics are so intimately connected with the basic values that they function as values by themselves. They have to be seen in conjunction with the other values and their appropriate fit. Having said this, we need to make sure that the 'means are not overemphasised losing sight of the ends' (Dewey 1929: 281–82).

1. Distributive justice and social contracts

This principle of ethics is much more than the term 'distributive justice' signifies. In fact, the term is misleading; it is used in this book only in the special manner of Rawls (1971). Few today would dispute that there should be equitable distribution of wealth. It is a trivial ethical statement to make. What is distinctive in Rawl's approach is that it is in no way a plea for state intervention, charity or even altruism. It sees this value as a most likely outcome of an ethical process of decision-making. The essential feature of this concept is transparency and full participation of those affected in the decision process. The poor or the minority would agree with only those decisions which would not worsen their own situation, even if those who are better off would gain more. If they entered into such a 'social contract', distributive justice would automatically get established (Rawls 1971). This theory of social contract is also known as contractarianism (Goodpaster 1983). There is a less recognised need for multinationals to be committed to such a social contract in their host countries, to prevent them from misusing the power of an exploitative economic imperialism (Hudson *et al.* 1995).

The history of economic imperialism in recent times is a travesty of this ethical principle; unfortunately, it can be camouflaged in specious ethical justifications, as in the case of the Bhopal gas tragedy. The ethical process of distributive justice was exemplified in the milk cooperatives in India that enabled remarkable cooperation between the rich and the poor.

Another well-known demonstration is found in water management at Ralegaon–Sidhi in Maharashtra under the leadership of Anna Saheb Hazare (Pangare and Pangare 1992). Distributive justice would also arise in personnel management at the micro level and the choice of social control measures on business at the macro level. Environmental practices in India are characterised by the singular failure to ensure distributive justice (see Chapter 13).

2. Democratic dispassionate discourse

The decisions that go through a process of distributive justice can never be well-informed unless there have been adequate and open public discussions where facts, beliefs and attitudes have been spelt out calmly (Habermas 1987, 1989). This ethical principle has four known supporters: Karl Marx for it being an instrument for the oppressed; Rousseau for it being a plea for freedom of discussion; Stevenson (1947–48) who emphasised the importance of linguistic, factual and attitudinal clarity; and of course, Indian tradition known for fair debate and discussion. Among others, the *Bhagavad Gita* preached removal of bias in discussions by detachment from personal benefits. This is more fully discussed in Chapter 2. John Woodal of the Harvard Medical School (quoted in Kolstoe 1995 and Schmidt 1997) commends the functional and practical rules provided

Democratic Discourse Among Buddhists

They held full and frequent assemblies. They met in concord, rose in concord and carried on business in concord.

—The rules of Buddhist Sanghas, 4th century BC (Murthy 1965: 224)

by the Baha'i faith for non-confrontationist consultative group discussions. Public policy in business ethics would require cultivation of institutions to enable this to happen. The crisis in confidence which besets Indian business can largely be attributed to the inadequate regard for this ethic.

3. Market systems

Most of the recent ethical writings on integrating greed, pleasure, efficiency, privacy and free choice rely on the existence of a market system considered to be a profoundly ethical instrument. Its ethical use has been accepted by many ancient cultures including India but with less enthusiasm and greater constraints. We will discuss this further in Chapter 3.

No Sin to Trade

It is no sin for ye to seek the bounty of your Lord by trading.

—Quran, 13th Surah II 198

Market systems can be viewed as value-neutral as they can only be vehicles for transactions. However, the relationships they generate have strong ethical overtones, and therefore the system can be treated as a value in ethics (Lunati 1996: 135).

4. Respect for processes of social adaptation

Respect for family and other institutions for socialising individuals in their ethical evolution is now understood as an important ethical value, equally valid for business. In fact, Alacrity Foundation of Tamil Nadu has made it a motto in their advertisements (see Chapter 5 for a more detailed discussion).

5. Respect for law

Institutionalising ethics through laws that can be enforced is a process as old as civilisation itself. Hosmer (1995) accords high value to this process. Thomas Hobbes and John Locke in England, and Kautilya, Thiruvalluvar and Manu in India have also been its proponents. As

Men are mostly led by punishments that is *dandaniti* the basis of all law. *Mahabharata*,

—Shantiparva 11 (Subramaniam 1993a)

was stated earlier in this chapter, the overzealous concern for the value of protecting the 'institutional means' should not supersede the basic need for ensuring that the outcomes are by themselves ethical (Dewey 1929:281–82).

Law is a convenient institutional means for implementing values. But if the laws were themselves a product of an unfair power game, respect for these would have an unethical outcome. Till recently the Indian lawmakers were neither benign nor democratic. Also, law has severe limitations because of its inherent logistical difficulties in legislating for the ethics of do's and is more comfortable with the ethics of don'ts (see Chapter 4).

6. Respect for professional codes

A major development in the ethical movement in the USA is the mobilisation of professions through professional councils, who develop professional codes which make it easier to reach across to organisations and provide a countervailing force to greed. This path of ethical control through professional guilds was quite common in ancient India. Professional councils and codes have played a major role in the ethical revival in the West. Respect for their codes as an ethical value is discussed in Chapter 6.

> Taking into consideration the law of guilds, a king should establish the particular law of each.
>
> —*Manusmriti, 5th century BC, 8.41*

7. Organisations as vehicles of ethical synergy

Large organisations that were not extensions of the state apparatus are relatively new to civilisation. An emerging ethical value in business is that they must synergise ethics such that their actions are the summation of individual ethical values and not of ethical disvalues. The respect for organisations and its ethical role is a major feature of much of Western ethical frameworks, and consequently becomes an ethical value by itself. We will explore this further in Chapter 7.

8. Respect for rituals and symbols

The last of the values is an enigma. A growing number of people now feel that rituals and symbols of every culture are strong emotional and psychological supports for ethical sustenance (Chakraborty 1991: 97, 138).

There are strong ancient Indian traditions both for and against this. Kabir ridiculed rituals but we will

> **Rituals As Instruments of Deception**
>
> The Hindus keep the eleventh day fast,
> The Turks pray daily, fast once a year,
> And crow God! God! like a cock,
> For kindness and compassion
> They have cast out all desire.
>
> —*Kabir, 15th century AD, Bijak Sabda 10*
> *(Hess and Singh 1985)*

see in Chapter 8 how they can have a powerful impact on business ethics.

Uses and Misuses of Disparity

This introduction to the speaking ethics of civilisation may make readers wonder if there are any major differences in ethical values among different civilisations and nations. They may find similar values across nations and across time. At the same time, these values may coexist with quite different and even contradictory ethical values. Many management researchers have however found subtle cultural characteristics and shifts peculiar to certain nations (see Chapter 5).

Less subtle and more gross are the kind of concerns which engage some in the West to write about ethical relativism (Donaldson 1996, Gergen 1995). These arise from issues such as copyright and piracy, patent violations, corruption and pollution standards. The issues posed by Western business executives relate mostly to ethical standards they should follow in the event of laws and conventions of the host countries being less stringent than those of the home country, or *vice versa*. An analogous situation can arise when Indian businessmen work abroad. One of the cases and several examples in Chapter 10 deal with such situations. Donaldson (1996) advises that in any event, core human values should not be compromised and the context of the local traditions must be grasped. It may be added that quite often these traditions are consistent with the core values.

Thus, piracy of computer software packages in India may actually be an economic compulsion resulting from monopolistic and unethical pricing practices of foreign companies (see Chapter 6). Similarly, Indians are unwilling to accept the sanctity of patents for the manufacture of agricultural products, e.g., formulations made from the neem tree now registered by the Americans. The root of this is in the core ethical value of property rights on common property resources, practised in India since time immemorial. Neem products ought not to be taken away from the Indian people using deceptive patent laws (see Chapter 4). Blatant unethicality should not be practised in the guise of cultural relativism. Thus it was unethitical of Union Carbide to have circumvented factory regulations under the dubious cover of cultural relativism.

Corruption is as rampant in the USA as in India, in spite of the normative ethics of neither country approving it (see Chapter 12). Western multinationals could serve the cause much better if they were to adhere to the social contract made in democratic consultation with the people of the host country (Hudson *et al.* 1995). The core ethical values would then be taken care of automatically in this process. However, no amount of self-righteous ethical sermons from political platforms and management schools can change the reality that Western business ethics is far from ideal.

Score Yourself on the Ethical Scale

As you come to the end of this chapter, you may like to test your ethical scores against a questionnaire used by the author on a large number of respondents—about 1500 as of date. The questionnaire is given in the Appendix to this chapter. It would be useful to compare your answers with one or more individuals and understand why they scored differently. Often, respondents to the questionnaire come to the conclusion that the answers are conditioned more strongly by the perceived consequences of the action proposed in the questionnaire, and less due to differences in the intrinsic ethical values. This raises hope for ethical amity, because a dispassionate discourse would eventually lead to a happy ethical solution. It would also be seen that in India the ethical standards in family relations are often not transferred to commercial transactions.

You may wonder if this is really correct. At the end of Appendix 1.1, the average responses of the 1500 or so of the earlier respondents are also analysed.

SUMMARY

This chapter defines ethics as a description of observed as well as desirable behaviour and conduct that attempt to articulate moral values. It is shown that ethical casual chains link values to behaviour and lead to consequences. The same consequences could emerge from differing values and the same values could result in differing consequences. There is a brief description of an inventory of 29 values which have been generated by human civilisation. They cover primary as well as instrumental, normative as well as descriptive, and analytical values. The values are all speaking in character and consequently overlap and/or contradict each other. The basic premise is that these values cut across cultures and time.

ISSUES TO PONDER OVER

- A company manufacturing condoms uses a sexually explicit advertisement for its products.

- A reputed computer manufacturer deliberately makes a computer incompatible with standard parts manufactured by others, so that only his parts are used if a machine breaks down.

- A pharmaceutical concern markets a product well-known and well-accepted in the world of *Ayurveda* (the Indian school of medicine), but not adequately tested by modern statistical methods.

- A managing director promotes A superseding B even though B is professionally more competent and loyal to the company. A has better contacts with foreign collaborators and this is perceived as being useful to the company strategically.

- Your friend Lata scored the questionnaire given in Appendix 1.1 as follows:

	What she would do	*What she thought others would do*
Ram	1 A	5 A*
Gopal	1 B	1 B*
Swaminath	5 Y	5 Y*
Raja	5 X	1 X*

(The alphabetical indicators refer to the corresponding figures in the questionnaire.) Ponder on Lata's moral values in comparison to yours.

- Select any religion of your choice and evaluate its emphasis on the 29 values listed in this chapter vis à vis business.

- Reduce the number of 29 values listed in this chapter to the least number you wish to have. Do this in three stages: (*a*) drop the values you disagree with, (*b*) drop out those that are sub-sets of more basic values already included, and (*c*) segregate values which are only a means to an end and can, in your opinion, be substituted by alternative means in the context you are familiar with.

APPENDIX 1.1

A Questionnaire to Record Responses to Ethical Attitudes

This is an effort to provide an avenue for free exchange of your ideas, feelings and opinions, and not an evaluatory exercise. This book does not wish to evaluate any ethical stand that anyone would like to take. It however hopes to stimulate openness and tolerance of diverse views.

The following two sections give a series of situations in business and family affairs. Your views on the appropriate action in each situation are solicited. The answers are coded 1 to 5, the meaning of which is given side by side. The responses are numbered A, A*, B, B*, X, X*, Y, Y*, C, C*, D, D*, W, W*, Z and Z*. The star-marked ones are the actions that you think are generally taken by other people. The non-star-marked ones are the actions that you would recommend corresponding to what you think is right and therefore would have taken.

Situational ethics: Commercial

1. Ram, an employee of a shopkeeper Krishna, tells lies about his goods and this enables him to increase his sales and Krishna's profits. Should/generally would Krishna (note recommended score)

Should	Generally would
A	A*

1. Sack him   2. Counsel him   3. Do nothing   4. Encourage him
5. Give him a promotion

2. Gopal, an employee of a shopkeeper Krishna, tells lies about his goods. He is found out and people avoid Krishna's shop. Krishna should/generally would (note recommended score)

Should	Generally would
B	B*

1. Sack him   2. Counsel him   3. Do nothing   4. Encourage him
5. Give him a promotion

3. Raja, an employee of a shopkeeper Krishna, always tells the truth about the quality of his goods. This results in people avoiding the shop and going to another shop where the salesman tells lies. Krishna should/generally would (note recommended score)

Should	Generally would
X	X*

1. Sack him   2. Counsel him   3. Do nothing   4. Encourage him
5. Give him a promotion

4. Swaminath, an employee of a shopkeeper Krishna, always tells the truth. As a result more people trust him and sales increase. Should/generally would Krishna (note recommended score)

Should	Generally would
Y	Y*

1. Sack him   2. Counsel him   3. Do nothing   4. Encourage him
5. Give him a promotion

Situational ethics: Family

1. Ravi is the eldest son of Lakshmi. He was always selfish, never helped in the house, always asked for money for his studies knowing full well the sacrifices it entailed for the family. He single-mindedly pursued his studies, and got a job in the USA. He made Lakshmi search for a rich bride for him in India and then migrated to America. He has three cars, a lovely bungalow and takes holidays all over the world. He still does not send any money home. When he does visit India once in two years, he publicly gives expensive presents to his parents. Should/generally would Lakshmi (note recommended score)

Should	Generally would
C	C*

1. Disown him   2. Advise him   3. Do nothing but keep quiet
4. Encourage him for greater success in his career   5. Show him up to his brothers as a very successful man who concentrated on his studies and won a rich wife, three cars, etc.

2. Sivakumar is the second son of Lakshmi. He was exactly like Ravi in his selfishness. But he was not as lucky. He therefore landed a very mediocre job in India. Lakshmi fixed his marriage in a rich family, but the family had a financial disaster and are now poor. He often demands money from Lakshmi which she gives, sacrificing much herself. Should/would generally Lakshmi (note recommended score)

Should	Generally would
D	D*

1. Disown him   2. Advise him   3. Do nothing but keep quiet
4. Encourage him for greater success in his career   5. Show him up to his brothers as very talented but unlucky

3. Satyam, the third brother, is extremely devoted to his parents. When Lakshmi was unwell during his critical examinations he looked after her, but this had a disastrous impact on his educational career. He landed a low-paid job. Lakshmi fixed his marriage with a girl from a poor family. Satyam and his wife stay with Lakshmi to help her even though it means long commuting to work for both Satyam and his wife. Lakshmi has advised Satyam several times that she is not helpless and that he should look after his own career and move to a house closer to his place of work. But he refuses to do this as he and his wife feel that Lakshmi is saying it out of consideration for their comfort.

Should/generally would Lakshmi (note recommended score)

Should	Generally would
W	W*

1. Disown him   2. Advise him   3. Do nothing but keep quiet
4. Encourage him for greater success in his career   5. Show him up to his brothers as very talented but unlucky

4. Kamlakar is Lakshmi's fourth son. He was also selfless like Satyam. But he was luckier and he got through the civil services examination and became a top bureaucrat. Lakshmi fixed his marriage with a top bureaucrat's daughter. He refused a foreign posting as he wished to be near his parents. He visits them once a month and is trying for a posting to his hometown. He supports his parents with a sumptuous contribution.

Should/generally would Lakshmi (note recommended score)

Should	Generally would
Z	Z*

1. Disown him   2. Advise him   3. Do nothing but keep quiet
4. Encourage him for greater success in his career   5. Show him up to his brothers as devoted, talented and successful

Computation of scores of family and commercial ethics

Go back to sections A1 and A2, note here as also in your notebook the scores recorded by you and compute overall scores as follows. We will discuss the meaning of the scores later.

Ethics Commercial	$EC = (Y - A) + (X - B)$	$\{\ \} + \{\ \} = \{\ \}$
Trust Commercial	$TC = (Y^* - A^*) + (X^* - B^*)$	$\{\ \} + \{\ \} = \{\ \}$
Success Commercial	$SC = (A - B) + (Y - X)$	$\{\ \} + \{\ \} = \{\ \}$
Distrust Commercial	$DC = (A^* - B^*) + (Y^* - X^*)$	$\{\ \} + \{\ \} = \{\ \}$
Ethics Family	$EF = (Z - C) + (W - D)$	$\{\ \} + \{\ \} = \{\ \}$
Trust Family	$TF = (Z^* - C^*) + (W^* - D^*)$	$\{\ \} + \{\ \} = \{\ \}$
Success Family	$SF = (C - D) + (Z - W)$	$\{\ \} + \{\ \} = \{\ \}$
Distrust Family	$DF = (C^* - D^*) + (Z^* - W^*)$	$\{\ \} + \{\ \} = \{\ \}$

Recheck calculations and reflect on the scores. Compare them with someone with whom you can freely discuss why they filled the scores the way they did. Only after this is done and you have come to your own conclusions, turn to the guide to analysis of your ethical scores and see one useful (but not necessarily the most appropriate) framework for analysis of the score and information on how 1500 other Indian respondents have scored.

Guide to analysis of your ethical scores

If you have discussed your score with your friends, you would have understood that even if your core values are quite close to each other your scores may be far apart. Your understanding of the consequences of an action may be different from that of your friend(s) due to your experiences having been different. But as a manager you would be concerned with these differences in perceptions. This analysis would help you to develop action plans which would be acceptable to others.

You could start with the scores of Ethics Commercial (EC) and Success Commercial (SC). On an average, the 1500 respondents before you have had their EC scores about 1.40 higher than their SC scores. This means that they think they value ethics moderately more than success achieved at any cost. But if one is a shopkeeper or an engineer without an MBA background or a senior executive, one is likely to have a higher SC score. Quite importantly, if you are a US MBA your SC score is likely to be higher than your EC score.

You could then see if a similar pattern exists in the difference between Ethics Family (EF) and Success Family (SF) scores. This difference is usually 2.40 or so, meaning that in family affairs, ethics takes a strong precedence over achievement. The larger the gap between this and the previous calculated difference between EC and SC, the more pronounced is the split in your personality between family values and commercial values. If you find that this difference is more than one (2.40 minus 1.40) which is the average, you could try to examine your attitudes and see why. Is it proper? Will this hurt you?

At the next step examine the absolute scores of EC/EF. If EC is much above 3.00 and EF much above 2.5, you are more volatile and vehement than average. Why? Are you natural, or pretending and playing to the gallery?

Let us then look at the star-marked scores of what you think others think. The average population has an EC score which is 1.60 more than Trust Commercial (TC), i.e., they feel that other people are much less ethical than themselves. Higher the difference, lower is the trust you have in others. This is different from being trustworthy which can be assessed by either the absolute scores of EC or the difference between EC and SC.

A similar analysis can be done of the family scores.

If you have a high trust in family matters the difference between EF and TF should be near zero. Normally it is about 0.70 as against 1.60 between EC and TC.

The degree of trust is obviously inversely related to the degree of distrust. The degree of distrust can also be gauged by the difference between SC and Distrust Commercial (DC) for commercial matters, and SF and Distrust Family (DF) for family matters. Normally DC minus SC is about 2.00 and DF minus SF about 1.00. This typically shows that distrust in the family is less than in commercial matters.

This analysis is very tentative. It gives some leads which may help you to explore your personality. Most students using the analysis have reported that they have gained much by it.

If you are interested, you could use this questionnaire on a large community and come to some conclusions about the way their minds work. You can also devise your own stories and situations for eliciting responses; these can capture the ethical issues more relevant to the community. However, do remember that while this exercise is useful, it cannot be uncritically relied on.

2

AMIDST THE
MADDING CROWD
Decision Processes of Groups

Analysis Leading to Paralysis

All of us take decisions that often have ethical implications. If we had no choice at any point of time, it would be easy to plead that ethics be damned, our hands are tied. On the other hand, getting embroiled in complicated choices requiring intense analysis could completely paralyse functioning. Sommers (1994) and Chakraborty (1995b) rightly point out that ethical decision-making usually follows neither extreme. Both complain that most current writings in business ethics assume that the latter situation of multiple choices prevails and that business ethics is akin to a lawyer's game—able advocacy in which clever and often specious arguments are marshalled by contesting lawyers.

Both believe that to a large extent, patterns of ethical behaviour are inbuilt into what one learns instinctually as a child. And what the child learns, usually from the mother, is in the context of family relationships and the result of profound social processes. Although it is a useful edifice to build on, its extension to business ethics is not so easy. To understand the more structured decision-making in business situations, we need to examine some general features of ethical decision processes as also of interaction between individuals and groups.

Ekla Cholo Re

Most people believe that while they are ethical by themselves, those around them are unethical and wicked. Reinhold Niebuhr (1932), a noted American theologian, held that they were indeed correct (as quoted in Henry 1995). He felt that ethical standards fall when individuals work together in a group because their egoistic impulses get compounded. Thinkers such as Gandhi realised this and often had to tread the lonely path, believing as they did in the ethics of the means rather than of the ends. Tagore too admired this heroic quality and extolled it in his famous Bengali poem 'Ekla Cholo Re' (Strike the Lonely Furrow). On the other hand, Karl Kautsky (1906: 100), the Marxist philosopher, observed that the larger the conglomeration of people, the higher is their ethicality.

There can be complex psychological reasons for the varying levels of ethicality of groups. Thus Gandhi's feeling of despair on being unable to control the consequences of his actions is a direct result of the complexity of modern societies; many of his methods were developed in simpler and less atomised societies. The absence of feedback on one's actions and the breaking up of one-to-one relationships which can help ethical behaviour are the bane of modern societies. Weber (1995) found that in contrast to sales personnel, production personnel felt less compelled to behave ethically as they did not interact with customers. Consequently, they needed a law or rule imposed from the top rather than an ethic from within to ensure customer satisfaction.

The alienation due to an absence of the softening effect of contacts could make people non-caring and callous; market systems by their anonymous character can do precisely that. But non-market-driven forces can turn groups against each other. The emotional gap between 'we' and 'they' can become much more violent and unbridgeable than the one between 'I' and 'he'. Group hostilities can be sustained more easily through self-righteous legitimisation; the bloody episodes of this country are the evidence.

Contrarily, if we expand on Kautsky, larger groups having higher ethicality would have greater security from isolation and despair. Since transparency is collectively ensured, the individuals can afford to behave in a more benign fashion. Mutual help within larger groups would demand much lesser individual sacrifices of individual members for effective social good. The Truth and Reconciliation Commission in South Africa under the chairmanship of Desmond Tutu demonstrates that in an ambience of transparency and trust, long-term enemies open up to speak the truth; a spontaneous mutual compassion appears to be emerging among the whites, the blacks and the browns (Verwoerd 1997).

Both Niebuhr and Kautsky may be right in their own way. The tendencies noted by them may come into play in different circumstances. Suffice it to say that just because large global systems have a greater possibility of becoming ethically callous, it is necessary to discover and encourage processes in which the psychological and other benefits of groups are obtained. Large organisations and global market systems are required if we want to rapidly improve the basic material well-being, an ethic which we also value. We may as well use them fully to achieve this goal.

Blundering One's Way Through

Ethical decisions cannot be cut and dry or exact as in engineering or physical sciences. These are slow adaptive processes with a mix of hard analysis, gut feeling and compromises. The more forthright and decisive a decision-maker is, the more ethically vulnerable his decisions may turn out to be. This would be even more so if the decision is to be acted upon by a group. It is only on rare occasions

> The myth of simplicity has sprung reverence for elegant solutions praised for succinctness; the idea breaks down when applied to behavioural sciences.
>
> —*Martin Kenneth Starr (1964)*

that the ethical pathways are so clear that decisions can be spontaneous. Only prophets appear to take decisions like that; their facade of infallibility is a necessary feature of the ideological drive for a new core ethic that attempts to replace a historically obsolete one (Gore 1993).

Against Bias

It is easy to say that clarity and objectivity are critically important to all decisions. However, more profound insights are needed to understand the conditions required to ensure objectivity and the impediments to it. Western thinking has two polarised views (Sinopoli 1995) on the means to ensure this objectivity, both of which are listed in the inventory of values in chapter 1. Rawls and Habermas suggest an approach of democratic dis-

> **The Role of Detachment**
>
> Without attachment do your duties always; a man who works without attachment attains the highest.
>
> —*Bhagavad Gita, Chapter 3, Sloka 19*

passionate discourse in a peaceful atmosphere. On the other hand, John Stuart Mill suggests aggressive polemical debate which emerges quite disconcertingly from the ethic supporting righteous pride. Indian thought and practice were often participatory and benevolent, rarely democratic. But the style of discussions range from peaceful debate to fierce polemics. The *Kural* advises that taking decisions should be like enjoying good food— chewing it properly rather than gobbling it up (Verse 417, 420, 462). But the most profound advice comes from the *Bhagavad Gita* which says that the decision-maker must ensure that he has no conflict of interests. He can do this by detaching himself from the benefits that may accrue to him as a result of his decision.

Ethicality of decisions would gain from the dictum described in the *Bhagavad Gita* as *nishkama karma* (action without attachment). Those who practice *nishkama karma*—and such people are not as rare as made out—can become surprisingly effective managers by maintaining an optimum balance between the ethics of achievement and the other dimensions of ethics. This approach can be useful even when the individual has to take personal decisions, but its benefits can be perceived better when group or organisational decisions are involved.

The Unfortunate Scapegoats

A typical characteristic of the functioning of a group or an organisation is that each member has a different role to perform. This is true even of animals. Since this imposes different functional compulsions, everyone cannot be evaluated by the same yardstick. In the caste-ridden times of the *Mahabarata*, it was accepted that traders would cheat. However, as we aim to develop into casteless societies, we cannot continue to think the same way. Hunt and Vittel (1993), in a bold acceptance of situational ethics, say that marketing personnel have this functional problem and that we should 'judge not the go-getters as we need them'. Such a functional problem would not be faced by, say, a professor or a housewife. Significantly, the normal and balanced jurisprudential conventions have till now been kinder to those who are caught in this ethical gap than harsh judgements of inflexible, logical and self-righteous moralists. This is hopefully how it will continue to be in India unless judicial activism goes 'the-heads-must-roll' way and refuses to recognise the grey areas. None today would however accept the caste-linked ethics of the *Mahabharata*.

Another type of ethical gap occurs in group activity. In a hierarchical arrangement, those lower down the hierarchy have to function within the constraints of unethicality of the decisions taken at the higher levels. Whereas this unfortunate situation is common today, the escapist attitude of many business managers is sad. Rhetorical pleas such as 'if only capitalism can be thrown out', 'if only people followed integral yoga', 'if only law is enforced more ruthlessly', etc., become convenient alibis. They should instead try to achieve maximum ethicality within the constraints, using an optimum mix of values. As in the previous type of ethical gap, jurisprudence (national and international) has a way of ensuring fairness. That Indian ethical and legal treatises have a good understanding of this was demonstrated by Justice Radha Binod Pal in his dissenting judgement in the trial of Japanese generals involved in the Second World War; he let them go, quoting from Indian ethical and legal texts (Nandy 1995).

Ethics does pay

Some like Mother Teresa hold that the true test of ethics is when it does not pay and we still follow it. The more comfortable view held by many current Western writers on business ethics is that ethics will pay, at least in the long run (Clutterbuck *et al.* 1992), unless it is fouled up by other failures in management (Jones 1995). Thiruvalluvar, who in the first century BC wrote for a people having a strong ambience of trade and business, felt the same when he said, 'If one has a reputation of speaking the truth, it will on its own give wealth' (*Kural*, Verse 296). Many leading Indian business houses believe in this; the majority however do not (Dutta 1997: 106–109, Monappa 1987). A closer approximation to reality is provided by Noe and Rebello (1994) who say that in a capitalist society ethics would ebb and flow and with it will change the relationship of profits with ethics.

In Chapter 1, while discussing trust as an ethical value, we described the possibility of trustworthy persons lacking mutual trust. In an ambience lacking ethics and trust, and trustworthiness, the ethical and trustworthy would be seen as ideal to transact with. Ethics will then pay. A large number would then begin to feel it is better to be ethical. Both trustworthiness and trust will grow. At this point the unethical and untrustworthy will exploit the situation and make profits on unethicality. Slowly a larger number would turn unethical till the ethical would again find it worthwhile to be so. And so the cycle will go on. What is important is that there could be long periods when people may be quite trustworthy, yet there would be a lack of trust in society due to various reasons. This is probably the present Indian situation.

There is a lesson in this for group decisions. Instead of depending on the fickle movements of the market forces to establish ethics, the ethical managers and policy-makers can take the bull by the horns and pre-empt these unpredictable changes. Activism, education, and political and institutional development should attempt to achieve levels of ethicality and trustworthiness as high as human nature can comfortably sustain. Even if we were to be ethical only because it would benefit us, these efforts should not be disqualified as evidences of selfishness, and consequently, unethicality. And most of all, the basic assumptions of the capitalist rules of unbridled market systems must be questioned.

Deciding for Oneself

Every management school teaches its students how they ought to take decisions. They follow a logical five-step analytical structure (Kitson and Campbell 1996):

1. Identify the problem
2. Generate alternate solutions
3. Evaluate alternatives using cost–benefit approach
4. Select the solution
5. Implement the chosen solution

The alternatives would be constrained by ethical preferences from among the 29 inventoried in Chapter 1. Many ethical discourses have implicitly assumed that ethical decision-makers are individuals who bear the responsibility for their decisions. A decision-maker may consult his/her spouse, children, parents and friends but the final decision and its responsibility rests with the individual, who has to innovate, develop ethical options and choose between them. Example 2.1 deals with a common real-life situation to help the reader to follow this reasoning.

EXAMPLE 2.1   Balaji Electro Treatments

Balaji Viswanathan, the sole owner of Balaji Electro Treatments (BET), was lost in thought. A Tamilian, he had been disowned by his strong-willed and rich father Viswanathan Mudaliar, for marrying Sheela Karanth, a brahmin from South Kanara. He had to seek employment and was lucky to be employed by Modi Chemicals, a nationally reputed concern, that spotted his talent in spite of his poor academic record.

Three years at Modi Chemicals saw Balaji establish himself as one of the rising stars among the electrochemists in the country. He decided to leave Modi and start his own business of electroplating at Bangalore, putting all his savings into this venture as also borrowing heavily from banks and some of his friends. He now had a problem and wished his father was there to help him. He would have liked Sheela to discuss this with his father. They would have formed a good team, he with his ethics and she with her practical sense, he thought.

Balaji had perfected a technique to electroplate reaction vessels for highly corrosive chemicals, which could work out cheaper than the available alternative technologies. But there were some snags. The surfaces had to be cleaned and replated from time to time. But the optimum usage time could not be predicted; it would depend on the nature of chemicals used. Only Balaji knew how to check the optimum conditions for replating the surfaces, which if not carried out timely could lead to leakage and a serious accident. The thicker the metal deposited on the surface, the longer the time it would take for safe usage and the less the probability of an accident. However, this would increase costs considerably.

He also had a clear idea of the instruments which could make this checking easy and foolproof. But these were not available in the market. The government factory inspectors had no clue as to how to prescribe safety standards for this process. His clients however advised him that he should not worry about it as they would 'look after these inspectors' and ensure that no objections were raised.

He found that with his reputation he could charge a price double his costs if he did thin deposits with a one-year guarantee. This would enable him to repay all his loans in two years. He was reasonably sure that any chance of an accident within one year was not more than one per cent. The probability of accidents increased beyond one year. But was it ethical to take this risk even for one year? Should he not warn his clients about the increased probability of risk after one year?

Sheela heard his dilemma and could think of at least 11 options open to him. All that he had to do now was to assess the likely consequences of each and choose the one that suited his philosophy of life. Balaji found a solution but he still missed his father's ethical vehemence and his quotations from the *Kural*.

Analyses for the reader

What are the realistic options available to Balaji and what are their consequences? What options would fit well with his family background and approach to life?

1. He could do as suggested in the last portion of the case. If a serious accident did occur, he would have to pay very high damages and face criminal prosecution under law. He may be willing to take this risk and find the means to wriggle out of paying the damages by using legal loopholes, as was attempted by Union Carbide in the Bhopal gas case. But would it be ethical to expose his clients, the workers and those living nearby to this risk without their knowledge and acceptance? (Refer to social contract and contractarianism discussed in Chapter 1.) Second, when others got to know about his profit margins, would they also not enter the field?

His high reputation and the trust others had in him may be destroyed if the truth of his 'skimming the market' became known. This would result in a business disaster in the long run.

2. On the other extreme, he could consider it his moral duty to perfect the measuring instrument to check the condition of the lining. He could educate the factory inspectors and prevail upon the government to publish safety standards for this type of equipment. All this would eat into his profits. Also, who would bear the cost of developing such an instrument? (Since writing the case, an electronic instrument to check the lining has come into the market. But the case can be dealt with as if this had not happened.)

3. He could offer to inspect the lining periodically, without letting others know how it was done. He could ensure safety and inform only those affected about the consequences of not checking the surface periodically. He could provide them with information on the cost of increasing the thickness and its effect on the risk of failure. They could all take a joint decision as to how risk and costs could be balanced to benefit all. The trade union leaders would discard his technology and prefer to play safe, and would expect the management to meet the costs.

The readers can now develop more alternatives and suggest criteria for realistically evaluating this decision, using some of the 29 values described in Chapter 1. They must put themselves in Balaji's shoes and empathise with his values in life. Readers keen on practising ethical decision-making must develop the ability to empathise.

Mixed Results from Professional Groups

As mentioned in Chapter 1, professional peer groups are intermediary organisations whose help and protection are sought by the individual decision-makers. On a large scale, decision processes become even more complex and ambiguous, but should not be given up as a hopeless task. Let us place the same Balaji Viswanathan in the midst of professional peers, the Association of Chemical Engineers. The case is much more fictional than Example 2.1; facts from some other real situations have been added on for pedagogic convenience.

EXAMPLE 2.2   The Association of Chemical Engineers

The situation and facts are the same as in Example 2.1. Additionally, there is a professional body called the Association of Chemical Engineers (ACE) of which Balaji Viswanathan was a member. Its membership was open to chemical engineers who could be academicians, consultants, entrepreneurs, employees in the industry, and government servants (including factory inspectors). There were a few experts in electrochemistry like Balaji, but they were all from academic institutions.

Dr Puri, President ACE, Bangalore branch, was a conscientious professional. Balaji liked Dr Puri and so decided to share his problems with him. He also explained the complete process to him, as he felt that without this information Dr Puri would not be able to advise him. He was sure that his confidence would not be misused. Dr Puri was not a businessman but a professor. Balaji had mentioned this in his welcome address to Dr Puri's second term of presidentship, for which Balaji was chiefly responsible. Dr Puri wondered if he should advise Balaji only at a personal level or if the Association should get involved in its member's personal problems.

Analyses for the reader
What options does ACE have?

1. Keep itself as a non-controversial social group that enables developing contacts.
2. Attempt a strong code of conduct for its members, with disciplinary action if they do not follow it. The code could encompass situations such as the one faced by Balaji. The disciplinary committee could go into the details of each case and pronounce its judgement on whether a member acted in accordance with the spirit of the moral code. This could result in splitting of the ACE into splinter groups with their own sectional interests. That could be worse than not having an ACE.
3. Set standards for electroplating in addition to the above.
4. Attempt a code of conduct and leave it to the good sense of the members to follow it. However, the ACE may then become the laughing stock if the members did not follow it.
5. Use the ACE as a political lobby for chemical engineers to gain social prominence and career advancement.

Readers may ponder over these alternatives and many more, and relate them to the real-life happenings in the behaviour of professional groups. Do they make things ethically worse as Niebuhr had predicted?

Organisational Decisions: Everyone Matters Equally

The nature of alternatives needing the working out of ethical trade-offs in business organisations is varied: product development and product choices; pricing policies; process choices; environmental issues; employment practices; career advancement decisions; customer policies; purchase decisions; financing decisions; acquisition and amalgamation; advertising policies; information-sharing policies; internal control policies; etc.

The more recent writings in business ethics (Kitson and Campbell 1996) have clearly seen the inadequacy of using the five-step decision processes described earlier in this chapter. They have recognised the need to use more loosely structured processes and analytical arguments within the ground realities, drawing on the range of ethical norms that different persons in the group believe in. A consensus on practical action plans, which inter alia involve ethical decisions, is easier to obtain than a consensus on abstract moral values (Hare 1986). Thus, all the features of ethical experience and knowledge described by the acronym DNA: descriptive, normative and analytical (Goodpaster 1995), have to be explored.

The six logical models discussed in this book are not all as different from each other as would appear on first reading; they have been discussed to provide a richer repertoire for managers to choose from. The repertoire starts with a highly normative Cavangah–Valesquez–Moberg model (Koontz and Weihrich 1988: 612–13), and goes on to the Hunt–Vittel model which is strongly descriptive and close to the speaking ethics expounded in the book. The last of the models presented in the book is a sharp reversal to the normative style of some Indian ethical thinking, which believes that preoccupation with descriptive ethics may lead one to ethical wilderness.

The application of the Cavangah–Valesquez–Moberg Model (Figure 2.1) is best illustrated in Example 2.3. The example is largely fictional but true to a somewhat professionalised Indian business and has echoes of a situation which the authors of the model have themselves used.

EXAMPLE 2.3   **Arvind Iyer, the Social Climber**

Arvind Iyer was an outgoing but not a very bright officer in Krishna Organics. His close friend Lewis Chandy was a very conscientious and brilliant scientist. It was somewhat embarrassing therefore for them to be competing for the favours of the Managing Director. The MD Gopal Iyengar was result-oriented and wishing to provide the right climate, had budgeted an amount of Rs 10 million for R&D for a high-tech project for the manufacture of a new environment-friendly pesticide. Arvind and Lewis were the only two to reach the final round of the selection. Gopal constituted a committee to review their performance. In the first sitting of the committee every one felt that Lewis was by far the more capable of the two. Their assessment was that they could not, at that

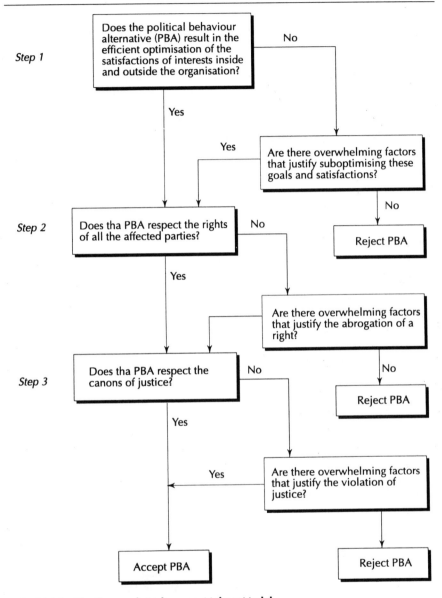

FIGURE 2.1 **The Cavangah–Valesquez–Moberg Model**

point of time, judge whose project was more likely to succeed. From the environmental and profitability point of view both projects seemed to be equally good.

But Arvind had openly lobbied for the project by meeting the committee members at their homes and befriending their wives. He told Lewis Chandy about this and advised him to do the same. Lewis believed that the dignity of a scientist did not permit him to adopt such tactics. The committee, by its second sitting, seemed to have succumbed to Arvind's pressure and recommended his case knowing fully well that this recommendation may be a stepping stone for him to move up the hierarchy. As a first step he would become Lewis Chandy's boss.

After great deliberation Gopal Iyengar decided to approve Arvind's project in preference to that of Lewis Chandy. One of the dissenting committee members felt that this project would not fully exploit Arvind's capabilities of public relations and aggressive salesmanship. On the other hand, being a technical project, it required the more sober qualities of Lewis Chandy. Gopal saw this dissenting note and, while not entirely disagreeing with it, decided to ignore it.

Analyses for the reader

The steps in the CVM model may be worked out in three alternative patterns:

The First Alternative Line of Thinking

Step One

> Yes, as the benefits to society would be the same in both projects. We are also considering a go-getter whose value is more than the other alternative's technical edge. Thus the proposal should be considered only after the consequences are ascertained to be decidedly positive and we are sure that we are not suboptimising.

Step Two

> Yes, neither party has been denied a chance to pursue his ambitions. Therefore neither's rights have been affected. Lewis can go on to greater scientific achievement and Iyer can achieve his ambitions too. Note that this does not talk about consequences.

Step Three

> Yes, both parties were given equal opportunity to explain and distributive justice is established. This again does not talk about consequences but only about ethical principles. Therefore we can accept Arvind Iyer's project as it has more value for the organisation than just a technical advantage. He can be a potential leader and is being encouraged.

The Second Alternative Line of Thinking

Step One

> No, we may be deeply disappointing Lewis. Also, the technical project is more likely to do well with Lewis as the boss, and not as a frustrated and disheartened scientist. Are there overwhelming reasons for suboptimising? Possibly yes, because the organisation may like to risk this possibility of Lewis's lower levels of achievement for the probability of throwing up Arvind as a new dynamic leader.

> Then go on to Step Three which checks on distributive justice, etc.

The Third Alternative Line of Thinking

Step One

> Same as in the second alternative but the answer to the second step—acceptance of the suboptimisation—is in the negative. Then accept Lewis's proposal.
>
> Now proceed to Steps Two and Three to check if Arvind's rights have been violated or distributive justice has been done.

The model, being partly descriptive, also has a prescriptive set of values. These are the greatest good for the greatest number, and ethics of rights and distributive justice. But the highest priority goes to greatest good for the greatest number. Significantly, the perception of 'good' is that of the decision-maker and not of the affected parties. We may also note that the entire model has no ethical values other than the aforesaid three. This would, for example, exclude the importance of stoic dignity of Lewis Chandy as an ethical principle, irrespective of its consequences at the first step.

The next model is that of Malloy and Lang (1993) which owes its inspiration to Aristotelian thinking but is descriptive beyond Aristotelian recognition. It also incorporates consideration for employees' perceptions, whereas Aristotle never gave any place to the slaves in his ethical world. It is therefore more benign and less severe than the ways of Aristotle. The model is in the nature of questions to be asked:

1. What is the stated purpose of the organisation?
2. What is the unstated purpose of the organisation?
3. What are the organisation's official goals?
4. What are the organisation's operational goals?
5. Is there a stated organisational philosophy?
6. Is there an unstated organisational philosophy?
7. How do the employees, management, clients and society perceive these purposes?
8. How does the organisation socialise its new members?
9. What are the organisation's rituals, myths, unique language and slogans?
10. What are the explicit standards?
11. What is the leadership style?
12. What is others' perception of the leadership style?
13. What is the preferred style of the organisation?
14. How do employees perceive the organisation?
15. What is the employees' value orientation towards work?

Goodpaster's (1983) model brings in a variegated weightage for the core ethical values from among the 29 inventoried in Chapter 1. He also poses questions:

1. Are there ethical norms involved? Centrally or peripherally? Is a decision required?

2. Do ethical issues involve internal or external environment?
3. From a descriptive perspective, what are the critical assumptions?
4. From the point of view of maximising utility of those affected, which is the best course of action? Support with facts.
5. From the point of individual rights, which is the best? Support with facts.
6. Priorities? Why?
7. Do the different criteria of ethics result in convergence of results? The chosen three are utilitarianism, pluralism and social contract.
8. If they diverge, which should one choose?
9. Are there any other considerations not captured so far?
10. What is the decision or action plan?

It may be seen that the Goodpaster model is broader than the CVM model, but still structured close to a few values with an escape route to include more.

The Laura Nash (1989) model is a subtle way of directly jumping into action, avoiding tedious theoretical discussions. It is in close interaction with the affected parties. It looks at issues very strongly from the perspective of universalisability (Kant 1985), i.e., the other person's perspective discussed in Chapter 1. The questions are as follows:

1. Have you defined the problem accurately?
2. Would you define it the same way if you stood on the other side?
3. How did the situation occur?
4. To whom and what is your loyalty as a person and as a member of the organisation?
5. What is your intention?
6. How does intention compare with probable results?
7. Whom will the decision injure?
8. Can you discuss with the affected party?
9. Will the decision stand the test of time?
10. Can you disclose the problem to your boss, your CEO, your board, your family and society.
11. What is the symbolic effect if the action is understood/misunderstood?
12. What are the exceptions you will allow to the decision?

The Hunt–Vittel model (Figure 2.2) is an elaborate descriptive diagram of how organisational decisions should be taken as if every one mattered equally. It advocates distributive justice and the social contract view of ethics. The extreme position of the ethics of democratic discourse in the Hunt–Vittel model can result in complete pandemonium if we also proceed with an implied high weightage to 'selfish greed', 'pleasure' and 'righteous anger'. While discussing the concept of democratic discourse, we had mentioned the rules followed by Buddhist *sanghas* to ensure that the

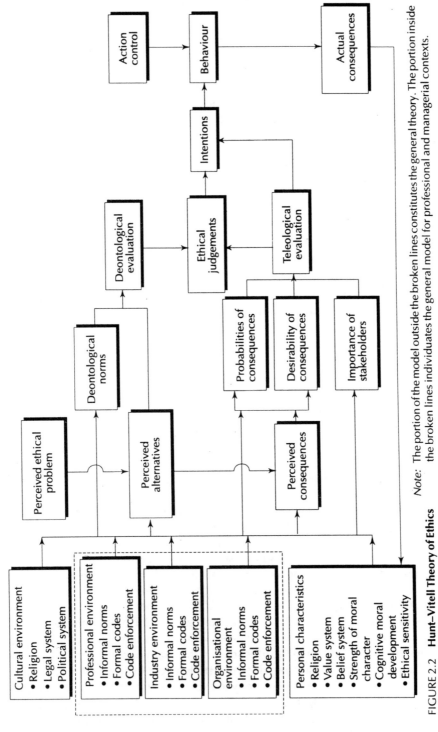

FIGURE 2.2   **Hunt–Vittel Theory of Ethics**

Source: From Hunt and Vittel (1993).

Note: The portion of the model outside the broken lines constitutes the general theory. The portion inside the broken lines individuates the general model for professional and managerial contexts.

discussion was held in an atmosphere of amity. This is critical if one has to use the Hunt–Vittel model for group decision-making. This is also realised in the West now. The functional and practical rules of the Baha'i religious order (Kolstoe 1995) for preventing pandemonium were also alluded to. If order is not restored even then, practical wisdom would require an ethical monitor to set things right (Hosmer 1987). This concept is close to the Indian one of an ethical *raj rishi* and is a departure from democratic processes which were one of our important values. Such an ethical monitor would be acceptable only if he practises *nishkama karma*. This ethicality of the concept of an ethical ombudsman is discussed further in Chapter 8 on human resource management.

Contentious Rules for Making Rules

Respect for the laws of the land is equally applicable to rules of conduct or codes within organisations. The complex organisational processes for the development and choice of ethical norms are required to lay down rules that should regulate business transactions. These could be evolved through a process of distributive justice using democratic discourse or could be imposed by the power structure from the top.

The second thinking would be quite consistent with the ethical norms of a large section of the managerial class in India who are largely drawn from the so-called higher castes. A more detailed discussion on this will follow in Chapter 4. But the problems of balancing the ethical needs of a diverse population are evident in Example 2.4. It deals with a non-business situation, but one familiar to students. By and large true to the facts of an actual happening, the example demonstrates the process of making laws.

EXAMPLE 2.4 **Beating the System**

The three professors of the Badami Institute of Management had very different perceptions of the nature of their students. Their control systems for detecting and punishing copying in the examinations were therefore different. Professor A believed totally in the honesty of his students. He therefore took no precautions against copying. Professor B believed that the students were normally virtuous but could adopt unfair means under strong temptation. Therefore, he had 10 sets of questions so that copying would be difficult if not impossible. Professor C distrusted the students totally and therefore supervised the examinations personally. The slightest whisper was viewed seriously by him. He would not allow the students to even go to the toilet during the examination.

The rules of the Institute provided that students could be expelled for copying, but after they had had an opportunity to explain their point before a disciplinary committee comprising professors. The director of the Institute received an anonymous letter saying that the students were in fact using unfair means in the examination. He therefore initiated a thorough review of the papers.

Of a total of 200, evidence of copying was discovered in the paper of four students of Professor A, three of Professor B and two of Professor C. One of the candidates was common to all the professors, and one between Professor A and Professor B. Thus, a total of six were found guilty: one in all the three subjects, a second in two subjects, and four in only one subject.

The issue of disciplinary action arose. Professor A wanted all the six to be dismissed so as to send the right signal and prevent recurrence. Professor B wanted the students who had copied in Professor C's paper to be dismissed as their action was premeditated and deliberate. Professor C said that since this was a failure of the invigilation system, the students should be let off with a warning.

The director left the decision to any one of the professors the students may choose. But the chosen professor's style of control would then have to be accepted by the students. However, the already high tuition fee would have to be hiked to accommodate the cost of increased invigilation.

Analyses for the reader

What are the alternatives available?

1. The class could decide to adopt the values of democratic discourse and distributive justice. The 'good' students, troubled by an unduly detailed and oppressive invigilation system which they may be willing to suffer only up to a point, may suggest that there be no continuous vigilance but only surprise checks. If these checks reveal copying, punishment could be exemplary. The 'bad' students, believing that the lack of vigilance may tempt them too much and computing the probability of their temptation decreasing with better in-vigilation, may be willing to pay higher fee. They may all ultimately agree with Professor B's method as being the best compromise.

2. Some may feel that the whole business of copying is unethical according to absolute standards, that there should be total invigilation but if someone does copy in spite of it, he should be pardoned. They would ignore the consequences altogether and instead rely on conscience.

3. A third group may believe that concepts of democratic discussion are unrealistic, and individual conscience is deceptive. They may feel that the faculty and the Institute must be bold enough to make their own rules and enforce the same strictly and impartially. They may feel that this is more con-sistent with the Indian traditions of Kautilya and Manu (see respect for law discussed in Chapter 1 and its implications in the past). If this happened, a systems approach could be adopted and a mathematical model be constructed. This would show the probability of copying and of being caught with different combinations of invigilation and levels of punishment if caught. The system chosen thereafter would minimise the cost of invigilation. These three options describe the basic approaches to the political processes of law-making, including business laws.

SUMMARY

The chapter describes the processes of ethical choice. It distinguishes between intuitive ethics and considered analytical ethics and describes the negative and positive impacts on ethicality of individuals as part of a network of groups. It suggests that managers should provide structural correctives to the negative factors and support the positive ones. The Indian concept of *nishkama karma* in avoiding bias in decisions is explained. The ethical gap that traps some segments of society as scapegoats for ethical failures of society as a whole is seen in the context of modern ethical thinking as well as ancient Indian writings. The dangers of simplistic approaches to ethics are detailed. The question of whether honesty will pay is discussed— it probably would, but this should be a less compulsive reason for being ethical. The processes of ethical decisions at the individual, professional, organisational and political levels are discussed with detailed examples. Some well-known models for ethical decision-making are explained. A consensus on practical ethical decisions is easier to obtain than one on abstract moral values.

ISSUES TO PONDER OVER

- Reflect on your experience as to whether the ethicality of individuals improves or deteriorates in groups.

- Reflect on the newspaper reports for the past one week. Could any of the problems have been due to the gap between trust and trustworthiness?

- Reflect if it is possible for you to prepare, all by yourself, a 10-point onepage moral code of conduct for all members of your business organisation.

- Reflect as to whether the lack of trust around you is a result of the inherent unethicality of individuals or of their inability to create mechanisms that could enable building trust.

CASE 2.1 Gurgaon Foods

Gurgaon Foods had a proposal for an international collaboration with Maxim Foods, USA, for exporting beef to the USA. The Managing Director Maxwell Jones was not sure if it would be sensible to start a beef factory in the area where the Hindu fundamentalists had a powerful hold. He gave the project to Rita Sharma, Govind Menon and Rusi Satarawallah for review. Rita was a devout Hindu and believed that the cow was sacred. She refused to be a party to the project. Govind had no such beliefs but was aware that the Directive Principles of the Indian Constitution mentioned that cow slaughter should be banned. Rusi was a total non-believer. He told Rita that it was well known that Aryans used to eat beef and that Hindu scriptures nowhere proscribed beef-eating. He also told Govind that the Directive Principles were not the law and cow slaughter was neither illegal nor unethical. He felt that even if such a law was moved, the company should bribe the legislators to see that the bill is not passed.

Maxwell was aware of the views of the three officers and hoped that Rusi would be able to convince the others. He was however surprised when they unanimously recommended that the project should not be taken up, even though they had found the project otherwise feasible and capable of yielding much better results than the company's financial cut-off norms. Maxwell asked Rita and Govind how they had managed to convince Rusi. He was intrigued to discover that they had been converted by Rusi and now agreed with him, except that they wished to draw the line against bribing the legislators.

Govind said that Rusi's facts and arguments had been logical and rational, and had made him review his own ethical approach. The company had in fact got the project cleared by the government on the assurance that only old cows would be slaughtered. 'Old cows are dying anyway on the wayside—neglected, starved and diseased,' he said. But their meeting with Sakhlani, General Manager Procurement, made him and Rusi reconsider the matter, each for his own reasons. Sakhlani said that the argument of old cattle was a facade and the beef would meet international standards only if young cows were used. He saw no problem in assuring the company of a supply of young healthy cows as they were willing to offer much higher prices than normal. Govind was worried that this would result in loss of nutrition to the rural population, especially children, as milk production would come down.

Rita resisted this sudden and abrupt change in Govind; she believed that this was not necessarily bad as milk was too expensive a source of nutrition for the poor children, and milk products were being exported by the National Dairy Development Board and anyway not available in abundance. Rusi could foresee in this contentious issue a major public relations problem all along the 'cow routes' and a threat to the company's credibility and survival. He was not concerned with the social consequences but switched sides for pragmatic reasons. He again swung them all to his stand that the project should not be supported. Rita and Govind found this pragmatic approach irresistible and their earlier ethical foundations of little consequence in taking the decision.

(This case is fictional but the issues are real and have been developed on the basis of newspaper and television reports of several multinationals working in India. The most explosive of them involved the Kentucky Fried Chicken outlet at Bangalore and the most recent interview on television was with the chief executive of McDonald, USA.)

Analyses for the reader

1. What ultimately decided the recommended action in this case?
    — Ethical principles and values
    — Fuller facts as they unfolded themselves as a consequence of reiterative democratic discourse
2. From your experience, rank the following for their ease of application for a manager:
    — Evolving and choosing ethical values

   — Pronouncing ethical values inducted in him by his family or earlier upbringing
   — Gathering facts and analysing them carefully in different ethical frameworks, his own and of those with whom he interacts

3. Rank in order of importance the three alternatives in the previous question.
4. Which of the six models described in this chapter on organisational decisions did you find the best to use in the case analysis?
5. Would you feel that the concept of *nishkama karma* would help this organisation to make a sounder decision?

3

THE SAINT AND THE DEVIL
The Liberating Impact of
Market Systems

The Sage Vision and Savage Suspicion

Western writers in business ethics accord a high value to market systems
(Hosmer 1995). Even ethical writers who do not believe in this institution
being the supreme value give it respect (Lunati 1996). Its overpowering
influence on Indian policy of recent times makes it important for Indian
managers to have a clear understanding of its ethical importance.

The institution of free markets (hereafter also markets) may be defined as
one in which goods and services are exchanged at rates and in proportions
which cannot be determined by a single person but by a self-regulating
mechanism of demand and supply. Adam Smith called this mechanism the
'invisible hand' (Samuelson and Nordhaus 1992: 40–41, 286–97).

The role of markets is central to the applied ethics of the future. Market
systems have existed from time immemorial in India and all over the world,
and are poised to become all pervasive in the 21st century. Indian markets
had developed their own norms to perform the ethical function they were
designed for (Bardhan 1996). Their dominance is however a very new
phenomenon.

Market systems are close to capitalism, but the two are not synonymous.
Capitalism is a system in which the means of production are owned by individuals and not jointly. It is believed
that such a system can perform effectively only with free markets.

The Sage Vision

Commerce is a pacific system
operating to cordialise mankind
by rendering nations as well as
individuals useful to each other.

—*Citizen Tom Paine*

The sage vision on the ethics of market systems is propounded by Paine
(1792) who looked upon capitalism and democracy as benevolent release
from the rigid constraints of feudalism.

On the other hand, Chakraborty (1991), drawing inspiration from the Indian tradition, does not regard it as one of the essential values. The reasons are obvious. Some Indian traditions, led by the *Arthashastra*, which survive to this day, look upon free markets with suspicion. The *Arthashastra* (4.2.28) not only warns us against merchants but also against pricing by market mechanisms. It lays down the margin on all internally made goods to be not more than five per cent and on imported goods not more than 10 per cent. There are however other stronger Indian traditions as in the *Panchatantra* and the *Kural*, which have a more lively appreciation of the benefits of markets. In neither case were market systems the last word on ethics. However, accumulation of wealth was considered perfectly ethical and legitimate.

The Savage Suspicion

Merchants are all thieves in effect if not in name; they form cartels and make excessive profits.

—*Arthashastra, 4th century BC*

The market system is one of the available means to integrate several values—controlled greed, pleasure-seeking, efficiency, individual choice and privacy—so that it can do the greatest good for the greatest number. It can also support tolerance and pluralism. In Coleman's (1992) opinion this mechanism allows mutually advantageous exchanges even though market participants may disagree in matters of fundamental importance. Thus, at least seven of the 29 values for which human civilisation has regard are induced at one stroke by market systems.

The Invisible Hand

An understanding of the features of market systems can help to perceive its ethical consequences.

1. Everybody has utility preferences among various goods and services, including the choice between leisure and work and supplying their own labour.
2. This preference can be expressed quantitatively as X units of A is equal to Y units of B, etc.
3. If we convert the preference into a common unit of money, it can be called the price one is willing to pay or charge.
4. This would indicate quantities one would be willing to exchange at different prices.
5. Aggregating all such demand and supply potential would form typical curves as in Figures 3.1 and 3.2. In a free market, the resultant market price will be formed as in Figure 3.3.
6. Consequent to these market prices and the shape of the demand and supply curves described earlier, sellers of goods would increase or decrease their production so that their marginal costs will be equal to

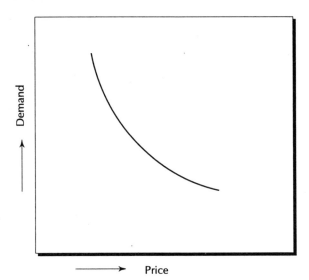

FIGURE 3.1   **Demand Curve**

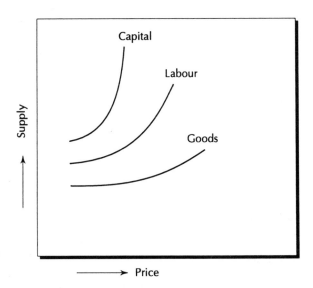

FIGURE 3.2   **Supply Curve**

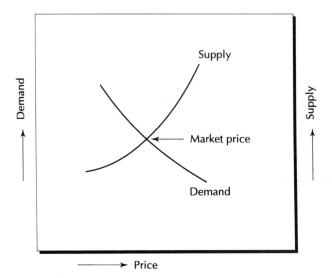

FIGURE 3.3   **Market Mechanism of Price Formation**

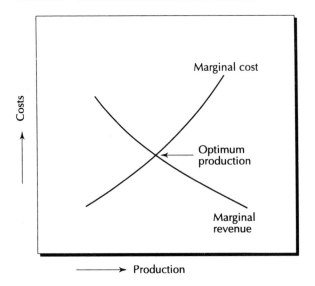

FIGURE 3.4   **Optimum Allocation of Resources**

their marginal revenue, i.e., the last extra unit they produce will give an incremental revenue equal to what they have incrementally spent; the last but one unit produced earlier would have then given them incremental profits. Production capacities would not be irrationally wasted (Figure 3.4).

7.   Human nature will be inclined to increase surpluses, and innovate to increase efficiency and reduce costs, which will automatically benefit society. These surpluses could be applied as per people's desires expressed through prices.

8. Those with a passion for innovation will attempt to improve society. They will take risks if they expect larger benefits. If the innovations fail they alone would be responsible; society will not bear the cost of such wrong decisions. It is up to the individuals to devise ways to guard against such risks. They will usually form large organisations to withstand shocks. They could sometimes form monopolies too (Schumpeter 1942) which would not necessarily be harmful to society.

9. Every human relationship can be accommodated in this mechanism with mutual benefits.

With the breakdown of feudalism in 19th century Europe, this way of looking at things captured the imagination of economic thinkers.

But contrary to the views usually held, Amartya Sen (1987) shows that the founders of this line of thinking were not naive to believe that market systems would automatically result in ensuring ethics. It is only the current crop of the Chicago school of economists who believe that the entire scheme is not only 'what is' but also 'what it ought to be' with as little modification as possible (Friedman 1962, 1970, Becker 1976). Thus market economists today, far from being indifferent to ethics, believe that the highest ethics are inherent in the market mechanism. But even they seek strong legal support for ethical synthesis, one of the basic values in Hosmer's (1995) select list of values but not in that of Chakraborty's (1991).

> **Law Plus Market Equals Ethics**
>
> The major test of every move in business, as in games of strategy, are legality and profits and not ethics.
>
> —A.Z. Carr (1968)

The understanding of the ethics of law through economic analysis is an interesting area of modern thinking. We will look at ethics of law and corruption in greater detail later, after examining if there are some obvious limitations to the thinking that market systems ensure ethics.

The God with Clay Feet

Having attempted to establish that with an effective legal system, market systems can be the key to ethics, let us look at some limitations of this approach.

1. An unequal distribution of resources between the poor and the rich could be further accentuated by the use of force by the rich against the poor. This is a situation that exists in modern times. In this situation distributive justice cannot be achieved only through market mechanisms, but also requires political action, taxation and administrative measures, supported by special legal procedures.

2. As per Noe and Rebello (1994), markets would oscillate between ethics and non-ethics, which can sometimes destroy the genuine innovator who can thrive only in an ethical ambience. Recent events in Silicon Valley, USA, show how this happens and the finest entrepreneurs are devoured by industrial and financial sharks (Herbig and Golden 1992). Perhaps a different type of ethics is needed to deal with these situations. Foong and Oliga (1992) call this 'emancipatory construction' as contrasted to Schum-peter's (1942) 'creative destruction' of uncontrolled market mechanisms.

3. Market mechanisms tend to be highly destructive of environment as they tend to concentrate on short-term benefits. This is one of the major ethical drawbacks of unbridled market mechanisms.

4. Free choice in market mechanisms has meaning only if the parties engaged in a transaction have symmetry of information, i.e., all parties in any transaction are fully and correctly informed. This cannot be ensured or induced by mere laws, and needs more basic ethical values. The inability of Western capitalist societies to ensure such a transparency has been a continuing threat to the survival of the system.

5. One of the essential conditions of ethics for minorities is that their rights and interests are protected. Market mechanisms have no means of ensuring this; only political processes can do so.

6. Market mechanisms can result in an unequal distribution of risks and rewards. They also presume that it would be ethical for some to trade risks for rewards and expose others to inordinately high risks. Islam considers this unethical.

7. Market mechanisms on their own fail to obtain benefits of cooperation that could lead to efficiency and consequently to profits. Cooperation would emerge naturally if one believes in compassion or camaraderie.

8. Market mechanisms can be used by developed countries selectively and deceptively against developing countries. They can mask their unethicality with perversely specious arguments supported by their economic and military power. This can be disastrous for developing countries.

9. The power structures always ensure that market mechanisms are conditioned to favour those in power. Nowhere in the world do we have a peaceful situation governed primarily by market systems not distorted by power struggles.

Controlling Greed Within Market Systems

Intense efforts have been made in the last 70 years to correct the unethical practices in market systems through economic, administrative and legal instruments devised by political processes. Lunati (1996), writing on the relationship between economics and ethics, believes that the surest way to develop an ethical conscience among businessmen is through government intervention. Hosmer (1987), on the other hand, is suspicious of government intervention. He feels that the crux of Lunati's proposition is unrealistic as it presupposes a Jekyll and Hyde psyche of the businessmen who behave benignly and abide by government regulations as a group even if they are wicked and greedy individually.

A running theme of this book is that it is possible to develop and nurture institutions that would conserve and cultivate the 'Jekyll' aspect of people and therefore moderate market systems. Gandhi's concept of trusteeship (Dantwala 1996) which borrowed from the Jain traditions is another such hope. Hirschman (1982: 1463–84), in a masterly analysis of the ethical philosophies of market systems over the last three centuries, shows that the philosophy has varied from a total belief in the system's ability to provide civilised choices to total horror at its potential to destroy decency and liberalism, as also how both the assertions could be true for some situations and in some societies. Today we may be witnessing a possibility of a dialectical synthesis of several features of market and non-market civilising institutions, and of the methods of both the precision of economics and the breadth of sociology, without depending solely on either of them (Baron and Hannan 1994). Whereas this synthesis would be eagerly sought for in economics, a similar synthesis would also be necessary in organisational theory and is discussed in Chapters 7 and 8. Hirschman's plea is that if all this calls for complexity in thinking and analysis in economics, so be it. And so be it in ethics.

Learning from the Other Side

Textbooks of business ethics now dominated by American writings assume that no systems other than capitalism and free markets exist anywhere in the world. This is not true. Today's managers must not have such a myopic view of reality; they must understand the ethical values in various alternative systems they would have to deal with at some stage in national and international business. We will discuss briefly the three systems of socialism, cooperatives and Islamic business systems.

At the start of the Russian socialist revolution in the early 20th century, it appeared that a new ethics was available as a realistic option. There had been several alternative visions earlier, most of them utopian and unrealistic. The collapse of the erstwhile Soviet Union has now given credence to a feeling that socialism is one more of these utopias. But more recent developments in Eastern Europe, China, Vietnam and Cuba show that whereas market systems are important, they can be used in more ethical ways than is done in the capitalist countries. Thus China even after liberalisation uses the ideas of Marx, Lenin and Mao to ensure a more balanced society (Nathan and Kelkar 1997). Poland has gone back to communist leadership with a more human face. Cubal, in spite of several impediments, is wary of slipping back to the horrors of its pre-revolutionary days. Vietnam is not giving up its communist philosophy altogether. Mintzbergh (1996: 49) sees in all these efforts an understanding of the social advantages of retaining the ownership of some factors of production in the hands of the community.

Marx would say that market mechanisms bring out the Hyde in a person as money, prices and commodities become proxies for real things. Marx (1932) and Engels (1878) call it commodity fetishism and there is an alienation in that system; alienation between the worker and production processes, between art and reality, between the public rhetoric and ground realities. Self-realisation can be attained only through communal activity (Kautsky 1906, Brenkert and Cambell in Simmonds 1985) and that is true ethics. This can be done if the means of production are communally owned. Lenin and Mao Tse Tung found it necessary to re-educate human beings to the new ethics, as contrasted to the ethics of greed. Swami Vivekananda (1962: 469) repeatedly declared the moral superiority of socialism. However, he felt that as long as *nishkama karma* and the Brahmanical qualities of *satvika* were not inculcated in the leaders, the system would be ethically fragile. Simmonds (1985) felt that allowing extensive discretionary powers to officials, which socialism implied, would damage all the ethics of rights. There is however little doubt that the attempts to remedy the obvious shortcomings of capitalism and free markets owe much to the intellectual and moral inspiration of the Russian revolution and that socialism cannot be condemned as totally unrealistic.

The second concept of cooperatives is an ethical cross between capitalism and socialism. This does not totally give up individual ownership of means of production, but visualises individuals working together in long-term arrangements for a common purpose. Some means of production may be commonly owned. Cooperatives use structural devices to develop trust relationships in market mechanisms; they cultivate the ethics of democratic discourse and distributive justice in political and group processes (Reddy and Sekhar 1993). Thus the individual members of the milk cooperatives in India and the collectives in socialist countries have long-term relationships as sellers and buyers, and develop the ethical quality of trust. At the same time, rights and justice are ensured through the member's direct control on the decision processes of the cooperative. Thus cooperatives use features of market systems to retain some of the latter's ethical outcomes. The philosophy of cooperatives owes much to Robert Owen, a contemporary of Marx and Engels (O' Toole 1995). Owen criticised both Marx and Engels on precisely the same lines as Swami Vivekananda criticised socialism as described earlier in the chapter. As in Gandhi's concept of trusteeship, Owen underlined the ethics of duties. The later offshoots of cooperatives swerved more towards the ethics of rights and gave up much of the ethics of duties. Cooperatives driven by the

> Trusteeship provides a means for transforming capitalist societies . . . . human nature is never beyond redemption.
>
> —*Gandhi's draft deed*
> *(Dantwala 1996: 39)*

concept of rights are widespread throughout the world and exist even in orthodox capitalist countries. Some, like the successful ones in Mondragon of the Basque region of Spain, continue to be inspired by their fight for democracy against the dictatorship of Franco and Hitler. We have however no living examples of economic systems based on Gandhi's concept of trusteeship; only some individual organisations have adopted this.

The third system is that of Islamic economics. The Islamic injunction on usury which we have described in Chapter 1 is the crux of the ethical world of Islamic economics. The basic ethics of Islam is based on camaraderie and brotherhood, and that usury amounts to exploitation of a brother's weakness. Also, gambling is considered unethical as it is obviously not useful; it gives a kick followed by a terrible depression to the gambler.

Islamic Injunction Against Gambling

They question thee . . . on games of chance. . . (it) is great sin and some utility but the sin of them is greater.

—*Quran, Surah II 219*

Lynch (1991) gives an account of the efforts being made by Islamic and other religious groups to practise ethical banking which avoids the concept of interest. The Islamic practices described are:

Madrada: Money given in trust and invested in ventures in which profit and loss is shared equitably
Murbaha: Goods given for resale
Ijara: Leasing
Mushabara: Joint ventures
Takahasi: Mutual funds

He also describes the Local Employment and Trade System (LETS) which is close to the concept of barter in that it has a nexus with production. The exchange is of real goods, which avoids speculative profit on the cost of capital.

However, a legislation or a religion that prohibits an asymmetric distribution of risks in exchange for asymmetric rewards can be ethically questioned on the basis of the right to free choice. If one is willing to take risks, are we ethical in preventing them? We may be accused of being paternalistic and of breaching the ethics of rights, but it can protect society from disasters. Thus, if Islam prohibited interest and commended the sharing of profits and losses, those lending moneys to others would ascertain the wisdom of its end use. The decisions on the use of moneys would therefore be wiser and more balanced and would protect society from the mad and the crooked (Samuelson and Nordhaus 1992). Consequently, it could be very ethical (see Chapter 11).

SUMMARY

The chapter provides the rationale for according market systems a high position in respect of ethical values in current writings. The unethicalities prevailing in market systems are also detailed. The chapter suggests that there are portents to show that the ethics of marketing systems would dialectically synthesise with the values of non-marketing systems to give a rounded benefit to humanity. The ethics of alternative systems to capitalism, namely socialism, cooperatives and Islam, are briefly discussed.

ISSUES TO PONDER OVER

- Ponder over the reasons for the strong differences between the views of Tom Paine and *Arthashastra* on the ethics of commercial activities.

- Considering the present situation in India, list the ethical values market systems are likely to foster and those which they are likely to hinder.

- What are the industries in which, in your opinion, multinationals would be highly tempted to be unethical and tend to harm the country in the long run even as appearing to benefit in the short run?

- One of your close friends wishes to start a new business and seeks financial assistance from you in the form of a loan. He is willing to pay you a high rate of interest at 30 per cent per annum. You feel that it would be more ethical to get into a partnership with him and share the profits and losses, but he feels that this would be unfair to you. Your friend has no other source of financing and no employment, and is desperate to start this business. What other facts and assessments would be required to ethically resolve this impasse?

- Ponder over Gandhi's concept of trusteeship and clarify if it would be relevant, whatever be the economic system—capitalism, socialism, cooperatives or Islamic.

CASE 3.1 The Bhopal Gas Tragedy

The version of Union Carbide USA

(As extracted from Hosmer 1987 and corrected for factual errors and supplemented at some places by Srivastava 1994.)

On 3 December 1984, some 2,000 people were killed and 200,000 injured when a cloud of poisonous methyl isocyanate gas was accidentally released from the Union Carbide plant in Bhopal, India. Methyl isocyanate is used in the manufacture of Sevin, a plant pesticide that is distributed throughout India for use on corn, rice, soyabean, cotton and alfalfa crops. Sevin was said to increase the harvest by over 10 per cent, enough to feed 70 million people.

The accident apparently occurred when 120 to 240 gallons of water was introduced into a tank containing 90,000 pounds of methyl isocyanate. The tank also contained approximately 3,000 pounds of chloroform, used as a solvent in the manufacture of methyl isocyanate; the two chemicals should have been separated before storage but this had not been done for some time in the operating process at Bhopal.

The water reacted exothermically (producing heat) with the chloroform, generating chlorine ions, which led to corrosion of the tank walls. The iron oxide from the corrosion in turn reacted exothermically with the methyl isocyanate. The increase in heat and pressure was rapid but unnoticed, because the pressure gauge on the tank had been inoperable for four months. The operators in the control room, monitoring a remote temperature gauge, were accustomed to higher-than-specified heat levels (25 °C rather than the 0 °C in the operating instructions) due to the continual presence of the chloroform and some water vapour in the tank. The refrigeration unit built to cool the storage tank had been disconnected six months earlier. The scrubber, a safety device meant to neutralise the methyl isocyanate with caustic soda, had been under repair since June. An operator, alarmed by the sudden increase in temperature, attempted to cool the tank by spraying it with water, but by then the reaction was unstoppable at a probable 200 °C. The rupture disc (a steel plate to prevent accidental operation of the safety valve) broke, the safety valve opened (just before, it is assumed, the tank would have burst), and over half the 45 tons of methyl isocyanate in storage was discharged in the air.

Following the accident, Union Carbide officials in the USA strongly denied that their firm was responsible for the tragedy. They made the following three statements in support of that position:

1. The American firm owned 50.9 per cent of the Indian subsidiary, but the parent corporation had been able to exercise little control. All managerial and technical personnel were citizens of India at the insistence of the Indian government. No Americans were permanently employed at the plant.

2. Safety warnings from visiting American inspectors about the manufacturing process of Sevin had been ignored.

3. Five automatic safety devices that had originally been installed as part of the Sevin manufacturing process had been either removed or replaced by manual safety methods by the time the accident occurred—allegedly to increase employment, or for repair, or as part of a cost-reduction programme. Automatic temperature and pressure warning signals had been removed soon after construction. The repairs on the automatic scrubber unit had extended over six months. The refrigeration unit to cool the tank had been inoperable for over an year. There were evidences of sabotage. (However, even on repeated requests they did not come out with concrete evidence of sabotage.)

4. The Bhopal plant had been built to increase employment in India. Union Carbide would have preferred to make Sevin in the USA and ship it to India for distribution and sale, due to substantial economies of scale in the manufacturing process.

Warren Anderson, Chairman of Union Carbide, stated that while he believed that the American company was not liable for the tragedy due to the points above, it was still morally responsible, and he suggested that the firm should pay prompt financial compensation to those killed and injured in the accident.

The culpability in the choice of designs

Praful Bidwai (1984), the well-known Indian journalist, mentions several obvious defects in the design of the plant. The control systems were radically different in the Virginia plant of Union Carbide with multi-stage electronic controls and back-ups. The Indian plant had inadequate controls, the standards not even satisfying the Indian specifications for other chemical plants.

Ramaseshan (1984) mentions that the process used by Union Carbide was banned in other parts of the world. Germany had prescribed an alternative process to manufacture the same product with much greater safety. This was known to the Indian authorities who allowed the plant to be established. Srivastava (1994) mentions that the parent Union Carbide was in a bad financial situation throughout this period and was being compelled to cut costs. Immediately after the Bhopal incident the Virginia plant was closed down. There had been a series of accidents in the Virginia plant too and Union Carbide was not given permission to install plants in other countries.

The charge of criminal negligence by the Indian Union Carbide

Mr Mukund, the Indian Works Manager, stoutly denied Warren Anderson's charges of negligence. Ramaseshan (1984) mentions that several accidents had occured prior to this incident. Other reports show that the factory inspector never stepped into the factory on his monthly trips, though there was one major objection raised both by him and the municipality which was overruled by the state and central governments. It was well known that political parties and influential persons got favours from the Union Carbide in several forms like employment, contracts and lavish entertainment.

The state's culpability

The state's culpability lay in permitting the slum dwellers to stay close to the factory, apart from permitting it to operate within city limits. The state said that Union Carbide never warned them about the nature of the chemicals.

The procedures of law and the uneasy settlement

The action in the case could be either criminal or civil or both. If it was criminal, *mens rea*, i.e., intentions would be involved. The question then was: does a company have a mind of its own, to have intentions?

Indian civil law provided little scope. Damages could be claimed under tort, which was based on case law which was poorly developed in India. That was one of the reasons that the Indian government (with the authority of the affected) sued Union Carbide in the USA where tort was taken more seriously, and appealed under the case law precedence of Ryland v. Fletcher, an English case. The case meant that if a person is foolish enough to bring, say, a tiger into a house, he cannot then plead that the owner of the house was negligent in letting it out.

Under civil law, if the Ryland v. Fletcher case had not been invoked, the case would have been smothered by the corporate veil. The poisonous substance was like the dangerous tiger. It was proven beyond doubt that it was brought in by Union Carbide USA. If the Ryland v. Fletcher case was not applied, it was no concern of Union Carbide USA as they only owned (even if partially) Union Carbide India as shareholders, and shareholders are not responsible for the management's faults in the company law concept that the corporate veil hid Union Carbide India from its shareholders Union Carbide USA. This veil cannot be torn asunder by law, was one of the multi-pronged pleas of Union Carbide USA.

Justice Keenan of the USA remitted the case back to the Indian courts with the condition that Union Carbide USA could not escape the provision of discovery, meaning an investigation in the internal documents of the company. Meanwhile, the suffering of the Bhopal victims continued unabated; all the while the Union Carbide officials were saying that this was all exaggerated.

The Supreme Court wished to put an end to the misery and awarded a damage of US$ 470 million which the company paid. They were absolved of all criminal charges. Subsequently, the revocation of criminal proceedings was withdrawn. A new twist was given to the case by the Supreme Court in 1996 when it held that no one from the company could be considered for punishment under the charge of manslaughter as they found no reason to believe that this was wilful negligence.

This judgement has been questioned as being too naive (India Today, 15 October 1996). According to them it was quite clear that the company officials were playing with fire. The maximum punishment for normal negligence under the Indian Penal Code would be two years' imprisonment which could be waived if the verdict was inordinately delayed. Due compensation has still not been paid to the victims because of incomplete documentation. The precise extent of the damage is still not known, though the Union Carbide doctors claim it is not as much as the Indian doctors estimate. The quantum for each death victim cannot be more than Rs 100,000 at the most. Union Carbide would have had to pay at least hundred times more if the accident had happened in America.

The Indian government did not take into consideration any damages to be paid to the victims due to its error in judgement or ineffective controls required under the Factories Act. They protected themselves under Article 300 of the Indian Constitution. This provided that the Government of India can be sued only to the extent the British government could have been before the Indian Constitution was promulgated. This meant that the protection available to the British Raj was available to the Government of India and Government of Madhya Pradesh. Since the Indian Constitution was passed by the representatives of the people, the formalities of judicial processes were apparently gone through. According to the Supreme Court, claims of damages under the laws of tort do not lie against the government if it was performing a sovereign function. This was decided in the case Kasturi Lal v. the State. The strict interpretation of Article 300 of the Indian Constitution was gradually being eased in recent judgements. But in the Bhopal case, the courts did not demand this accountability of the State. They were apparently worried that it would open up a Pandora's box. Every action by a government servant could raise a litigation and become a cause for claiming damages.

Analyses for the reader

1. How do we evaluate ethically every actor in this sordid and tragic drama?
2. If you were to join a company manufacturing or distributing a dangerous chemical, what steps would you like to take to be on the right side of the law and of your own personal ethics?
3. What would be your assessment of the ability of free market mechanisms to be systemically ethical *on their own*, with adequate safeguards provided by the state through legal and administrative means as an arbitrator? Would your answer be the same for India and America?
4. What are the specific steps one would need to take in dealing with foreign multinationals doing business in India, to ensure their ethical conduct?
5. Do you agree with the ethics of the Supreme Court judgement in the Kasturi Lal case and in the Bhopal case judgement of 1996 absolving the company of manslaughter?
6. If the ethical concepts of distributive justice, democratic discourse and social contract, discussed in Chapters 1 and 2, were to be a reality in India, what steps should have been taken before installing the plant at Bhopal?

4

THE PROTECTIVE DEITY
Law as an Instrument of Ethics

Is Law such 'a Ass'?

Respect for law as an ethical value is highly regarded by Hosmer (1995). As with all instrumental values, it is understood to be a proxy for the prime values it seeks to further. Going beyond the first-order analysis it is important to note whether the proxy always furthers the prime values faithfully. Law, according to the ungrammatical Mr Bumble, the immortal character in Charles Dickens' *Oliver Twist*, could be 'a ass'. Is this true sometimes? To understand this, we need to do a second-order analysis of the relationship between law and ethics.

Law is a code of conduct which the authority in power prescribes for society. It basically differs from ethics in its option to use force if and when necessary and by the fact that it is backed by power. These twin features of the orientation of law make for complex results that have varied over time and across nations. The relationship can be depicted as in Figure 4.1.

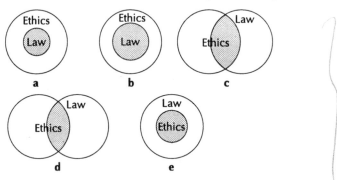

FIGURE 4.1 **Law and Ethics**

Source: Sekhar 1996 b

The patterns are true for both general law and business law and can be explained roughly by eight factors.

1. Law can represent the interests of the exploitative class in power, whereas ethical norms of society can be perceived differently by the exploited class.

2. Law can represent normative ethics (the ought to be) of the society as a whole, but can be so administered by the power structure as to render it short of ethics.
3. Law represents the minimum agreed ethical standards by common consent but the ethical norms of a large number are higher.
4. Law can more easily cover the overall boundaries of behaviour. Its intricate contextual details can be exhausting. Ethics can fill in the gaps and fulfil the spirit and intention of the law.
5. There may be a time lag between society recognising an ethical norm and its incorporation in its statutes. Some may believe that society's ethics are superior to law. There can be situations when statutes may be perceived as precursors to ethics. The same statutes can also be perceived as destroying ethics by some others if they feel that these fail to honour sanctified norms of the past.
6. Law can be structured somewhat inappropriately and clumsily making it an easy tool for unethical operators. Thus, though laws may be well-intentioned, they may have disastrous results in reality from an ethical point of view. Ethics may require such laws to be repealed so that they do not indirectly help spread unethicality.
7. Law may be designed for perfectly amoral purposes of just coordination and logistics, e.g., driving on the left or right side of the road. Ethics is not involved here.
8. Force is involved in law as also surveillance and monitoring. Law is therefore logistically better equipped to handle the fewer don'ts of ethics than the larger do's, and concentrates on the don'ts and not the do's of ethics.
    Let us now discuss how these eight factors lead to the results given in Figure 4.1.

He Who Wields the Rod

Marxists gave much weightage to the first and second factors (Tumanov 1974). Typically, they would say that Figure 4.1a was the situation among tribals where there were no class distinctions. Business was conducted on trust and for mutual benefit. Figure 4.1b would represent an advanced state of feudal system such as in the days of Manu or Kautilya. Business ethics was openly casteist and obviously partial. But the law ensured that the system would not collapse due to over-exploitation. Figure 4.1c represents bourgeois economy where law was respected to ensure private profit. Figure 4.1d shows the decay of the implementation of the bourgeois law and may correspond to the present situation in India, accor-ding to the Marxists. They see the Indian state as an alliance of vested interests who function as bandits rather than tyrants (Bardhan 1996). Figure 4.1e would represent Nazism as in Hitler's Germany or Ne Win's Myanmar. It has all the evil design of a Manu-driven law but much greater brutal strength and technological wherewithal to enforce it. We will now examine the situation in India as in Figure 4.1d somewhat independently of Marxist dogma and more in line with our 29 values.

Law as it is now structured in India has two branches—civil and criminal. Civil law primarily deals with transactions that have to be settled between individuals (or entities). They can, if need be, use institutions of the state. They usually have conditions for performance and damages for non-performance. The Contract Act is a typical civil law. Any breach serious enough to be of direct concern to the state comes under the purview of criminal law. It is usually dealt with by penalties and punishments rather than by damages. The Indian Penal Code is a typical criminal law.

Both these branches have both substantive and procedural law. The latter indicates how the laws will be implemented, keeping in view several ethical principles such as natural justice. Natural justice requires that no judgement be passed without hearing the affected party and there be no preconditions before hearing them. These laws have to be passed by a democratically elected legislature and have to be consistent with the Indian Constitution. The law that is thus passed is known as an Act. Administrative authorities are delegated powers by the legislature to prescribe rules and orders under these Acts. Often, the Act provides for consultation with the affected parties before the rules and orders are prescribed. The law is administered by the bureaucracy but disputes are settled by the judiciary which is independent of the bureaucracy.

Business—and business ethics—is concerned with both civil and criminal law. The workings of the Indian legal system would show that Indian law is now designed, at least in theory, to incorporate the ethical values of distributive justice, democratic discourse and rights. Why should there then be a dichotomy between law and ethics on account of the first two factors? What are the typical instances?

A typical instance even in substantive law is the Negotiable Instruments Act. It holds that once a promissory note is signed it will be presumed to have been done with mutual consent. This presumption is ridiculous as a poor person in India in need of money can be forced to sign an unequal condition on the note. A second problem arises because legal procedures involve very complicated arguments. The wealthy can engage expensive lawyers and have the lasting power to wait for delayed settlement and judgements. In such situations, being kind and considerate would be an ethical value in the non-hatched portion of the circle of ethics in Figure 4.1d.

Indian society is in the process of evolution and turmoil. The new spirit of the ethics of rights has yet to come to a practical understanding of the means to optimise ethics. Contrary to Bardhan's (1996) stand on the present Indian situation, this analysis is closer to the philosophy of speaking ethics.

Holier Than Thou

Many look at the relationship between law and ethics from a 'holier than thou' perspective. They derive their logic from factors three and five. 'We give better specifications in our products than the ISI or PFA', 'We give better perquisites to our workers than in the Minimum Wages Act', 'We take back goods from the customer even if law is categorical that sales once made are final', and so on. Insider trading as in the recent Reliance case is still not treated as a serious legal offence in India calling for stern criminal action but is extensively considered unethical. Ethical organisations take adequate precautions against this. They look upon law with reverence. Stevenson (1984) notes that the Jain traditions are chary of breaking the laws of the land; they could however do better than law. Since Jains are highly represented among the Indian business class, this observation is very pertinent to Indian business ethics. But this can lead to odd results.

Again, a female employee who is adulterous is legally not culpable as adultery if committed by women is not a crime in the Indian Penal Code. Only men are culpable under Section 497 of the Indian Penal Code. Yet the organisation can 'do better than law' and hold her unethical and dismiss her under its code of conduct. Conversely, an organisation which does not think adultery is unethical may not take action even against a man who is adulterous, though it is a crime in the Indian Penal Code. Similarly, business ethics in America is deeply concerned about homosexuality and lesbianism. Homosexuality is a crime with a penalty up to life imprisonment under the Indian law which was drafted by Macaulay who took up a typical Victorian attitude. Manu also treated both these sexual behaviours as crimes. Many however would consider these within the bounds of ethics. Being a victim of AIDS is no crime by law but would be considered a travesty in ethics; these impinge on personnel policies. Such may therefore be the cause of crowding on the white portion of the circle of ethics in Figure 4.1d.

Hell Paved with Good Intentions

The most prevalent view among the business community in India on the Indian legal system is that it is 'the road to hell paved with good intentions'. Thus they see the legislation on fiscal measures of taxation, foreign exchange and industrial relations as having had disastrous ethical consequences in India. They therefore have little compunction in breaking laws.

They consider evasion of income tax or custom's duty or dodging foreign exchange rules as something perfectly ethical. As far as they are concerned, these only enable the government to either squander resources or stop the benefit of free trade from reaching the Indian people. Taxation, according to them, results in resources being appropriated by the government who fritters it away. These could be used more effectively by private individuals. Taxation encourages the government to increase unwise, unplanned expenditure. Non-payment of taxes would therefore force the government to husband its resources better. Lastly, since free trade benefits the largest number of persons, to be ethical, government regulations preventing this need to be infringed upon.

Ethical Benefits of Breaking FE Laws

They could not have conducted business with limited foreign exchange . . . these have to be accounted for by subterfuge . . .The Reserve Bank turned a Nelson's eye because it is for the overall interest of the country . . .

[A senior Indian business executive responding to the prosecution of the ITC bosses]

—*Business India*
(18 November 1996: 72)

Mahatma Gandhi breaching the Salt Act by extracting salt without paying duty was an illegal act. But he considered it totally ethical. Likewise, many would consider it ethical to pay less than the minimum wages and provide some employment to a starving population; but they can be prosecuted for it. The much-vaunted South-East Asian tigers and Japan had no legal minimum either when their economies bloomed. Donaldson (1996) gives this as an example of 'local ethics' being different but not 'wrong'. Indian labour economists, even of Gandhian persuasion such as Hiraway (1992), feel that such minimum wage regulations have actually harmed the poor since as a result, industry switched to capital-intensive methods. The laws may have, according to some, contributed to massive unethical outcomes (See Table 4.1).

TABLE 4.1   **Wage Distribution Patterns in India (1990)**

	% of working force	% of national income	Average worker earnings ratio
Public sector	12.30	37	5.73
Organised sector	11.46	23	3.80
Unorganised sector	76.24	40	1.00
Total	100	100	

Table 4.1 shows that on an average 12.30 per cent of the population in the public (government) sector receive about 5.73 times the earnings per day of unorganised rural and small-scale sector workers. The workers in the organised sector (usually medium- and large-scale industries) including multinationals earn about 3.80 times the unorganised workers. The wage differentials are not market driven, nor skill- or effort-based, but the combined result of labour legislation and militant trade unions. The consequent effect on prices is usually felt more by the workers of the unorganised sector. Is this an ethically satisfactory result?

Do as the Romans Do

The seventh factor causing apparent differences in the areas of operation of law and ethics is related to the establishment of standard dimensions for the Indian Standard Institution under the Act as also the Standard Weights and Measures Act and Packaging Rules which are intended to improve coordination. If one is in Rome it is best to do as the Romans do! Apparently, these laws have no moral significance and would normally not give rise to moral dilemmas. Hosmer (1987: 71) therefore concludes that these are ethical non-issues. In fact, they are really not so, because on close reasoning they would seem to be important factors for increasing efficiency which was one of our 29 ethical values. Their absence may actually be detrimental.

The Don'ts of Law and the Dos of Ethics

These seven factors, important as they are, do not characterise the differences between ethics and law as clearly as the eighth one. This factor sees laws as primarily concerned with the don'ts of ethics whereas ethics is at its strongest in the dos. The required ethical behaviour may not be covered by the law at all. 'Look after the aged', 'Be affectionate to your wife', 'Be considerate to your workers', 'Teach your students well', 'Ensure good after-sales service', 'Take participative decisions with all employees', 'Do not tell lies', etc., will come within the circle of ethics but not within that of law in Figure 4.1c and therefore will not be in the hatched portion. Some of these dos are far more important for society than most of the don'ts of law.

More Law or Less Law

That laws are always intended to prevent chaos and disorder is true of all times across cultures and countries, whether in Hamurabi's Mesopotamia, Kautilya's or Manu's India, and Hobbes's or Locke's medieval England. They are necessary for the stability of any system of values. But more the laws, greater are the chances of an intrusion into the ethics of free choice and market systems. Ancient Indian law-givers were not worried about the multiplicity of rigid laws and instead seemed to thrive on them.

> Taking into consideration the law of each caste . . . a king should establish the law of each. The king should establish the prices for each sale.
>
> —*Manusmriti, Chapter 8.41, 402, 403*

But the moderns who rely on the values of free choice, pluralism and market systems would like to have only minimal uniform laws. They also lay more stress on laws that ensure symmetry of information among all persons,

> The state shall endeavour . . . a uniform civil code.
>
> —*Indian Constitution, Article 44*

transparency in all transactions, and strong punishments for breaching trust and withholding information. Becker (1964) has even worked out a formula for the penalties to be provided by law: Penalty is equal to loss of net social value by breach divided by the probability of being caught. To keep the cost of surveillance low, if the probability of being caught is low, the penalty would be high. Thus Kautilya and Khomeini kept extremely high penalties, including death. This argument misses the ethics of compassion.

On the other hand, those who recognise the failures of market systems seek more extensive corrective laws. It is possible that the two extremes in Indian politics both seek a larger number of laws. The traditional right of feudal origins or capitalists propped up by government support, holding on to Manu and Kautilya, are suspicious of a totally free-market capitalism. They are interspersed across several political parties. The radical left look for the ethics of minimum standards of living at any cost, and will seek many laws to achieve this.

The Ethics of Compassion and Anglo-Saxon Law

Contemporary Indian law is imbued with more compassion than ancient Indian law. The quality of mercy is more visible and the underprivileged are more protected. In criminal law, the accused unless proved guilty by the prosecution is now treated as innocent. In ancient Indian law, the pronouncement on the charge was 'guilty' or 'not guilty' with nothing in-

> Throughout the web of . . . law, the golden thread is that it is the duty of prosecution to prove the guilt.
>
> —Justice Sankey in the Woolmington Case (1935)

between. The concept of benefit of doubt never existed. The absence of this streak of refined institutionalised compassion is significant. Compassion was what an individual in India had to show, not systemically provided as in Anglo-Saxon law. Chinese law and continental law, for example, was like the ancient Indian law; a person was guilty unless proved innocent. Nevertheless, ancient Indian legal theory saw law as a means to protect the weak from the strong, the small fish from the big fish (*matsya*

> Judges not punishing the guilty will go to hell. Every part of the body of the low caste will be cut off if any part of the upper caste is cut.
>
> —Manusmriti, 8. 128, 8.228

dharma). *Danda* (punishment) was the last resort if *sama* (counselling), *dana* (reward) and *bheda* (manipulation) did not succeed.

An Overview of Indian Law

To appreciate the enormous range of Indian law, we will look at some Indian laws which have an impact on business ethics. These include laws on taxation, banking, finance, stock markets, professional councils, corporate governance, marketing, purchase, personnel, environment, and gender equality.

Taxation laws covering income tax, sales tax, excise, customs and octroi are powerful. These appear unethical to those who have to pay and there is always a strong temptation to break or circumvent these. Economic analysts and vested interests of international origin are only too quick to point out inequities in some of these laws thus providing a support to the unwilling taxpayer.

Banking, finance and stock exchange regulations are brave efforts to ensure that individual greed does not destroy society. We will see this in greater detail in Chapter 11.

The laws regulating professional councils such as those of doctors, accountants and company secretaries are dealt with in Chapter 5.

The laws of corporate governance are recent developments, some of them products of late capitalism. They cover the Indian Companies Act, Cooperatives Acts and Societies Registration Acts. In Chapter 7 dealing with organisational ethics we will see how powerfully they have affected the ethics of a network of relationships, and have made the consistent application of the simpler ethics difficult in modern times.

Several ethical principles that society has evolved in the areas of marketing and purchase have now been converted to laws which make implementation less ambiguous. This is more true abroad than in India. However, several recent enactments in India have reduced the gap between the law and ethics of sellers (producers) and purchasers (customers). The Contract Act, Sale of Goods Act, Standard Weights and Measures Act, Seeds Act, Food and Adulteration Act, Consumer Protection Act, Monopolies and Restrictive Trade Practices Act, Trade and Merchandise Mark Act, Drugs and Cosmetics Act, Indian Penal Code, Bureau of Indian Standards Act and the judicial pronouncements under the written and unwritten laws of tort are some examples.

The ethical aspects of advertising continue to be beyond law. Only if one is scandalously obscene or defamatory can one be apprehended under the Indian Penal Code. The issues involved are too nebulous and contentious to be contained in legal enactments. An alternative method of controls through advertisers' councils is referred to in Chapter 6. But there are still many grey areas which can be tackled only with an innate sense of ethics rather than through the external controls of law. The field of industrial relations is replete with regulations—the Industrial Disputes Act and Industrial Employment Standing Orders Act that govern conditions of service, Contract Labour Act that governs the limits to short-tenure contract appointments, the Minimum Wages Act, Payment of Wages Act, Employment Insurance Act, Workmen's Compensation Act, Provident Fund Act and various industry-specific legislation. The Factories Act and the Shops and Establishments Act govern the conditions at work as well as basic perquisites for industrial and non-industrial labour. Legislation for affirmative action for the underprivileged has so far covered only employment by the state. In this respect the Indian legislation is not as bold and far-reaching as the US legislation.

Environment Protection Acts, Air and Water Pollution Acts, Forest Acts and several other legislations have enormous scope for regulating those activities of business that affect the environment. Gender protection is enshrined in the Indian Constitution but only in employment by the state. The Equal Remuneration Act provides for equal pay for equal work in private sector employment as well. But this protection is available only to workmen as defined under the Industrial Disputes Act. Women managers do not get the benefit of this protection.

The Open Ends of International Law

The relationship between international law and ethics is distinguishable from that relating to domestic laws. Since the concept of sovereignty covers only individual nations, laws that apply across nations cannot be enforced unilaterally and are valid only on the basis of 'contracts' between nations. These contracts are sought to be established on ethical principles of distributive justice and democratic discourse. However, military and economic power have played a greater role in these contracts.

Dubey (1996) represents a large number of intellectuals who believe that the North is using its military and economic powers to force unequal contracts on the South. Once these contracts are made, the North uses the facade of legality and ethics to pin down the South. The make-believe ethical issue of the sanctity of law camouflages the unethicality of the entire transaction, which is a travesty of the ethical concepts of the greatest

> The new trading order is unequal and ... unjust ... the developing countries have accepted far-reaching commitments in key sectors without getting returns ... they severally limit policy options in crucial areas.
>
> —*Muchkund Dubey (1996)*

good for the greatest number, distributive justice and democratic dispassionate discourse. Thus it suffers from the flaw pointed out by Dewey (1929) that law—one of the useful means to implement ethics—has fouled the ethicality of the ends. In such circumstances, breaking the law may not be unethical.

But once the international contract is made it becomes a law to be followed by everyone. If one does feel as strongly as Dubey does, where does one draw the ethical line? Example 4.1 narrates the experience of Sir Sokhey, when he was Director of the Haffkine Institute, Bombay.

EXAMPLE 4.1 **Sir Sokhey's Theft of the Penicillin Spores**

Sir Sahib Singh Sokhey was one of India's most famous scientists in the field of immunology. Extremely socially conscious, he noticed that the multinationals were cornering the results of research and pricing penicillin abnormally high. Penicillin had immense potential as a life-saving drug. His friends in the erstwhile Soviet Union also said that their researches in antibiotics were not progressing satisfactorily. Much as they would have liked to help India in setting up the indigenous Hindustan Antibiotics, their penicillin spores were not as efficient as those of the West. Sir Sokhey invited himself to a drug laboratory in Switzerland belonging to a famous multinational. When nobody was watching he slipped a test tube containing the high quality spores into his pocket. He gave this to Hindustan Antibiotics and to the Russians. The price of penicillin fell and millions of lives were saved. Was his action ethical?

Controversial patents have been registered by firms of developed countries using the basic scientific corpus of developing countries (Ramu 1997: 101). This scientific corpus has grown from time immemorial, treated as a common property in their law. Breach of common property in this manner could be considered ethically wrong. King Jr (1995), however, has commended the example of a firm placed in similar circumstances, which expiated this unethicality by funding liberally to the infrastructural development of the communities thus abused. In the capitalist developed world, such an attempt to preserve the sanctity of the patent laws appeals to the ethics of duties. This gratuitous action however undermines the basic ethics of the rights of the affected community. The utter disregard of the rights of the South was highlighted at the Rio Conference, when the South's right to be recompensed by the North for polluting the environment and common property was reconfirmed.

The Ethical Law Breakers

The arguments given so far do not mean that the ethically conscious can break the law as a matter of course. If this is encouraged or condoned there could be a complete breakdown of trust which we have identified as a major ethical value. This is the reason that Indian Jain traditions never wish to break any law (Stevenson 1984). The truly ethically conscious would usually wait till the law is corrected for ethicality. Till then they may suffer it but not break it. There could be many other more ethical issues awaiting action, that one need not seek situations where one may need to break an unethical law. This follows the ethics of meliorism (see Chapter 2). However, if after due deliberation, one finds a strong conflict in ethics one may break the law. Thus Kohlbergh (1981) describes a situation where Dr Heinz has no money to pay for his wife's medicine and the pharmacist will not give it to him on credit. The wife would die if she did not get the medicine. There is a conflict of two ethics, one of saving a life and the other of not stealing and breaking the law. He then applies the ethics of universalisability: how would I react if

I were in the pharmacist's place? He would not have minded if someone else in such a situation broke into the shop. So this is what Heinz does—steals the medicine. This was Gandhi's argument in defying the Salt Act or Krishna's when he made Yudhishtara tell a lie in the *Bhagavad Gita* to ensure that the unethical did not capture the world. Conscience can be a double-edged sword that can justify breaking the law.

SUMMARY

The chapter describes the support that votaries of market systems seek from law. They seek simple and minimal laws that can be strictly and uniformly enforced with stringent punishments. The laws they desire are however less restrictive than the laws of ancient India. The inherent element of the ethics of compassion in Anglo-Saxon laws now adopted in India can be seen from the principle that no one can be pronounced guilty unless proved so conclusively. The cause for divergence between law and ethics is described. The most important of these is that ethics concentrate on the dos and laws on the don'ts. The ethical dilemma experienced by the highly ethical who are compelled to break unethical laws is discussed.

ISSUES TO PONDER OVER

Reflect on where you would put these pronouncements in the Venn diagram in Figure 4.1c or 4.1d (inside or outside). These relate business ethics to law. You need not presume that the pronouncements are *ipso facto* ethical.

- Do not tax low-count cotton yarn used by handlooms (presently they are taxed).
- Do not market baby milk food (presently there is no bar subject to stipulations in the Infant Milk Food etc. Act which prohibits sale without warning).
- Do donate to Mother Teresa's Christian charities (IT Act permits this as deduction from income).
- Do donate only to Hindu charities (IT Act permits it as deductions from income).
- Do pay your domestic household help a minimum living wage (there is no legislation in India).
- Separate the degradable and non-degradable waste in your house and keep them in different bins for the waste collectors (there is no legislation in India).
- Do *yogasana* every day (there is no legislation).
- Do not lust for your secretary (there is no legislation).
- Do not refuse employment to homosexuals (this is a crime under Indian law and refusal is legal).
- Never buy smuggled goods even if it be a life-saving drug for your very ill father (it is punishable under Indian law).

- Avoid paying income tax somehow as the money collected will be wasted (this is punishable by Indian law).

CASE 4.1 Cannanore Handloom Exports

Elizabeth Verghese (Lizzy) was the sole proprietor of Cannanore Handloom Exports, a successful export-oriented concern, supplying fabric to several top hotels worldwide. The industry was highly competitive and Lizzy had to strain herself to cut costs. Some cost reductions could be obtained from better designs but labour cost control was critical. Only because her designs could not be mass-manufactured and were exclusive, could she manage to be in business. Lizzy was an alumnus of the National Institute of Design, Ahmedabad, and was an expert computer-based textile designer.

She had 100 weavers working at any given time in her factory at Cannanore, Kerala. But her workforce was double that. Half of them worked for 150 days a year and the rest for the other 150 days. None of them could claim permanency as this required a minimum attendance of 240 days a year. That way she was not obliged to give them the provident fund and other benefits due to permanent employees. Thus she was paying about Rs 46 per day, which was 15 per cent higher than the legal minimum wage of Rs 40 per day. She was however denying them about 30 per cent extra as benefits coming from permanency; this would have amounted to Rs 13.80 at the basic wages of Rs 46 that she was paying. The workers accepted this grudgingly, as her wage rates were considerably higher than the market rate which was Rs 30 per day. On the days they were not employed with her, they managed on these market rates; usually they were able to get employment for 90 days a year at these lower rates. The arrangement was considered perfectly legal and was being extensively practised in Kerala. The practice however was universally recognised as unethical. No wonder industrial relations were not always cordial.

Elizabeth's husband, Thomas Verghese, was an MBA and occasionally helped her. At his suggestion, she introduced a scheme whereby she could assure work round the year for those who chose that scheme. She sold the looms to the workers against a long-term loan and had the weavers install them at their homes. She offered them an equivalent of Rs 40 per day in wages but full year's employment; this in actual practice was 300 days employment as against 150 days in the previous arrangement. Since this arrangement was construed as a contract for supply and not a contract for employment, her lawyers advised that she need not pay them the minimum wages nor the perquisites as for permanent employees. Those who chose the scheme were happy as their yearly wages increased with 300 days' work. But Lizzy soon found that it was less foolproof in dodging labour laws than the previous arrangement.

The Supreme Court in a recent case came down heavily on such 'masks or facades' and directed that such arrangements should be discontinued and the true nature of the contracts as that of employment and not of supply should be revealed. The Kerala government was threatening to prosecute her for this breach of law. Because of the difficulty of supervision at distant villages, the quality of the product also suffered and some supplies were rejected by the foreign purchasers. Thomas's idea was turning sour on Lizzy.

Thomas now came out with a bolder idea. He suggested they close down the business in Kerala and shift to Tamil Nadu, where the minimum wages were much lower at Rs 25 per day and the market rate was even lower at Rs 20 per day; the skills in weaving were at par with the best in Kerala. The labour machinery was 'more understanding' of the handloom situation. 'We can give employment to more Indians. With lower wage rates, we can employ more persons. We can expand our sales and exports with a little more elbow room for flexible pricing. That is doing the greatest good for the greatest number', said Thomas.

Lizzy was also a member of the state-level tripartite committee which fixed minimum wages from time to time. The committee had equal representation from the government, the industry and trade unions. The committee followed the 'need-based' concept of fixing minimum wages, deriving it from minimum nutrition, clothing, housing and medical standards. The industry representatives did not take a realistic stand in the meetings, as the deliberations were never confidential and they could be branded anti-labour.

They also scored negatively with the politicians in power. On the other hand, the union leaders were not worried about the problems of unemployment as they felt that their accountability was to those already in employment. The next meeting of the committee was due within a month.

Lizzy, a devout Christian and strongly attached to her native Kerala and its people, was less enthusiastic about this suggestion. 'It does not seem ethical. May loyal workers in Kerala will starve to death', she told her parish priest.

Analysis for the reader

1. If you were Lizzy what would you do and why?

5

THE JOY OF LIVING TOGETHER
The Indian Processes of Socialisation

The Several Ways to Public Trust

Fukuyama (1995) sees socialisation as a key process in the development of trust. We have seen trust as a key value in business ethics in all the preceding chapters of the book. But socialisation without individuation can be psychologically destructive (Garg and Parikh 1995). Individuation is a process whereby individual identity and its relationship to the social milieu is established. Psychological processes for establishing socialisation and individuation are subtle and varied, and can be personal and individualised, or made public in successive stages within the family, within institutions and organisations and across larger communities.

In this chapter, we will explain the unique features of the Indian practices of socialisation. Two of the most important streams of descriptions and analysis of the individualised processes owe their origins to the West and to India respectively. Much as the two streams differ in their terminology and their philosophic moorings, they are similar in their structure and approach. While Western descriptions have scientific and empirical moorings, Indian thinking is rooted in its intuitive and spiritual traditions. But on closer analysis, this liberal modernity of the West can be surprisingly close to Indian religiosity (Pande 1991: 15).

Kohlbergh's Six Stages of Moral Evolution

The Western description is based on the works of Lawrence Kohlbergh (1981). After decades of empirical research he now maintains that it is universally true that ethical adaptation is a six-stage process (Thomas 1993). These six stages are at three levels of two stages each for easy identification:

Level A: Pre-conventional
Stage 1: The stage of punishment and obedience. Here the individual behaves in a manner akin to that of the Pavlovian dog.

Stage 2: The stage of individual instrumental purpose and exchange. One does what is of one's own interests, but acknowledging others' interests; the individual uses the instrument of exchange of services and thereby resolves conflicts.

Level B: Conventional
Stage 3: The stage of mutual interpersonal expectations, relationships and conformity. One is able to put oneself in the other's position and empathise. (The family is an example where we find such an interpersonal expectation.)
Stage 4: The stage of social system and conscience maintenance. One is loyal to one's social institutions (say, religion, college, professional council, organisation, etc.).

Level C: Post-conventional and principled
Stage 5: The stage of prior rights and social contracts. One recognises rational perspective according to which there are values and rights. One needs to note that till Stage 4, this broadening vision where one can think of abstract social values and rights, is absent; the horizon is limited to a smaller circle. Therefore at this stage the person can face an ethical dilemma between different affiliations: organistion v. professional goals, professional goals v. community welfare v. professional goals, and so on. It needs a little more than common sense to resolve these (Beteille 1996).
Stage 6: The stage of universal ethical principles. This is the deontological stage according to Kohlbergh (1981, Chapter 1 Universalisability).

The six stages are twofold in character: the intellectual stages of cognition, i.e., understanding reality and fixing it in one's mind, and the stages of moral development to match the intellectual stages. Interestingly, Kohlbergh believes that if the environment is not conducive, a person can intellectually reach Stage 6 but deliberately remain morally at Stage 4 as she or he

> I know what is right and wrong. I know not why I am driven to always do the wrong.
> —*Duryodhana in Mahabharata*
> *(Dadaji 1908: 302)*

may find that she or he has to sacrifice too much to reach Stage 6. This would have been the case of General Rommel, who thought Adolf Hitler was unethical. Rommel was therefore in Stage 6 intellectually. But he behaved as if he still continued in Stage 4 as he would otherwise have been shot by Hitler. Duryodhana, the anti-hero of the *Mahabharata*, who confessed to being ethically wrong, but lacked the emotional conviction to overcome it and felt that his envy drives him to unethical behaviour.

Society and social institutions should be such that everyone should be able to reach Stage 6 both cognitively and morally. Kohlbergh clarifies the difference between Stages 5 and 6 in his story of Heinz's dilemma (Thomas 1993) on the ethics of thieving and breaking the laws in extenuating circumstances discussed in Chapter 4. Stage 6 involves the ability to universalise in complex situations involving conflict of ethics. Since there is no coercion in the entire process, individuals in well-organised societies can choose from various alternatives so that individuation can take place (Garg and Parikh 1995).

The Indian Ways of Introspection

Perhaps the most comprehensive view of evolving ethical values from the Indian perspective is that of Aurobindo as described by him in *The Yoga of Divine Works—Karma Yoga* (1986). The following quotation from his book shows how his socialising process is similar to Kohlbergh's: 'There are four main strands of human conduct that make an ascending scale. The first is personal need and desire. The second is the law and collectivity; the third is the ideal ethic and the last is the divine law of Nature . . .'

He goes on to describe how Patanjali's yoga, and yoga as expounded in the *Bhagavad Gita* can help this evolutionary process. Patanjali's *Yoga Sutra*, a more polished version of the *Sankhya* philosophy, looks at moral and ethical development as also the development of the intellect to grasp the totality of the ever-increasing social context. The benefits of reflection on moral development are repeatedly driven home. The ability to empathise is considered to be the first step in moral development. 'By being friendly he discerns the power of friendliness, by feeling compassion he discerns the powers of compassion, by feeling for joy of others he discerns the power of joy' (Wood 1992, translation from Patanjali: 252).

Patanjali goes on to list the practical steps to maintain equanimity and avoid the disturbances of *kama, krodha, lobha, moha, mada* and *matsarya* (lust, anger, greed, delusion, intoxication and envy). The similarity of Kohlbergh's scheme with Eastern thought has also been noted by the Chinese (Ma 1997). But, somewhat more pronouncedly than Patanjali and Aurobindo, Chinese thoughts emphasise the affective and emotional part.

Yoga practices may seem merely physical and mental to a superficial observer. But Patanjali describes these as interactive processes with ethical and spiritual development. The *Bhagavad Gita* also recommends a fine balance of these multiple physical, ethical and spiritual processes.

> He who by likeness to himself sees equality in all is deemed the highest *Yogin*.
>
> —Bhagavad Gita, Chapter 6, Sloka 32
>
> A man who is fallen from yoga is not lost.
>
> —Bhagavad Gita, Chapter 6, Sloka 40

More importantly, the *Bhagavad Gita* never offers anything as singular advice. Thus the physical features of yoga—as also the formalities of the scriptures— can be dismissed as not being the be all and end all.

It is much more important to contemplate on one's own self (*Bhagavad Gita*, Chapter 2, Sloka 3) and learn to laugh at oneself (*Kural*, Verse 304).

Transcendental meditation (TM) as developed by Mahesh Yogi claims to have improved ethical attitudes tremendously and has been extensively adapted by several institutions and management programmes all over the world (Gustavsson 1995). Mahesh Yogi's followers claim to have established the physiological basis of these practices through formal evaluatory processes (Orme-Johnson *et al.* 1997). But these have not been universally accepted except among those who are already converts, which is of course a very large number. The essence of this meditative process is to enable a person to reach 'pure cosmic consciousness'.

Chakraborty (1993b) has developed a process of meditation which gives a heightened feeling of ethicality. Many organisations in India and abroad have adopted his methods. He reports on their sustainability in organisations at least for a two-year period with very salutary effects on ethicality.

His meditative methods are goal-directed whereas TM is not. But promoters of both methods claim to produce spontaneous ethical behaviour. In the case of Chakraborty's methods, there is a suggestion that it is somewhat Indian culture-specific (Hixon 1995), perhaps specific also to the Sanskritised sub-cultures in India. An attempt to broaden the psychological reach of meditation to more heterogeneous groups is explained in Appendix 5.1.

Zen Yoga goes even deeper into meditative practices with similar arguments. There is however one very important difference between the two. Zen Yoga is 'not administered in an artificial condition but in actual life of daily living in this world' (Saher 1989: 189). Herman Hesse's (1971) Sidhartha gets his vision of Gautama Buddha and of Truth by reflecting on his turbulent and unconventional life and sensitising himself to the deep murmurings of a running forest river. Articulated in words his conclusion, 'love humanity', seems trivial. But as a process of psychological adaptation, profound changes are recorded in him. Not words and ideas but processes are shown to be the true stuff of ethical development. Krishnamurthi (1971), a highly controversial maverick among modern Indian philosophers, scoffs at almost the whole of ancient Indian thinking, but reaches out for experiences as in Zen to sensitise people for a more beautiful world.

Yoga as restricted to a set of exclusive ritual practices is not the basic meaning of the *Bhagavad Gita*. It has a surprisingly open and universal view of several equally effective processes. Aurobindo also takes the same position (1994: 373). Gandhi attached very little importance to the physical exercises associated with yoga and did not ever practise them. His yoga consisted of 'action' (Parikh 1987). The *Bhagavad Gita* also visualises more public and community processes for socialising.

Other Indian Public Ways to Private Trust

Some ethical thinkers, both from the West (Sommers 1994) and India (Chakraborty 1995b), have been unhappy with current discourses. They think ethical dilemmas are overdramatised and that little attention is paid to building up instinctual ethical responses in young children and budding managers. In this chapter we will look at some more important but less self-conscious cultural instruments that societies have developed over time: myths, legends, poetry, literature, music, etc., which are as potent as they are unobtrusive. Their ethical import is learnt naturally, as part of growing up, within the family environment. Not necessarily learnt by extensive bookish learning, the depth of our understanding does not grow with literacy or higher education. These instruments are however too multi-faceted and comprehensive to be neatly encapsulated in a limited and oversimplified logic. We will deal with attempts in this direction later in this chapter.

Six types of influences on the culture of the Indian people contribute to their ethical responses.

1. Rule books of ethics, typical examples being the *Thirukural,* Bhartrihari's *Nitishathaka* (6th Century AD), *Arthashastra* (4th Century BC), *Manusmriti* (5th Century BC) and Patanjali's *Yoga Shastra* (2nd Century BC).

2. The case-study type of ethical discourses which are not explicitly didactic. They are experiential-cum-analytical, such as the *Bhagavad Gita* (2nd Century BC) and the Vedantic *Upanishads* (4th Century BC).

3. Epics and literature which are fashioned with elegance, such as the *Ramayana, Mahabharata, Bhagavatham, Panchatantra, Naganandham* and the *Jataka* tales. The epics were translated in all the regional languages. Each of these translations had a distinct ethical message to give in modification of the original Sanskrit version.

4. Regional works from the medieval period such as those of Kabir from Uttar Pradesh (15th Century AD), Nanak from the Punjab (15th Century AD), Alvars and Nayanmars of Tamil Nadu (8th Century AD), and Basaveswara of Karnataka (12th Century AD).

5. Foreign emigrants and invaders. The most profound influences were Islam and Christianity.

6. Myths, legends and songs of the tribals, as well as the hymns of the Vedas (5000 BC), which celebrate the exuberant joy of nature and are close to the concept of speaking ethics advocated in this book.

How much of these influence the instinctive responses of the present generation? If their popularity is any indication, they must be influencing the people immensely. B.R. Chopra's *Mahabharata* and Ramanand Sagar's *Ramayana* were blockbusters on the Indian television. On the days they were telecast, there was hardly any traffic on the roads. The Indian business class often speak 'in parables peppered with folk wisdom, mythology and scriptures' (Dutta 1997: 186). Tharoor (1989) quotes the German writer Gunter Grass, 'I think in India some stories should be keptalive ... Literature must refresh memory'. The past is not easily removed from the ethos and Indian managers of today must recognise this. However, its influence and pervasiveness even though profound and extensive is not necessarily consistent. The language of the mythologies is ambiguous and is interpreted differently by different people. Hirayanna (1958) sees the ethical values as being under constant change throughout history and being modified by several authors. A 'running tale' by its very structure would show life as it flows along, with all its contradictions. Its very ambiguity is its merit. Mythology is very relevant for socialising processes and its contemporary impact is described vividly by several insightful writers (Kakkar 1996, Tharoor 1989). Though a broad and generally accepted message, a well-researched comprehensive understanding of this has yet to emerge.

The ethical directions in the *Ramayana* are more obvious. Ramachandra, the hero of this epic, is the role model adopted extensively not only in India but in several parts of South and South-East Asia (Iyengar 1994). His steadfast monogamy, his righteous anger, his sweetness of speech, his truthfulness, his filial affections, all combine to epitomise all that is good and desirable in man. Seen in this model role, the very aberrations he exhibits on a few occasions are classic cases of 'ethical conflict' or 'dilemma ethics' (*apat dharma*—as described in the Indian texts of ethics).

Unlike in the *Ramayana*, in the *Mahabharata* and *Bhagavatham* one single character does not personify all ethically desired qualities. The characters have a mix of endearing and negative qualities making them more true to life. Nevertheless, the stories provide unmistakable ethical signals. Ramakrishna Paramahamsa, of early 20th century Bengal, is known to have used these stories to convey positive ethical messages. The audience related the messages of *Bhagavatham* to themselves effectively. The 29 ethical values inventoried in Chapter 1 are vividly portrayed in these two epics.

The *Mahabharata* has many ethical models—Karna's graciousness, Yudhishtara's truthfulness and fair-mindedness, Bhishma's steadfastness and stoic sacrifice, Eklavya's single-minded intensity of desire to learn and his respect for his teacher, and the righteous self-assertion of Draupadi. Similarly, we have role models in other legends and epics: Prahlada's devotion, Sudama's pride in his poverty, the message of the power of repentance in the story of the fallen brahmin Ajamila, the sacrifice of Dadhichi who gave his own ribs as a gift, the trusting affection of Shabari, the compassion of Sibi, the chastity of Sita, Savitri, Sukanya and Damayanti, the single-mindedness of Dhruva, and the humility and trustful nature of Bali even at the time of his destruction (Subramaniam 1981, 1993a, 1993b,

Krishnamurthy 1994). Ancient and medieval India's literature ranged from the romantic poetry of Kalidasa of the 5th Century AD to the extremely didactic and self-righteously pious *Naganandham*.

The ethical messages of the *Panchatantra* (1st Century BC), and *Hitopadesha* unlike Kautilya's are human documents and at the same time hilarious. Children therefore take an instant liking to them. They sometimes come close to being bawdy and appeal to adults alike. As the name indicates, the *Panchatantra* suggests five 'tricks' for success—How to avoid conflict among friends, how to win friends, how not to slip into wrong friendship with the traditional enemy, and how not to act foolishly without due consideration. But there is a gentle reminder that 'unethical conduct' can lead to disaster with none to sympathise or help. The *Jataka Tales* (Jayakar 1982) bring out the Buddhist idea of compassion. Spread far and wide in the world wherever Buddhism was adopted as a religion, they are the subject matter of the glorious paintings of Ajanta Caves (8th Century AD).

The ethical history of India is usually described in its Sanskritised track. It is only now being realised that myths and legends of the tribals and the dalits also contribute to it (Omvedt 1995). Their perspective could be very different from the later-day Sanskritic cultures. But as mentioned earlier in this chapter, their similarity to earlier Vedic literature is unmistakable. The *Vedas* are now either sanctified as the words of God by the fundamentalists, or disliked as apostles of oppression of the upper classes. If one read them without these prejudices, one would notice that they are spontaneous responses to life and nature by a vigorous, optimistic but aggressive people. In their description of life, there is no self-consciousness of their foibles. The overemphasis on hating and killing the dark-skinned enemies, namely the Dravidians, is all too obvious. But all this is no reason to deny their robust ethics of practical commonplace life described as speaking ethics in the book.

The potential use of piety or *bhakti marga* for socialising has been demonstrated in several social movements. Thus Panduranga Shastri Athavle's efforts in transforming a whole group of villages has been made into a moving film by Shyam Benegal called *Antarnad* (The Inner Voice). The impossible task of getting diverse castes and classes to work together for collective watershed development was miraculously achieved by Anna Saheb Hazare in Ralegaon–Sidhi of Maharashtra, basically by using the Hindu concepts of *bhakti* (piety). The international and widespread appeal of even admittedly quixotic movements like the Hare Krishna and that of Acharya Rajnish shows the potential hold of the Indian concept of love in the processes of socialising. As was observed earlier, the explicit expression of love in an exuberant form was not one of the characteristics of Patanjali's methods. The Chinese methods had a more restrained expression of love (Ma 1997). Kohlbergh was even more cerebral than Patanjali. Thus, we had a variety of methods of socialising in India, each with its own typical features and fitting into its pluralist approach.

Sado-masochistic Caricatures of the Indian Situation

Several pronouncements on Indian culture tend to make sweeping statements to prove a favoured framework or sustain reader interest by using caricatures. Moralist writers tend to caricature to make a point or win a debate. These caricatures may make important points and serve as useful leads. As Gore (1993) points out, they serve the purpose of replacing or moderating existing obsolete ideologies. But if one relies on them for framing one's philosophy, one would come to total grief.

One of the early caricatures was by Lord Macaulay. This attitude of a confirmed imperialist can be laughed away, but for the fact that many a time this has become a part of the mind-set of managers. Obviously, Macaulay was way off the mark.

Indians are Deceitful

What is horn to a bull, the sting to a bee, deceit is to a Bengali.

—*Lord Macaulay (1898)*

The second caricature is by D.D. Kosambi (1964), the brilliant Marxist who is quite unable to accept the peculiar philosophy of speaking ethics systematically cultivated in India. His caricature of the Indian tradition is one of deliberate ambiguity and double-think, to cover up the ugly truth of exploitation and class suppression inevitable with the low surpluses of the primitive means of production. His attack on the Krishna legend is now a focal point of an assessment of whether the Marxist analysis genuinely aids understanding of the Indian psyche. As a counterpoise to Kosambi, Garg and Parikh (1995) consider the Krishna legend the acme of the Indian style of individuation, the escape route to get away from the conformism imposed by a caste society. But Kosambi is devastatingly critical of it all!

> The *Gita* with its brilliant Sanskrit and superb inconsistency is a book that allows the reader to justify almost any action ... Its many-faceted god [Krishna] is likewise inconsistent, though all things to all men and everything to most women ... most promiscuously virile of bed-mates; yet devoted to Radha alone in mystic union ... the ultimate manifestation of eternal peace, but the roughest of bullies ... the very fountain-head of all morality ... nevertheless ran counter to every rule of decency, fair play, or chivalry. The whole Krishna saga is a magnificent example of what a true believer can manage to swallow, a perfect setting of opportunism for the specious arguments of the *Gita*. It reflects ... a primitive level of production and its religion.

Does this diatribe make sense to the reader? Does it enable the reader to see the world as it is? This task is indeed very difficult if we are already wedded to a dogmatic school of thought.

Garg and Parikh (1995) see Indian culture in a manner different from that of the orthodox Marxists. However, their caricature of modern managers is inspired by the fundamentalist view that everything was right in ancient India and that current Western thinking has spoilt it all. But they are not consistent with the more patient empirical and quantitative findings of Kaur (1994), who found Indian mananagers optimistic and positive. The managers considered three factors as most important for success: (*a*) ambition, capability and broadmindedness, (*b*) beauty, peace and equality, and (*c*) work ethics. Inner harmony just scraped through as an also-ran, but family and caste affiliation did not count—an observation that may sound counter-intuitive but is consistent with other works in Indian villages (Reddy and Sekhar 1993). Kaur's managers were in no way frustrated as were those of Garg and Parikh (1995).

> **The Ten Tenets of Indian Managers**
>
> Success in beaten path; Power games; Manipulate organisations; Hold back innovations till backed by power; Not recognise merit; Aim at results and not quality; Expediency; Wait for orders and assignments; Reward oneself at any cost; Do not experiment.
>
> —*Garg and Parikh (1995)*

Lastly, we must now see the well-intentioned efforts of Chakraborty to bring Indian managers to their Indian roots. But one wonders if he has overdone his efforts to show how ethically inadequate the Indian manager had become due to Western influence (1995a: 110-11). Research indicates that Indians are more balanced than these caricatures depict. Data from a survey of the cultural attributes of 677 respondents from all over rural India (Reddy and Sekhar 1993) and another of ethical attitudes of 800 respondents (Sekhar 1995) confirm the generally more sympathetic account of Indian perceptions of ethicality.

Ethical Passions of the Young

A recurrent theme in this book is the similarity of patterns of human experience across nations and ages. If the managers grasp this universal commonality, they will find it easier to deal with persons from varied cultures. This is the critical socialising need of today's managers. Example 5.1 demonstrates this universality of ethical patterns.

EXAMPLE 5.1 **Susan Shapiro**

Susan Shapiro was a Jewish girl with a troubled record of brilliance and conflict. A masters in chemistry from the prestigious MIT, she joined the research division of Parke–Davis but left them in a huff as 'they were not ready for women as yet'.

She concluded this after 'being asked by a male to fetch him coffee'. Having to choose between a Ph.D. and an MBA, she whimsically concluded that a chemistry laboratory was the wrong place for an angry and violent person like her as she might destroy expensive equipment around her in a fit of fury. She joined the MBA programme of another well-known university at Michigan, but soon felt that 'marketing' was a manipulative, unethical subject. She liked finance and economics more. Further, being a Jew she would not work on Saturdays. During the summer she made a trip to Israel to work in the communal farms (kibbutz). As the Arab–Israel war broke out, she overstayed her summer-break working at a hospital in Israel. 'I had to do my duty,' she said. She joined back late at the university. All this resulted in her getting poor grades. She was in the bottom half of the class. She could not therefore get the placements she desired. Finance jobs were available to only those with higher grade-point averages.

Close to the end of the placement period she did get two job offers in marketing from pharmaceutical companies. They chose her primarily because of her M.Sc and her experience in Parke–Davis. Further, it seemed that by that time there was a swing in favour of hiring women. 'And I hope my being a Jew did not hurt, but one never knows,' she said.

She and 19 others who joined the firm were taken on training trips. She felt superior to the others who did not have a background of chemistry. She also thought that the training was superficial and not satisfactory. 'What can you learn just by seeing chemical plants', she said. She was also cold to all the information on the organisational structure of the company.

At one of the divisions of the plant she noted that the benzene concentration must have been a 1,000 in million parts, as against the US permissible standard of 10. It smarted her eyes. Her professor at the MIT never allowed the concentration in the laboratory to go beyond 100. He had told her that there is a positive correlation between benzene concentration and the incidence of leukaemia and disabled children. She asked one of the foremen in the plant why they tolerated it. He good-humouredly said that the posting to the plant was a sign-on job for temporary employees till they got permanent assignments. It was a transit camp so to speak. She complained of this situation to the personnel director back at the head office. He was more polite than the foreman but told her that 'she could not hope to change the company within a month of her joining and that she should not be a troublemaker'. She posed the question to herself, 'I do not want to continue in this job at the expense of people getting leukaemia and disabled children. What should I do?'

(This example has been adapted from Hosmer 1987.)

Analysis for the reader

It would be inappropriate to straightaway apply any one of the six descriptive-cum-analytical models of group decision-making or the strictly logical fivestep decision model in Chapter 2. Before we do that we must clear our minds of all analyses and be empathetic. These models would fail to capture the dilemma

Susan is facing. It is easy to show that her every step was irrational from the point of 'greatest good for the greatest number'. We would fail to understand Susan as a person responding ethically in a manner she understands.

We may see her as many of us are: emotional, well-intentioned but driven by the limited ethics of our intimate social groups. She is driven by her loyalty to her Jewish cause, or the codes of professional conduct learnt at the MIT. Overwhelmed by the emotional pull of these ethical ideals, she slips into rhetoric when she says her existence in the company would cause disabled children and leukaemia. This is an absurd assertion unless it is meant to be a rhetoric. Her too-high an opinion of her place in the universe is obvious to all except herself. This ego is resulting in her complete loss of a sense of humour. The *Bhagavad Gita* addresses itself precisely to this undesirable emotional state. It appeals to people to look inward. The *Kural* also marks the damage one does to onself by the loss of one's sense of humour. Only after Susan gets over this state would she be able to pose the issues with clarity and find a happy outlet for her undoubtedly ethical instincts.

India as a Tower of Babel

It would be overambitious to attempt to survey the entire Indian culture in one sub-section of a chapter. However, we will attempt to suggest a broad outline of Indian culture as part of world cultures, keeping in view the values inventoried earlier.

Cultural studies are notoriously controversial, whether at the micro or macro levels. Studies at the micro level, either using quantitative techniques or qualitative 'thick' descriptions, can never be sufficiently conclusive for a country as a whole. Nevertheless there is some use for such studies: in describing how efficiency and work ethics are induced in a different way in the East (Kao *et al.* 1994), and aggressive individualism is eschewed in favour of gratitude and respectfulness. The most oft-quoted study on organisational culture and the difference between the East was the West was done by Hofstede (1996). He classifies cultural attributes into a four-by-four matrix.

1. Small power distance — Long power distance
2. Collectivist — Individualist
3. Feminine — Masculine
4. Weak uncertainty — Strong uncertainty.

If Hofstede is correct, the emphasis among the 29 values mentioned in Chapter 1 will undoubtedly be conditioned by these attributes. Hofstede argues with great vehemence that these cultural characteristics can be noticed only in behaviour, and that the superficial symbols used cannot capture them. Thus, two groups having the same symbol, say the sign of *namaste*—bringing the palms together—may actually have two different associated cultural attributes. He also believes that these cultural attributes would persist and cannot be changed for a long time. Hofstede's (1984) instruments have not been used in India to the extent that they yield reliable results. He has however classified Indians as comfortable in uncertain situations, but not so in the absence of hierarchies. They also think as 'I' and not as 'we'. America and Denmark are comfortable with the absence of hierarchy whereas Pakistan is uncomfortable with uncertainty.

Having said this, one must be clear that it has not been possible for any researcher to say with confidence where India lies in Hofstede's matrix. The reasons are simple. He will get all the varieties in India. Also, Hofstede's cultural attributes do not still disprove the commonality of ethical values that transcend these cultural trends. The superordinate ethical values as much transcend these cultural characteristics as they in turn transcend mere symbols.

We would therefore still attempt to understand Indian culture as a flesh-and-blood cover over a skeletal structure universal across human civilisation. Many would be unwilling to concede this universality. On the other hand, any intellectual attempt to grasp this universality is considered a wicked devise to hegemonise and suppress the underprivileged (Thomson 1961), as any attempt to recognising universality is usually that of a dominant people who force their thinking on others and attempt to obliterate the identity of the minorities. Ambedkar (1949) saw the concept of Indian unity as an attempt to impose Brahminic culture on the dalits.

In this philosophy of universality, let us contrast the contrary approaches of two famous Western thinkers. The first is the French social anthropologist Claude Levi-Strauss and the second, the Swiss psychologist Carl Jung. Both saw cultures 'holistically' and not piecemeal. But Claude Levi-Strauss (1963) believed that there were basically universal structures of the human mind which threw up similarities. Carl Jung on the other hand believed that stories and myths live in 'racial consciousness' as 'archetypes' and drive its members along predetermined lines. Thus in a racial consciousness, if there is aversion for entrepreneurship or a glorification of laziness, this tendency will prevail whatever one does. These archetypes must be recognised, otherwise they can cause social and personal disharmony. He glorifies the mystic cult of the irrational (Reed et al. 1954, Morgan et al. 1994). He also establishes a myth of the ununderstandability of different ethnic cultures of each other. It is an intellectual legitimisation of the biblical story of the Tower of Babel wherein different people killed each other as they could not understand each other. This was also quoted in support of the right reactionary Nazis.

Quite alarmingly this Tower of Babel approach has also been extended by the much-acclaimed leftist Birmingham school of England, to the 'micro-politics of small groups' (Nandy 1994). They recommend fragmentation of nations. The culmination of this philosophy is the events leading to the dismemberment of Bosnia. It must be amply clear to the reader that the book is closer to the way Levi-Strauss looked at the eternal features of human society. But it does not ignore the 'historical approach' implicit in Jung (Reed *et al.* 1954, Morgan *et al.* 1994) and Hofstede (1996). The need for sustenance of individuals and small-group identities is recognised as also the empowerment of those denied a voice for long (Ghosh 1996).

If we assert that all cultures are essentially similar, we may ask if there is any point in attempting to understand Indian culture as distinct from others. Yes, there is a point. Even as we note the similarity in basic structures, a manager would benefit from understanding the dissimilarities; these could be in the flesh-and-blood cover of the basic skeletal structure. One could see some point in Carl Jung's observation without going overboard on the ethnic mystiques as in Aurobindo.

The exaggerated overstatement of the uniqueness of Indian culture comes from two extreme positions. The first is of the Western thinkers who have attempted to subvert it for imperialistic purposes. The second is from xenophobic Indian thinkers who are usually associated with the fundamentalist and feudalist right. We should beware of such exaggerations as also of being biased by the compulsions of the leaders of the national freedom movement to see total unity of values in India (Gore 1993). We must also avoid the contrary conditioning to establish a forced and fissiparous pluralism in India using the specious argument of caste, class and regional equity and justice (Ambedkar 1949 and 1950, Ghosh 1996).

The Ethnic Mystique of India

India profoundly differentiated from all surrounding cultures ... with great richness of variation but with a general unity.

—Aurobindo (1992: 379–392)

In believing we are a nation we are cherishing a great illusion.

—B.R. Ambedkar (1949)

India Seen as a Complex Challenge

This somewhat discursive review of Indian culture roughly seems to yield the following trends for India:

1. A finely developed system of individual psychological adaptation to society through introspection and minimising distortions born out of ego.

2. A vast repertoire of epics, fables, stories and legends which are on the whole predisposed towards bonhomie, truthfulness and trustworthiness. These can be learnt within the family. But this bonhomie could prove to be fragile under the pressures that will be described later.

It must be recognised that there has never been any common culture in India.

—B.R. Ambedkar (1950)

3. A healthy suspicion of institutionalised ethical dispensation which no authoritarianism can crush, typically in the spirit of Kabir, the Indian poet-saint belonging to the weaver class of artisans.

4. A great tolerance towards ambiguity and uncertainty, quite often wrongly understood by superficial observers as fatalism. Concentrating on the art of the possible is different from fatalism.

5. A formalised blueprint for 'organisational ethics' of two kinds, both highly stylised and idealised versions of the operations of a despotic state. The first is centralised, manipulative, oppressive and based on mistrust which can be euphemistically described as 'realistic'. This is typically as in Kautilya's *Arthashastra.*

The second is based on 'decentralised and delegated operations', benign and idealistic, working on cautious and guarded trust, as in the Dravidian traditions of the *Thirukural.* The British followed more or less the Kautilya model during their imperialistic rule over India. This decentralisation had conflict-resolution mechanisms, well-practised as in the *panchayat* systems. These were however severely constrained by the power structures of caste.

6. A difficult set of boundaries to communication among people, created by a racial consciousness fractured into a thousand sub-systems, divided now by caste, class and gender. They are now desperately trying to come to terms with the universal racial consciousness. This gives rise to a persisting feeling that 'we' are ethical, but 'they' are not. This also leads to breakdown of trust, and the paradox of 'awareness unaccompanied by action' (Rao 1996).

7. The near-total absence of the concept of a participatory process in decision-making with the people. This was expected of pronouncedly despotic structures, benign in their idealised versions, but by and large oppressive in most cases in reality. One can be discerning and see that the first four features would go well with the ideas we have developed so far in the book. Bardhan (1996) argues that the fifth feature was a positive one which has been allowed to go wrong by muddling up and substitution by a bureaucracy which was neither here nor there. 'It substitutes tyranny with banditry,' he says. The last two features are by and large hindrances. These past trends in Indian traditions have undoubtedly been shaken up by two developments:

1. The new awakening with the ushering of the Indian Constitution
2. The more dynamic contacts with other cultures and nations

These two influences spell new problems in applied ethics, harmonising differing signals from the five categories of institutions: market systems, law, family, professionalism and traditional cultures. The ethics of rights which were suppressed in the autocratic regimes of the Indian past would come on their own, hopefully balanced by the ethics of duties.

It seems indisputable that psychological processes for socialising individuals in society are one of the fundamental features of ethics. In this

Indian traditions are rich in technique and cannot be ignored. It would be important to separate these techniques from those which flow directly from the undemocratic, unegalitarian and exploitative features of the Indian past. Seen in proper perspective, Indian techniques are effective means to develop from the infant stage (Stage 1) to the fully mature stage (Stage 6) in Kohlbergh's schema. Spiritual thinking may see this as a prelude to Stage 7—the transcendental stage. The book does not dwell on that stage but has attempted to show that there is a common path for both streams up to Kohlbergh's Stage 6.

APPENDIX 5.1

Hymns for Harmony

This exercise closely follows the model of the ethical training methods developed by Chakraborty (1993a) and is based on the idea that a mind in harmony with nature and also reflective, is well poised for stimulating ethical clarity. The session has a set of hymns and songs to 'tune in' followed by mental exercises.

> Death or fear I have none Nor distinction of caste Everywhere I exist I am Siva I am Siva
>
> —*Shankaracharya, 8th Century* AD

Chakraborty usually commences the exercises with the well-known hymn 'Shivoham Shivoham' from Shankaracharya. It is based on the concept of divinity of all humanity and the universe. This expounds the philosophy of Advaita or Monism, no different from the philosophy of another great Western philosopher and ethical writer, Spinoza.

> All things are in God and follow from necessity His essence
>
> —*Benedict Spinoza (1898), 17th Century* AD

I however use the exercise to invoke an ethos closer to the present needs of the Indian managers. The exercise establishes an Indian identity. It recognises the growing need for power to deal with other cultures with a resilience born out of the understanding, strength and pride of being an Indian.

One must choose the music and lyrics most appropriate to the audience and the desired ethos; a wrongly chosen piece could jar the spirit and spoil the ambience.

My modification of Professor Chakraborty's methods is suited to a class of management students from all over India, with varying cultural and religious backgrounds, including the most Westernised to the hard-boiled traditionalists, the affluent to the poorest, and the conformists to the dissidents.

The modification is essentially in the choice of music and reduction of the duration of the meditation. If this exercise were to be done by a Western audience, young or old, the music has to be appropriately altered. It is not necessary that the music need be only classical or related to any religious ritual, though religious music is usually more adaptable for meditation. After the music, the mind-stilling exercise starts.

Step 1 *Breathing in the good and breathing out the bad*
This step is for you to consciously enhance your positive ethical pro-pensities. It is preferable to do this on a near-empty stomach. Completely relax either in a squatting position or in an erect chair. Loosen any tight clothing you may be wearing. Recollect dispassionately your good and bad qualities. Commence breathing slowly through one nostril, using your finger to close the other nostril. Breathe out a little quicker. As you do so, suggest to yourself that you are breathing in the good and breathing out the bad. When the rhythm is established, slowly revert to normal breathing. Sit still for a minute and await the next step.

Step 2 *Cerebral deconditioning*
Drain your brain of all thoughts by imagining that the top of the brain is open. Get into a mood of total serenity.

Step 3 *Getting beauty into the brain*
Imagine the awesome beauty of nature. Fix your mind on some inspiring sight, say, the lovely glow of the sun. Slowly allow this beautiful image to sink into your brain.

Step 4 *Getting the beauty to enrapture the entire self*
Allow your heart to rejoice in the beauty and enrapture your entire self.

Step 5 *The spirit of camaraderie*
Imagine you are sharing this wonderful feeling with the entire humanity; at this stage do this as an abstract compulsive thought without particularising individuals.

Step 6 *Translating bonhomie to work situation*
Convert this exuberant bonhomie to your usual work situation. Imagine yourself working with cooperative joy.

Step 7 *Relapsing into everlasting peacefulness*
Gradually slide from the work situation to everlasting peace felt by your entire self.

Step 8 *Return to normal*
Slowly come back to normal. Be silent for the next half hour.

Professor Chakraborty suggests a minimum period of 40 minutes exclud-ing the half hour of final silence.

I would however suggest a period suited to each individual as would come naturally to him or her. The effect would be best if it is adopted naturally and not as a self-mortification. A 15-minute period, including a short tuning-in period of ennobling and peaceful music to one's taste and cultural background, would suit most people.

SUMMARY

This chapter details two important streams of descriptions and analysis of socialising processes which develop trust as an ethical value. One is from the West owing to Kohlbergh and the second is the Indian process spanning Sankhya philosophy of two thousand years ago to Chakraborty. The chapter shows how the six stages of ethical development described by Kohlbergh are analogous to the stages described by Aurobindo as also to Chinese philosophy. Indian psychological traditions shorn of their exploitative features are shown to be very valuable in these processes, sought for by Kohlbergh. The superior understanding of psychological processes of ethical adaptation which Indian texts provide even for Western subjects is demonstrated in a case analysis.

A quick round-up of the stream of Indian cultural roots is provided. Some of the modern researches in inter-cultural studies are summarised only to reaffirm the essential oneness of human civilisation. The troubled soul of India is revealed as a tangled challenge to the Indian manager.

ISSUES TO PONDER OVER

- In your opinion, are literacy and higher education, necessary conditions for ethical development over the six stages of Kohlbergh and their analogous stages described by Aurobindo. Reflect on someone whom you know closely and intimately.

- Pick up the biography of anyone whom you admire. Have the greatest benefits to humanity necessarily come from those in Kohlbergh's sixth stage or beyond?

- Reflect on the following conduct:
  (a) Your classmate, whom you otherwise greatly admire for her talent, comes to a crucial test unprepared as she was attending to her ailing mother. She pleads with you to show her your answer-sheet for copying. This is against the rules of the educational institution. You feel that the rules of the institution are not flexible enough to accommodate such cases. You allow her to copy.
  (b) You have done badly in your examination. You suppress the information from your mother who has a heart problem. She has strained hard financially to educate you.
  (c) You had a serious neurological ailment as a child. The doctors say that you are all right now but there is no perfect guarantee that it will never recur. In your application for a job, which requires you to give your full medical history, you do not mention it. You know that if you do you will not get the job. Your parents will be financially unbearably burdened if you do not get the job.

CASE 5.1 **Air Tech Ltd**

Air Tech Ltd (AT) was one of the few companies in India chosen as vendors by Mysore Aeronautics (MA) for its newly designed aircraft. MA had pending orders from several foreign countries; these would lapse if supplies were not made in a year's time. AT was to supply the most critical part X.

MA had advanced money to AT but this would be settled against the final payment of the parts supplied only after the test runs by ace pilots. Before the actual flying tests were done, AT was expected to test the part in laboratory conditions. Sanjay Karlekar (SK), who was only 22, was on this job. This was his first job at AT. SK had chosen the not-so-popular subject of metallurgy at the Indian Institute of Technology (IIT), Powai, though with his marks in the entrance examination any branch was there for his asking. He had a reputation of seriousness and intellectual honesty at the IIT. He modelled himself on his professor who was a stickler for perfection.

His fierce loyalty to his subject almost turned into hatred when he found he was not getting any placements whereas others in electronics nowhere matching his abilities were getting cushy jobs. But this fleeting regret vanished when Dr P. Krishnan (50), the MIT-returned designer, chose him for AT. That was six months ago. Right now his cycle of happiness seemed to have again ended abruptly. Frustrated and angry, he felt that Krishnan was a false god whom he had worshipped.

Two months after he joined AT, he was checking on the design calculations made by Krishnan and found that there was an error. It meant that part X was still in the grey area between acceptable and non-acceptable limits of tolerance. He spoke about this to Col. Balasubramaniam (40), his immediate boss. He was an instrumentation engineer and SK found him lacking in knowledge about metallurgy. The chairman, Air Vice Marshal Nagaraj, PVSM, had advised him in his induction programme that the colonel had a lot of commonsense and he should heed his advice. The colonel asked SK to lie low on this. He explained the background of the order to SK. The chairman had assured MA that part X was perfectly safe and had been designed by one of the top scientists of MIT. Krishnan in a patriotic mood had offered to return to India and give his design to Nagaraj, sacrificing a spectacular career in the USA. This order was directly needed by AT; it had fallen into difficult days. 'A greenhorn even if educated in IIT cannot question a seasoned scientist,' said the colonel. SK had been used to a different culture and code of conduct in IIT, where students were encouraged to question ideas.

SK was hoping he had actually made a theoretical mistake somewhere, and Krishnan was right. He went about his laboratory tests. It involved putting the part through violent temperature fluctuations which would simulate the real-life ambience of the aircraft. SK's worst fears were confirmed when X failed the test. He panicked. The colonel suggested that the calibration of the temperature gauge may have been wrong and SK may be making the tests more severe than required. He said he would speak to the instrumentation engineer. The colonel advised him to try again. Very soon thereafter, SK was relieved that the part passed the test. The colonel suggested that it would be better if he had the test report approved by Ram Taneja (RT) (35) a senior hand; he himself was not technically well equipped to countersign the report. RT suggested SK take the full responsibility for the test readings and he would do the interpretation and draft the final report for sending it on to MA. The report was submitted to Krishnan for final clearance. Noting that the test results were signed only by SK, he asked RT to countersign it. RT wished to check the whole thing all over again and found that the temperature gauge had been tampered with. He questioned SK who confessed he had not checked it, but the colonel had given some instructions of which he was not aware. RT advised SK to be careful in accepting the colonel's advice lock, stock and barrel. The colonel had been prematurely retired by the army as he failed to make the grade of a brigadier. He was beholden to Nagaraj for this job. SK asked for the report back so that he could resubmit it. RK felt that things were going out of hand.

Whenever there was a serious problem it was usual for the officers of the company to seek the advice of Dr. V. Raman (75) who was retained by the company as Technical Advisor. He kept his confidence and was highly respected. 'He is like Bhisma Pitamaha of the *Mahabharata*,' said Nagaraj about him. RT took SK along with him for the meeting. Raman exuded warmth, but to their dismay, it seemed that as he tried to explain the situation of X, he was avoiding the issue. When they were leaving he remarked, 'Why do you worry, if the part is no good, it may show up in the test-run. If it does not, it is fine for AT. If it does, we will face the issue when it turns up. Technology progress is always a matter of trial and error.'

SK was horrified at the callous attitude of such a venerable person to human life. RT agreed with SK but he mentioned that test pilots were paid such astronomical salaries for taking risks that one need shed no extra tears for them. RT also confided to SK that he could ill-afford to displease Nagaraj. It was true that he could get a job anywhere, but these would not pay enough to support repayments of the substantial loan he had taken for his lovely new house in a posh area. Nor could it support his daughter's education at a famous public school at Kodaikanal.

He signed the test report as well as the readings recorded by SK giving SK no chance to correct them.

Nagaraj organised a public function dedicating part X to the nation. It seemed to have pleased everyone except RT and SK.

(This case though fictional has been discussed with senior scientists of the Air Force defence establishments. They have confirmed that the case is true to life.)

Analyses for the reader

1. At what stage of Kohlbergh's evolution are the different characters in the case?
2. If you were in Sanjay Karlelkar's position, what would you have done?

6

THE FICKLE MOB
Professional Councils as Intermediaries

Professionals Not Always Good

Respect for professional codes is an ethical value nurtured by human civilisation. In Chapter 5, we saw that the socialising processes of professionals came at the more advanced fourth stage of ethical development when the processes revolve around institutions other than the family; the horizons are widened at this stage. The term 'professionals' in this book underlines the concept of their 'selling skills' rather than being 'entrepreneurs' as owners of business. The later-day development of capitalism saw separation of ownership and management. Thus arises the need for professional ethics. Since owners are compulsively driven to make profits, they expect professionals to fall in line. Back-seat owners can be far more ruthless than those in the driver's seat. The professionals on the other hand may have other ethical considerations, which can cause considerable discord among them.

Professions can however be vastly different in the levels of skills they require as also the value attached to these skills by society. Some professions are bound to be esoteric and beyond common understanding. Others by their very nature may be more transparent and easier to understand. The services of some of these professions may be amenable to short-term assessment of performance, while others can be evaluated only by their results in the long term. Each profession also has a unique and distinct role in society. A combination of these factors governs the ethical interaction among professional groups and with society at large.

As societies undergo change, newer professions are born, while the older ones die out. The vast array of professions is illustratively classified roughly in the categories highly esoteric, moderately esoteric and comparatively transparent.

1. *Highly esoteric:* Doctors, scientists, accountants, classical musicians, knowledge engineers (the term is explained later in the chapter), etc.

2. *Moderately esoteric:* Engineers, lawyers, architects, jewellers, popular musicians, actors, etc.
3. *Comparatively transparent:* Schoolteachers, nurses, marketing professionals, advertising professionals, bricklayers, barbers, cobblers, potters, etc.

In this chapter, we will deal with four professions as illustrations—doctors, accountants, knowledge engineers, and public relations personnel. In several other places, we will examine the role of other professional groups, such as architects, engineers, advertisers and purchase managers. The special features of professionals working in multidisciplinary groups as members of the boards of directors of companies, are described as an important aspect of corporate governance.

Professional Councils as Builders of Trust

Is there something about these professions that would bring them together in 'councils' for collective action? Would this reflect on their ethics? Is this coming together a useful device to build trust? Are these councils more useful than formal law in governing ethical behaviour?

Fukuyama (1995) believes that such councils acting as intermediaries can bring about stability, efficiency and trust in society. However, he feels that they can, on occasions, also be dysfunctional. He cites Germany as having councils with, by and large, positive features while those in the UK, France and even the USA had played a negative role. The Institute of Chartered Accountants of India, for example, can ensure that its members do not falsely certify an account in a bid to get an abnormally high fee from those who they audit. It can then downplay the destabilising influence that greed can cause and provide transparent information to the public. Councils of advertisers can monitor and stem destructive competitive ethical abuse among themselves. On the other hand there are several instances of professionals banding together and holding society to ransom. Doctors in the USA ensure their continued monopoly by restricting fresh entrants.

Economic Compulsions Breach Idealism

In Chapter 3, we had discussed that one of the important requirements for ethical outcomes in a free market system is the symmetry of information between the buyer and the seller. The consequent complex interactions and the role an intermediary organisation can play could be illustrated in Table 6.1.

It is obvious that the more esoteric a profession, the less possible would it be to ensure absolute symmetry of information and more likely society would be to rely on intermediary organisations and peer pressures. This is typical of accountancy.

TABLE 6.1   **Conditions that Determine Ethicality among Professions**

	When professions can dictate ethics	When professions cannot dictate ethics
Nature of profession	Highly complex in knowledge base	Low or medium in knowledge base
People's perception of criticality	Medium	Very low or very high
Comparative value of service	Medium	Very low or very high.
Importance of client trust	High	Moderate

But if the buyers of the services of professionals have to pay too high a price to them, they would tend to get to know more about the profession and break the asymmetry of information. We have several instances now of patients demanding full details of their ailments and the line of treatment proposed by a doctor before they are willing to undergo treatment. They no longer allow a doctor to get away with a 'take-it-or-leave-it' approach.

On the other hand, if the 'value' of the product or service is comparatively low, the buyer may not mind discarding the product itself if he does not have adequate knowledge of its true worth. For example, if a jeweller is too secretive about his trade, the customer may just not buy any jewellery, since it is dispensable and not as valuable in his perception.

Thus in professions like medicine, accounting, audit, and architecture, ethical behaviour would be unique selling propositions. To take the example of an architect, his product costs are normally high. Also, the client has no means of verifying the quality of his products as the results would be known only over time. An engineering product, on the other hand, even if it is a consumer durable, would be 'found out' fairly quickly for its defects. Given the model in Table 6.1, we can argue that it is ethically beneficial for society to have intermediary self-regulating institutions among professions. We should however be cautious in relying solely on this mechanism as professional groups can have a tendency to promote themselves as larger than life.

Other supportive institutions are then necessary to complement the work of professional groups:

1. Judicial review, as is available in the Consumer Protection Act
2. Public discussion
3. Academic research
4. Free choice
5. A well-developed ethical norm for whistle-blowing (see Chapter 9)
6. A desire for decency which is the ultimate bedrock of pluralism

Professional Codes Not Magic Wands

Current ethical movements in the USA have seen an explosive growth of codes of conduct, with a touching faith in their appeal to regulate naked greed. Chakraborty (1995a) quotes from several American writers on ethics to show that this belief is not well founded. On the other hand, he argues that the socialising processes of more abiding and intrinsic strength are the psychological ones which Indians have practised for long. Olson (1965), an economist, argued from a different understanding that economic forces would overcome such fragile good intentions embodied in codes of collective action.

Current research however indicates that both Chakraborty and Olson may be overstating their case. Olson in particular has been severely questioned by several sociologists (Baron and Hannan 1994). Codes of conduct have a limited but salutary role to play. Vasquez-Paraga and Ali (1995) show in their study of sales personnel in Turkey that this is true of a culture that has a religious bias. A brief summary of several codes of conduct is provided in Appendix 6.1.

The Accountability of Accountants

The accountant, according to Ijiri (1975 and 1983), has two roles in organisations as the supplier of information—for decision-making and for accountability. He gives information to the manager inside the organisation, as also to different stakeholders such as employees, shareholders and creditors. Based on this information they take their own decisions. Ethical equity and fairness can be ensured only if there is no asymmetry of information, and the same information is available to everyone correctly and fully. The accountant's role in this is critical and ethically invaluable.

In the accountability model, which is distinctly different from the information-supplier model, his role is to provide information on the working of the accounter who is accountable to an accountee. The words 'accounter' and 'accountee' are coined by Ijiri (1975, 1983). The accounter is the agent of the accountee who is the principal. If we reflect on the basic concepts of the Law of Contract, the accountee will want information even if it is 'uncomfortable' to the accounter. The accountant will function as a score-keeper on behalf of the accountee. The accounter on the other hand will prefer to reveal as little information as possible that may reflect poorly on him. Control theory would show that neither too much information nor too little may be good for either the accounter or the accountee or the organisation as a whole; an optimum level has to be found. Moreover, the accountant can also be a problem-solver for the accounter rather than a score-keeper for the accountee.

When the accountee is the society at large and the accounter is the organisation as a whole, the scope of accounting would cover social accounting and audit, including environmental costs and benefits. Professional accountants will have to play a significant role in such social accounting in the future. The conflict of interests between 'ethics of privacy' and 'ethics of public disclosure' will then become even more acute. Caught in the crossfire, the accountant will have to contemplate on the dilemma of revealing the truth.

In both the above roles, more so in the latter than the former, the accountants and auditors have to protect themselves and be guided by their own ethical standards. Some of these norms can also be incorporated as formal laws, for it would be dysfunctional to leave these entirely to market forces (Chua 1986). They are never really free and often camouflage real and powerful struggles within and without organisations. On the other hand, many in the USA labelled as 'agency theorists and neoclassicists' have serious reservations on moderating market forces in any manner. In more authoritarian states like the Mauryan one in ancient India, it was considered unsafe to leave all this to 'voluntary norms'. Typically, the *Arthashastra* lays down several norms on them (Rangarajan 1987).

> All accounts should be in the form prescribed in the *Arthashastra*. Failure to do so will be punished.
>
> —*Arthashastra, 4th Century BC, 2.7.35*

The accountants in India often have difficulty in choosing an 'ethical path'. The stakeholder has often little option but to believe that the accountants have the highest code of ethics of truthfulness. He has to work on the assumption that the accountant is not under duress from either the accounter or accountee other than himself. Should the stakeholders rely on the state to protect the accountant from being coerced into not performing his ethical duties or should all of them jointly look up to the 'guilds'? The accountants in India have two guilds, both invested with powers of regulation, including penalty and withdrawal of powers to practise—the Institute of Chartered Accountants of India and the Institute of Cost and Works Accountants of India.

The ethical norms prescribed by these guilds have to ensure that their members do not display aggression or overzealous righteousness to strengthen their hold on organisations to achieve their personal career goals but discharge fairly the ethical role expected of them in accounting disclosures and audit practices. Appendix 6.1.B lists a brief resume of these norms.

Two American examples will help readers to understand the universal issues in the ethics of accountancy. The first is in respect of auditing and the second in respect of cost accounting.

EXAMPLE 6.1   A Fledgling Auditor's Threatened Career

This case from Hosmer (1987) has been condensed and rephrased. Roger Warsham had done on MBA a little late in life. He was 28 and had a wife and two children. He therefore had difficulties in getting placed. Further, he wished to do his Certificate of Public Accountants (CPA) to improve his career prospects. He could not get into any of the well-known firms. Only a small audit firm, Abramsons, with a local clientele offered him a job. They were having a tough time competing with bigger firms but prided themselves as offering personalised service to their clients, which the bigger firms could not offer.

In an audit of a manufacturing firm, Roger discovered that they had taken a loan from a savings fund. The firm was not doing well anyway. It was illegal for savings funds to advance loans to manufacturing firms. They could sanction loans only against mortgages of residential real estate. He checked the accounts of the savings fund, which had also been audited by him. He found that the loan association had not shown him the related file. He then attempted to reconcile the total of loans sanctioned as appearing in the accounts and the details furnished separately. To his horror he found that the figures did not reconcile. It was obvious that the savings fund had deliberately kept the information from audit.

He also found out that a wealthy lawyer was the president of the savings association and was also a director on the board of the manufacturing firm. He took photocopies of all the related papers, and took the papers to the partner who was furious. 'You put the papers through the shredder, or you will never get a CPA from Michigan or work in any accounting office in the state for the rest of your life.' Unlike in India, the CPA was controlled by individual states. This was not centralised in a national institute.

Analysis for the reader

What should Roger do?

There are several options open to him, one of which is being pursued in the analysis. The reader should also think of more options and pursue them to their logical conclusion.

Roger is in a comparatively easier position than his Indian counterparts. He could pursue his CPA in any other state. Knowing the competition among audit firms as also their vulnerability to scandals, Roger can shoot to fame by publicly exposing Abramsons. What would be the consequences? Will he get a job as an accountant elsewhere with a reputation of a whistle-blower? Is whistle-blowing a unique selling proposition for other audit firms? (see Chapter 9). The readers will find it remarkably appropriate to the ethics propounded in the *Gita* of the practical wisdom of action against unethicality.

Costing an Easy Tool to Cover Up

The two examples are abstracted from Horngren *et al.* (1994) and Taylor (1996) respectively. The first is based in the USA and the second in the UK.

They show how the subject of cost accountancy could get mystified to camouflage an unethical act.

EXAMPLE 6.2   **The Bulli Coal Company**

The Bulli Coal Company processes its coal in two stages. In the first stage, three products A, B and C emerge at the split-off point. A is processed further to make open-fire coke, B is processed to make closed-appliances coke. C is tar. Coal is bought at US $ 30. Every 100 tons costs US$ 1,000 to process up to the first split-off. The further processing of the output A out of the same 100 tons costs US $ 800. This cost for B is US $ 600. Every 100 tons produces 30 tons of open-fire coke, 40 tons of closed-appliance coke and 10 tons of tar. The sale prices of these three products per ton are US$ 100, 80 and 20 respectively.

Ralph Adams the manager tells Jim Murray the management accountant that he has struck a profitable deal with Kembla Construction that would justify their investment in a plant to convert tar to road tar. He hopes Murray will support him in his project. Without his support, the investment will not be sanctioned by the company.

Every 10 ton of tar yields 8 ton of road tar and the conversion costs US $240 for every 10 ton of tar. He now proposes to sell road tar to Kembla at US $ 50 per ton. Adams claims this gives him a 40 per cent gross margin. Ralph Adams ignores the cost of production of tar as computed by the company which distributes the pre-split-off cost among the products in proportion to their weights, i.e., 30:40:10. Tar would be shown to cost US $ 103 by this process. Adams ignores this costing practice and says that it is foolish costing as pre-split-off costs are not relevant for post-split-off decisions, quoting from an authentic book on Joint Costing.

He shows his version of costs as follows:

$$\text{Revenue} \quad \text{US\$ 50}$$

$$\text{Processing} \quad \text{US\$ 30} \quad (24 \times 10/8)$$

$$\text{Gross Margin} \quad \text{US\$ 20} \quad (\text{which is 40 per cent of US\$50})$$

Adams gives free tickets to Murray's wife and two boys for an important football match and arranges for the boys to be photographed with a football celebrity. This raises Murray's suspicion. He checks on the market price of road tar and finds it to be between US$ 65 and 75. He also finds out that Adams' wife is the chief marketing officer at Kembla which his father-in-law owns. What should he do?

Analysis for the reader

The maze of figures have been given deliberately to confuse the reader.

The accountant should be warned to be careful and wary of getting lost in involved calculations. He should learn to sift and analyse figures logically. He would then recognise that there is a gross loss of US $ 5 (50–30-25), i.e., 10 per cent if we take the opportunity cost of tar at US $ 20 per ton, i.e., US $25 for every ton of road tar (20 x 10/8). But this does not mean that the investment is not justified. Road tar could get a market rate of US$ 65–75. This would justify the investment.

He should also not commit the mistake of computing the cost of road tar starting with the cost of US$ 103 per ton of tar at the point of split-off. This figure is not relevant as it is a sunk cost once the decision to process the coal has been taken. The company may be using this method to value closing stocks of tar but this should not be extended to economic decision-making.

If Murray were not clear in his mind, he could very well rationalise his acceptance of gifts from Adams and agree to the investment in the new plant. On the other hand, if he were self-righteous, he may use erroneous logic to prove that the investment itself was unjustified. The reader may like to go over the code of conduct for management accountants in Appendix 6.1.C, which requires competence, confidentiality, integrity and objectivity—qualities compatible with Indian ethical tradition. It is also a lesson for accountants to keep their eyes and ears open for relevant information. This situation is not unfamiliar to Indian cost accountants.

EXAMPLE 6.3   **Angela's Cost–Benefit Computations**

Angela was employed as a management accountant in a senior position. She had to evaluate the different options of the location of a drydock for her company, considering costs of sailing to the port, charter fees lost due to the ship being out of service, dry-docking fees and repair costs. The estimates had to be based on several assumptions. Her MD was interested in one location and Angela could easily justify that location as the best choice. It was difficult for anyone to go through the maze of computations and assumptions and disprove her.

This is a familiar situation for many Indian accountants—to get away with a lot by using twisted logic and blaming the assumptions handed over by someone else. Professionalism requires that the accountant should realise the importance of both values and knowledge and not misuse the trust reposed in him. The attitude of *nishkama karma* discussed in Chapters 2 and 5 is the key to ethical behaviour.

Profits: Charaka and Hippocrates

The ethics of doctors and pharmacists are very relevant to Indian managers. Business managers can have many interfaces with doctors and pharmacists during the course of their business. What is special about these two is that the managers are inevitably drawn into the ethical issues that originate from the relationship of doctors with their clients.

The history of ancient Indian medical ethics is remarkable for being so different from the callous medical ethics and the precarious doctor–patient relationship in the USA. Doctors in ancient India seemed to have been remarkably strong ethically not only with regard to people but also animals and plants. Indians were the first in the world to have first-class hospitals for animals (Roy 1991). In spite of this, the *Arthashastra* prescribed punishments against any unethicality that may slip through.

Medical ethics in India is under the stress of free-market systems. The ancient ethical systems had different sources of stress that did not affect the doctors, namely, the caste system and the exploitative economic relationships.

In the USA, 'every fifth case of personal bankruptcy is due to megasize medical bills' (Kothari and Mehta 1988). The ethics in the medical profession are far more complex than in other professions and involve wide-ranging ethical issues. Three features of the medical profession make it extremely sensitive to ethicality (Bal 1993):

1. The subject is extremely complex and it is not easy to measure the impact of any medical treatment except in the long term.
2. The knowledge is highly uncertain—no two doctors agree and the limits of knowledge are forever expanding.
3. On the interaction between a doctor and his or her clients, a balance between the two can be maintained only by ethical principles and not by the market.

Ethical dilemmas of specialised professions like doctors can also be handled through guilds, provided there are appropriate alternative safeguards, such as the Consumer Protection Act. The courts have been ambivalent in accepting the Act as satisfactory in restoring ethics. They are worried about the consequent breakdown of trust between the patient and the doctor. The Act has at last been upheld by the Supreme Court (*Indian Medical Association* v. *V.P. Shanta and Others LA 258 SC*). The Supreme Court has obviously found the Indian Medical Council ineffective in coping with the strong pull of the market systems towards ethical disharmony and breach of trust. The basic understanding of the Act is that the relationship between the doctor and the patient is contractual, i.e., legal and economic; these are products of the market systems as an ethical value per se. The courts were worried that if too much value was placed on this narrow way of treating the relationship, other ethical values that are much more important in this relationship would be lost sight of. The patient may distrust a doctor thinking that his treatment is conditioned by the doctor's need for profits, and the doctors may mistrust the patient and feel that they are laying a trap for them for claiming damages. A summary of the code of the medical council is provided in Appendix 6.1.A.

The medical profession and the drug companies thrive on the breach of principle no. 33 of the Code of Ethics of the Medical Council: that the public should not be misled on the nature of drugs. A visit to any rural area would reveal the extent to which useless and ineffective tonics are prescribed by doctors. Obviously, such prescriptions are at the behest of drug companies. The situation is portrayed in the case of Dr Console of the USA. The facts are from published literature (Nader *et al.* 1972).

EXAMPLE 6.4   **Dr Dale Console**

Dr Dale Console, former Director of E.R. Squibbs, one of the famous pharmaceutical companies of the world, created a sensation in the medical world in
1960. Testifying before the congressional committee (the Kauffer Committee),
he indicted the promotional campaigns of pharmaceutical companies 'for increasing sales through the exploitation of physicians and manipulation of im-
proper prescription of drugs'. He described their promotional technique as:

1. Providing a barrage of irrelevant facts the physician has no time or expert
   knowledge to examine critically
2. Following the maxim 'If you cannot convince them, confuse them'
3. Not only advertising useless products but also indicating the effective-
   ness of drugs beyond the range of their utility

He criticised the physicians' unhealthy and often corrupt relationship with
drug companies whose sole aim appeared to be to confuse the Federal Food and
Drug Agencies.

He left Squibbs in 1957, as he could not stand the moral strain of working for
them. Being morally conscientious, he destroyed all documents he had from
Squibbs which could have enabled him to indict the company specifically.
Since 1957, he grappled with the morality of his exposing the pharmaceutical
companies. He felt deeply for those who continued with the companies and
suffered similar pangs of conscience.

In 1960, the committee asked for evidence and gave legal protection to the
informers. Dr Console was relieved that his morality had been supported
socially. His evidence created a sensation. But he said that he did not feel
morally superior to other doctors. He was otherwise well established in his
private practice.

Analyses for the reader

1. Why is it that Dr Console could not use the platform of the US medical
   councils to speak out against the drug companies?
2. Is it ethically right for the US Congress to expect Dr Console to complain
   against his own company?

The Confucian Expert on Computers

One of the profound outcomes of modern computers is a branch of knowledge described as 'knowledge engineering'. It deals with ways to capture
human intelligence and the intuitive methods of problem-solving using
hazy and fuzzy databases. The discipline is designed to distil the knowledge
gained by an expert over long years of experience into systematic rules
which can be used by a computer. The computer can then simulate the
expert. Once this is done, the organisations are no longer dependent on the

expert and he can be dispensed with. If we follow the capitalist rules of the game, an expense which does not contribute to profit should be done away with. Thus the experts who have given their best throughout their lives can be dispensed with. On the other hand, experts who do not share their knowledge would continue in service. This runs counter to the professional codes that one normally follows, namely, that knowledge should be fully shared. Thus there is a conflict of ethical values between work ethics, compassion, respect for old age and dignity on the one hand, and profit on the other. The professional codes of those who can devise such computer software sit badly with the shark-eat-shark policies induced and encouraged in countries with rabid capitalism. It is quick to appeal to such knowledge experts that they should freely make available their knowledge. So did the Nobel Prize winning economist Harry Markowitz feel when he refused to copyright his software packages for portfolio management; he gifted it to the academic world. But that is not the normal way of the US world. Once this invention is shared, an unethical company may find the author dispensable. However, in a culture where Confucianism prevails, such a short-sighted policy will not be culturally acceptable.

The Profession of Image Building

Public relations managers are extensively used by modern business organisations to build a friendly network that can help business interests. There is however a growing feeling among others that public relations executives can never be accepted at their face value as they only build up facades for their organisations.

In a most unlikely move, the profession now feels that it should develop a code of ethics for its professionals that would re-establish their credibility. There are several versions of these codes, the most famous of which is known as the 'Code of Athens'. The gist of this is reproduced in Appendix 6.1.J. The First All India Conference of Public Relations Practitioners found it necessary to adopt this international code of ethics and make a bold bid to wipe off their image as fixers and manipulators. The Indian PROs have several difficult ethical situations to contend with. Example 6.5 is a typical true-to-life example.

EXAMPLE 6.5   **A Fallen Angel Among Devils**

Sushmita Ray had just joined as the Chief Public Relations Officer of a major public sector undertaking. Innocent by temperament and upbringing, she faced a peculior situation—her chairman wanted her to somehow persuade a well-known newspaper to avoid reporting on a controversial corruption charge against him and instead write a favourable editorial. Sushmita was not convinced that her chairman came out clean in the case. The newspaper on the other hand was willing to accommodate him if the organisation released a spate of large-sized advertisements. Sushmita had got this job through her husband's colleagues in the Indian Foreign Service. Her husband Subroto Ray had suddenly died leaving her with three children in a disastrous financial condition. What should she do?

Codes of Corporate Governance

There is a strong interest in recent times in India to establish a code of corporate governance for companies. Corporate governance etymologically covers the whole range of systems of management in companies. But in practice, the term is restricted to the role of the board of directors of the company and the auditors, and their relationship with the shareholders. There has been a flood of literature and case studies on this (Chandra 1995, Murthy 1996, Sharma 1997, Seth 1997, Bhagat 1997, Shroff 1997). A committee of the Confederation of Indian Industries (CII) headed by Rahul Bajaj has floated a draft code on this subject (*Business Standard* 1997a).

As mentioned in Chapter 4, the norms of conduct for the members of the board of directors are extensively dealt with in the Indian Companies Act. It is now being realised that legislation alone cannot ensure ethical conduct; self-regulation is a more vital part in market systems. The spirit invoked by codes that are voluntarily administered is much more important than a mere formal enhancement of ethics over the normative provisions of the law, even though this could also be attempted. Thus the Bajaj Committee of the CII has a stricter norm in the codes than in the Companies Act, and requires the director to resign if he does not attend at least 50 per cent of the meetings. He cannot also be a member of more than 10 boards (*Business Standard* 1997b).

The codes could say, among other things, that the directors should ensure equity among different groups of shareholders, among foreign shareholders and Indian shareholders, among the shareholders of different companies involved in a merger or acquisition (as discussed in detail in Chapter 11). The ethical duties of the nominated directors to all the shareholders and beyond the sectional interest that they may represent could also be covered. Transparency is another requirement. The underlying philosophy in all these efforts is to enhance the accountability of the members of the board to the Indian shareholders. An equally compulsive requirement—to look after the other stakeholders—does not emerge clearly and boldly in these efforts, whereas this may be equally important.

APPENDIX 6.1

Extracts from some Codes of Conduct

A. Codes of the Medical Council of India

The codes cover 33 principles (Jesani 1993):
1. General principles (nine principles)
2. Duties to patients (four principles)
3. Duties to profession (four principles)
4. Doctor–doctor relationship (two principles)
5. Duties to consultation (eight principles)
6. Duties in cases of interference (three principles)
7. Duties to public (three principles)

Among these 33 codes, the industry-related ones are:

1. Doctors should not misuse patent laws to withhold benefits from the patients.
2. They should encourage the pharmaceutical industry.
3. They should educate the public on the correct and ethical use of drugs.
4. They should follow the law related to drugs.

There is a list for 'misconduct' as well, e.g., refusing to perform a sterilisation operation on religious grounds!

The corresponding US codes have a stronger emphasis on patient autonomy and of course the misconduct of refusing a sterilisation operation does not occur.

B. Ethics for Indian accountants

The First Schedule to the Chartered Accountants Act is an attempt to legislate these norms. In three parts, the first is for accountants in practice, the second in employment and the third as a general one.

Part I For Practising Chartered Accountants
Misconduct of a chartered accontant is defined as:

Clause 1: If he allows any person to practise as a chartered accountant if he is not one.

Clause 2: If he pays any brokerage or fee out of his remuneration to a non-chartered accountant.

Clause 3: If he shares the profit with a lawyer or broker.

Clause 4: If he enters into partnership with a person other than a chartered accountant in practice and shares the fees with him.

Clauses 5, 6 & 7: If he advertises on solicits work.

Clause 8: If he accepts a position held by another chartered accountant without communicating with him.

Clause 9: If he accepts an auditor's position in a company and if he is legally prohibited from doing so.

Clause 10: If his charges are based on a percentage of profits.

Clause 11: If he engages in a profession other than chartered account-ancy without the permission of the Council.

Part II For Employees

Misconduct of an employee would be:

If he discloses the confidential information of his employer.

If he accepts gratification from a lawyer, broker or customer dealing with his organisation.

Part III For all

A person would be regarded as indulging in misconduct if he gives wrong information to the Council.

The Second Schedule lists misconduct in the auditing function. The more important ones are:

Clause 1: He discloses confidential information about his client.

Clause 2: He certifies a statement without adequate scrutiny.

Clause 3: He lends his name to any financial projections for the future of a company.

Clause 4: He does not disclose his interest in any financial report.

Clause 5: He omits to mention any important fact which he is aware of in a financial statement.

Clause 6: He fails to report any major misstatement in the accounts of his client.

Clause 7: He is grossly negligent in his work.

Clause 8: He fails to attempt to get adequate information from his client for certifying the accounts.

Chartered accountants are expected to follow the guidelines and standards of the Institute in auditing, accounting and disclosure. If the standards are manda-tory (some are only recommendatory), not conforming to or breaching these is construed as 'misconduct'.

The Institute of Cost and Works Accountants of India also has similar norms. Both these bodies have councils that are the custodians and administrators of these norms.

C. The code of American management accountants

The Standards of Ethics for American Management Accountants has four basic stipulations: Competence, Confidentiality, Integrity and Objectivity. It is significant that competence is part of the code. Other than the obvious directive not to accept gifts, etc., management accountants are expected to adhere to the truth even it be unfavourable to the company. Objectivity must always be maintained.

D. The code for purchase managers

The ethics of the National American Purchase Managers visualises the ethical obligations to employers, suppliers and professional colleagues. It is summa-rised below:

1. To provide justice to those whom they deal with
2. To buy without prejudices and get the maximum value for money spent
3. Subscribe to honesty and truth
4. Respect obligations
5. Avoid sharp practices

E. The engineers' code

The National Society of Professional Engineers has a code which requires professionals to:

1. Dissociate themselves from organisations that are of questionable character
2. Further the cause of public good
3. Avoid engineeringly unsafe ventures
4. Maintain confidentiality
5. Advise clearly the consequences if a technical opinion is overruled by a non-technical person

F. The chemists' code

The code prescribed by the American Chemical Society spells out a chemist's duty to the public, to science, to his profession, to his employees and his students in idealised terms. With an employer, he should behave as if the company were his own.

G. The lawyers' code

The legal code of lawyers in USA (Nader *et al.* 1972) distinguishes between the lawyer as an advocate and as an advisor. In the former role, he acts as an independent person and his ethics is to argue for his clients and ensure that he is given the benefit of the doubt in ethics and law. In the latter case, he is close to being an employee and his ethics is in advising ethically and lawfully. Once the advice is given, the client is responsible if he takes the wrong ethical action. In extreme cases the lawyer should withdraw from employment.

H. Code for marketing managers

A code of ethics for marketing managers is issued by the American Marketing Association. It includes:

1. *Basic guidelines:* Not doing harm knowingly, accurate representation of their education and training, following the laws in letter and spirit
2. *Honesty and fairness:* Serving customers, clients, employees, distributors and public, avoid conflict of interest, employ equitable fee schedules of payments or receipt
3. *Follow the well-understood principles of rights and duties in the process of exchange:* Products should be safe, communications not deceptive, in good faith, adequate processes for redressal of grievances

4. *Product development:* Safety standards, any component substitution to be advised to the customer, extra cost and added features
5. *Promotion:* Avoid false, misleading, high pressure and manipulative tactics
6. *Distribution:* No coercion, ensuring free channels, etc.
7. *Pricing:* Neither predatory nor rigged
8. *Market research:* Prohibit selling under the guise of market research, research integrity, confidentiality and privacy of respondents
9. *Organisational:* Avoid adverse organisational behaviour

I. Advertisement codes

The codes of advertisers have been issued by the Advertisement Council of India. There is much overlapping with the codes for marketing. Additionally, advertisement codes incorporate the principle that moral, aesthetic and religious sentiments should not be offended. Thus stereotyping on the bases of gender, ethnic group, etc., would be considered unethical. Second, advertisements should not directly and adversely compare products with those of the competitors. Third, rhetoric like offering to refund money if the product is not good should be avoided.

J. The Code of Athens of public relations practitioners

1. The core philosophy of the code is to uphold the Universal Declaration of Human Rights of the UNO.
2. It upholds the free flow of information.
3. It requires behaviour in a manner as to develop the confidence of those with whom they come in contact, whether clients or employers.
4. The practitioners must avoid ambiguous language and maintain loyalty to the clients and employers.
5. They must protect the interests of the organisation they serve and the general public.
6. They must never compromise on the truth due to other requirements.
7. They must never manipulate to create subconscious motivations.
8. They must never impair human dignity and integrity.

K. Code of Ethics of the Association for Computer Machinery (ACM)

The ACM has five canons. An ACM member should:
1. Act with integrity at all times
2. Strive to increase his or her own competence and the competence and prestige of the profession
3. Accept responsibility for his or her work
4. Act with professional responsibility
5. Use his or her knowledge and skills for the advancement of human welfare

There are detailed ethical guidelines under each of these canons (Johnson 1985).

SUMMARY

The word 'professional' is used more in the context of individuals who sell skills than in the sense of entrepreneurs. The tendencies in the ethical behaviour of the different professions in a market economy are analysed. The positive role of intermediary organisations ethically binding the professions together is explored. It is shown that such an intermediary organisation can have both positive and negative impacts. A fuller exploration of the ethics of accountants, doctors, knowledge engineers and public relations executives is provided. Codes of conduct for several professions are indicated. The recent movements on establishing a code of corporate governance are critiqued as paying inadequate attention to stakeholders other than Indian shareholders.

ISSUES TO PONDER OVER
- What are the situations that would induce professionals to follow ethical codes of conduct if they bind themselves in collective bodies?
- Pick up any advertisement in recent times which you consider unethical and examine if this unethicality could have been better prevented by law or by self-regulation by groups of professional bodies.
- Is a code of ethics formally adopted by even a well-meaning business firm likely to have a conflict anywhere with codes adopted by equally well-meaning professional bodies? In which industry and situations is it most likely to give conflicting signals to managers?

CASE 6.1   **The Computer Whiz-Kid**

Dr P. Rajarathnam, hereafter called Rathnam—a name by which he was popularly known—had a wide variety of qualifications that included a doctorate in petroleum engineering and a Master's degree in computer science. He was a well-known authority in the application of knowledge engineering in the field of petroleum refining. He was a professor at the University of Texico in Texas. In 1986, a team of high-level executives from Colorado Petroleum Incorporated (CPI), an oil company in the Gulf, was on a study tour of the School of Petroleum Engineering at Texico. They were highly impressed with the work of Rathnam, particularly in the field of knowledge-engineering applications to solve process problems associated with petroleum refineries. The sequel was a fantastic offer of appointment by CPI to Rathnam, which he accepted, little realising the master plan of his new employers.

Rathnam was the Chief Executive Engineer of their computer installations which were primarily used for geological analysis, planning drilling programmes and trouble-shooting refinery problems. Soon after joining, he was introduced to Dr S.C. Bose, the Chief Geologist, who became his close friend.

They freely exchanged experiences over many hours of professional discussion. Bose was a true scientist who did not hold back any knowledge. Rathnam soon knew all about Bose's methods of investigation and developed an expert system that embodied this knowledge. The top management of CPI supported this project beyond the expectations of the two scientists.

The news that CPI had decided to give Bose the golden handshake was a terrible moral shock to Rathnam who had no difficulty in identifying the cause— the much regarded knowledge base of his own creation. Rathnam pleaded with the top management to change their minds. He reminded them that Bose was a heart patient and would find it impossible to get another good job, and also that this action of theirs would result in many brilliant persons shying away from the company's employment. They did not take him seriously. Much to their shock Rathnam resigned from his job.

As a permanent resident of the USA, Rathnam could have returned there after his stint with CPI. But he did not intend to return to Texico though he was welcome there. He had just turned 56 and he could have worked as professor for at least another 10 years. He chose to come back to India in spite of the offers from several universities in the USA, as he expected to be more 'comfortable with the ethical climate in India'.

Dr Rathnam had offers from several institutes of management in India. He decided to make his choice only after acquainting himself with each of them for a period of two to three days. He told them all that he 'would like to belong to the growing segment of early retirees who spent their time and expertise to serve the society at large and educational institutions are the best media he would prefer'.

However, Rathnam soon started showing signs of disapproval of the things happening in India. 'The Indian world seems to have changed from my student days, and I see much petty dishonesty and a permissive ethical climate though not as ruthless as CPI but saddening nevertheless,' he said. He was disturbed by three problems. There was large-scale use of pirated software. This weighed on his conscience. Second, there was hardly any spirit of knowledge-sharing among computer professionals. Third, Indian systems had little protection for ensuring privacy of information. Admittedly, this would require very high costs but he felt that the price was worth paying.

In one of the institutes, he had a heart-to-heart discussion with Professor Kulkarni who belonged to his generation. Rathnam was further bewildered by Kulkarni's views. Kulkarni felt that the ethics of piracy must also be seen in the light of the ethics of fair pricing by foreign software manufacturers. But it seemed that the Indian Copyright Act was now tightened and foreign manufacturers had posted representatives who could help police raids to capture evidences of piracy. Greater liberalisation had also provided greater opportunities for equitable bargains by educational institutions. Some others felt that the Indian legal system was unequal to the task of regulating piracy as corruption could destroy all semblance of law and order.

As for the reluctance of many Indians to share their knowledge, he found most heads of institutions unable to do anything about it as computer personnel were in short supply with a high turnover. He had hoped that the Indian culture would have been able to reassure persons that organisations would not behave in the manner that CPI had with Dr Bose after getting all his knowledge. But nowhere did he find such a relationship of trust.

Lastly, he found most institutions unwilling to go all out to ensure privacy of information using foolproof systems; they attempted to ensure this only by a better code of ethics among computer professionals. But with shortage of personnel in the field, strict enforcement of this code was not always possible. Rathnam was wondering if he had indeed taken a wrong decision in returning to India, or whether he should now give up his earlier ambition of 'serving the society at large through educational institutions'. He could also go in for business to avoid all these hassles. Or maybe his entire rationalisation had been a facade to cover his overwhelming self-righteousness and inability to view ethics as a means of larger good than the application of rigid codes of conduct.

(The case is largely true to the happenings in India; the foreign incidents are based on reports in computer journals.)

Analyses for the reader

1. If you were Dr Rajarathnam what would you do?
2. Do you think professional codes for computer professionals need to be different in the USA and India?

7

NOTHING LIKE THIS
HAS HAPPENED BEFORE
Discoveries in the Nature of
Modern Organisations

Who Cares for Lost Sheep

Modern organisations emerging from late capitalism are seen as positive ways of synergising the ethics of individuals to higher levels of ethicality. The ethic that only 'small is beautiful' is not an absolute value. Modern organisations, generally not small, should not be condemned as prone to unethicality merely on account of their size and the consequent loss of the 'human face'. What is it that distinguishes modern organisations from the older ones? Size is not the only criterion; the crux of the difference is that they are creatures of the ethics of free choice, one of the values inventoried in Chapter 1.

People may come and go but organisations will go on forever. The most striking demonstration of this phenomenon is the innovative concept of ownership in the Indian Companies Act, which is similar to company regulations all over the world. The shareholders (the owners as they are called) can sell their shares and their ownership rights freely in the market. They can opt out of the organisation in exercise of their right to free choice (Chandra 1995). As transience of ownership is assured by law, the free choice of the other stakeholders in the organisation is also obviously available in theory.

But the information on the basis of which this free choice is made is usually incomplete at any given point of time. This pushes stakeholders to trust the judgement of others in the hierarchy of the organisation. The larger the organisation, the less complete is the information available to each member; hence, the more necessary it becomes for the hierarchy to give ethical signals for values through a system of rewards and penalties.

Complexity of Modern Organisations

What did the New Yorkers know about the care of the flock, the lost sheep and black sheep.

—C.I. Barnard (Ryan and Scott 1995)

On the other hand, the ethics of Gandhi is largely based on every person depending on his own conscience and not relying unduly on the consequences of his actions. Is it a position of despair that ethical decisions would get confused if they depended on second-hand messages of consequences arranged in Barnard's hierarchy (Douglas 1995)? Barnard viewed this Gandhian approach with disdain and contempt. He felt that the whole schema was derived from a totally different economic milieu and would not lead us anywhere if applied to modern organisations, a view we may not share.

Older Theories of Bureaucracy not Useful Now

Organisations of the type we are discussing are no more than a hundred years old. Their structures and relationships cannot be understood only from the older historical theories, Indian or foreign.

The earlier theories on management of organisations were typically those of the state; comparing them with modern organisations is weak and can be deceptive.

Ancient states had little participation from the stakeholders, whether they were benign as in the *Kural* or oppressive as in the *Arthashastra*. Even as late as at the end of the 19th century, the ideas developed in the *Arthashastra* are repeated by Weber (1947) in some form or the other. His ideas were also based upon the state functioning as a fair arbitrator, even as individual entrepreneurs played their role, convinced of the glory of private effort and reward. But the rapid developments of largescale industry and late capitalism has made most of their ideas inappropriate and unhelpful in understanding the dynamics and ethics of organisations (Kennedy 1994). We must therefore not go 'back to the wisdom of Kautilya', and instead be guided by the ethics preached by Evan and Freeman (1988).

The Old Order

Industrious producers, good men forming the elite, and high-minded men of wealth are required for the state.

—*Kural, Verse 733*

The New Order

Each stakeholder has a right to be treated as an end in itself and not as a means, and must participate in determining the direction of the firm.

—*Evan and Freeman (1988)*

New Visions of Institutional Economics

Owing to institutional economists, the last few years have seen major changes in the understanding of organisations or firms to fall in line with economic literature (Kenneth Arrow quoted in Williamson 1995). These have given rise to varying definitions of the expression 'firm'. The uncertain theories span several disciplines, mainly economics and sociology. The subject is in a state of flux, attempting to synthesise different streams (Baron and Hannan 1994). These developments are relevant for understanding the ethics associated with them. The ethical analysis of the origins of trust by Fukuyama (1995) is based on the economic concepts of Coase (1937) and Williamson and Winter (1991). They view firms as the means of reducing transaction costs. If every activity is exposed to 'market systems', it would increase transaction costs. Firms shield internal transactions from market systems that are based on 'firm contracts'. Transaction within firms do not use firm contracts but quasi contracts allowing considerable flexibility of operation. Thus the boundaries of the firm are defined by the nature of the contracts: quasi contracts are inside the boundaries and firm contracts outside. Inside transactions extensively rely on ethical values other than market systems: the ethics of efficiency and values such as trust, compassion and dignity (Reddy and Sekhar 1993).

Cyert and March (1962), on the other hand, look at firms as common ground for a 'coalition of interests' of shareholders, lenders, borrowers, sellers, consumers, employees and the state. This conceives of a more open system which does not discriminate between the relationships with the shareholders, employees and other stakeholders. This also calls for a strong interplay of ethics other than that of market systems in all activities.

The third way is that of agency theorists. They look at firms as clusters of principal and agent relationships (Ross 1973, Eisenhardt 1989). The corporate entity of a firm is the principal and the managers its agents. Agents must be delegated powers but must also be monitored to ensure that they do not indulge in opportunistic behaviour. It is important to note that the principal in this theory is not the individual shareholder but the corporate entity. This means that the managers are trustees of institutions (with multiple constituents) rather than merely attorneys for shareholders (Dodd 1932, Donaldson and Preston 1995).

The Deceptive Methods of Science

One approach to a managerial utopia is to construct an organisational structure much like a civil construction, based on mathematical formulae. In practice the overall objectives of the organisation are developed, the different processes logically flowing out of the technology are studied and a structure is developed for optimum performance in fulfilment of the ethics of efficiency. One of the proponents of this approach is Thomson (1967). In this approach, the organisation can be seen as consisting of three types of departments: the technical core, the buffer and the boundary-spanning. Weber (1995) has researched the consequences of this division on the behaviour of the technical core to respond only to rules and law. But the behaviour of those in the boundary-spanning departments is more caring and ethical. They do not need a legal whipping stick. They get feedback on their unethicality, quick and strong.

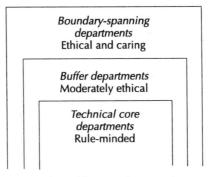

(Adapted from Weber 1995)

Weber's research has shown that it is useful to sometimes assess the ethicality of the different branches of the organisation and see if inadequacy of information leads to any loss of ethics. It would be incorrect to conclude from Weber's work that there is an inevitability in the unethicality in core departments like production and an ethicality in boundary departments like sales and purchase. This would be taking a mechanistic view of organisations and human behaviour. While there is need for greater pragmatism in these methods, they however provide some insights and raise some warnings and concerns.

The Battleground of Power and Class

The non-marketing systems within a firm are more fully explored by the sociologists (Baron and Hannan 1994); they however prefer to call the firm an 'organisation'. Ramaswamy (1984) and Pande and Pathak (1996) explain two existing alternative theories of 'power' in industrial relationships. Both are contrary to the collaborative features of the ethics of distributive justice and democratic discourse. Both look at three segments: the employers (capitalists), the employees (workers) and the state. The Marxists see the whole issue as one of conflict between two groups, the capitalists and the workers. The state could be a representative of either of these classes. In the second theory, that of the pluralists, there are several pressure groups, distributed over the employers, employees and state. They jostle together in various coalitions all the time. Both theories believe that each group is pursuing its rights and seeking an optimum compromise. The concept of pluralism pursued so far is one of allowing everyone to choose their own path and work for positive collaboration. The concept of pluralism used in this theory is that each group should fight for its rights and in this process the greatest good for the greatest number will emerge. The emphasis is on rights rather than on duties.

As we can see, some sociologists like to see organisations as battlegrounds for disputes, contentions, conflicts and power struggles, all in the process of developing self-esteem and self-fulfilment of social groups of society at large (Pande and Pathak 1996). We on the other hand see the same goals being achieved through social cohesion.

Ethics as the Last Resort

All the models we have discussed so far show the need for a full and total involvement of several ethical values other than market systems and law. These would mainly be the dos of ethics. We have come far enough to appreciate the difference between law and ethics and between the dos and don'ts of ethics. We must however recognise that these thoughts would not enable us to decide if ethics is the last resort or the first feature. That is largely a matter of personal choice.

Stakeholders First and Shareholders After

One of the most important features of a modern joint-stock company is that the shareholders have the total freedom to sell their shares in the market. They would do so if they found that their interest lay somewhere else. Thus if opportunism is the characteristic of an unethical relationship, such unethicality is fully legitimised by law. In such a situation, the shareholders would have no particular

> **Stakeholders First**
>
> The very purpose of the firm is to serve as a vehicle for coordinating stakeholders' interests.
>
> —*R. E. Freeman*
> *(Donaldson and Preston 1995)*

ethical right to bend an organisation to their benefit at the cost of others who have stakes in the company. The remarkable feature of the property rights of shareholders is that their opportunism can do little damage to the company as the transaction of buying and selling shares does not affect the financial books of the company itself. Recent theories on the ethics of organisations have taken full cognisance of these aspects. They would thus put the interests of the stakeholders first, the shareholders after.

The discussions so far have centered around rights. A more positive way of looking at the ethics of organisations is to see them as effective vehicles for the ethics of duties of the managements and stakeholders. But one must beware of the positive ethical propensities of individuals getting lost due to unseemly conflicts that may emerge from the inadequacies in organisational structure and style. Niebuhr's (1932) dismal prediction that individuals tend to deteriorate ethically in groups (Henry 1995) was discussed in Chapter 2. If Niebuhr is even partially correct, there is a greater need to ensure that this does not happen.

Mahesh (1993) has dwelt at length on the greater role of the employees as the main stakeholders. Having the most long-standing and abiding association with the organisation, their skills are specially cultivated to suit the needs of the organisation. Unlike anonymous shareholders, they tend to be less opportunistic. The implications of this understanding for human resource management is discussed in Chapter 7.

Finally, Kitson and Campbell (1996: 110) see competitors also as stakeholders. Thus, competitors could cooperate with organisations to mutual benefit in minimising the costs of research and development, etc. Several strategic alliances in the developed world have used this concept effectively.

Managers Be Not So Proud

We now come to an important question for managers in organisations: Is the ethical role of a manager really to be an arbitrator between the conflicting interests of the different stakeholders, and do so in an absolutely transparent manner? Cadbury (1983) claims that this is precisely the ethical role of a manager in an organisation. Transparency would be required if we have to work within the value framework of distributive justice. It would not be a precondition if we follow the path of egocentricism advocated by Ayn Rand (1968) or Nietszche (1924). All that could happen under this framework is that if a leader is no longer found good enough, he can be rejected. Let us now pause to consider if managers should therefore feel so important as to become arrogant; in reality they could.

The Risk of Conformism

Two cases in the book (7.2 Satyakam and 8.1 Excellent Pesticides) describe the risk of self-consciously ethical organisations falling prey to conformism. This damages several of the ethical values we have espoused in Chapter 1. Sinclair (1993) argues that the proclaimed ethics of many high-profile ethical organisations serve the interests of only those in power. They can undermine ethical conduct by removing dissent and rational debate on issues. Some highly ethical organisations in India fumbled with the passage of time. Some of these were founded by the gurus of modern India, Tagore, Aurobindo, Gandhi and even Swami Vivekananda who had apparently a keen managerial intuition.

Tagore's Shantiniketan is in complete doldrums now and has stopped producing outstanding students or scholarship. Aurobindo's asharm is riddled with strife between two warring factions. Gandhi's ashram at Sabarmati in Ahmedabad witnessed the management, with the help of bayonet-wielding policemen, forcing old inmates to vacate the accommodation given to them long ago by Gandhi. The Ramakrishna Mission founded by Swami Vivekananda had major strikes. Also, some of its hospitals were reported to be running very badly. Every one of these debacles could be traced to the inability of the organisations to creatively use dissent, even though moral values were otherwise respected in form, if not in spirit. Thus the full potential of the undoubtedly great contributions of these founders of modern India could not be realised.

Get On, Get Honour, Get Honest

Looking at organisations of varying sizes, would a unit in the small-scale sector inherently tend to be less ethical or more ethical? Several Indian managers who responded to a survey by Giri (1994) felt that the small-scale units which are usually on the brink of survival cannot afford the luxury of ethics. On the other hand, big companies cannot afford to be unethical. They feel that one must first get on with their task, then achieve honour and only thereafter can they afford to be honest. Kanitkar and Contractor (1992) show in their study of small women entrepreneurs that corruption is the most difficult problem they have to handle. The only way some women can cope with it is to 'contract out corruption' through agents. On the other hand, several other respondents of Giri (1994) believed that ethics is the main sustenance of small entrepreneurs. Kanitkar (1995), based on a second extensive survey of micro-level rural entrepreneurs, has not reported a single case where success can be attributed to unethical practices. It is well known however that the wage rates in small-scale units are below those of bigger units. This by itself cannot be the damning evidence of bad ethics; some wages is better than no employment and no wages (Donaldson 1996). On balance, one may say that in a freer economy the chances of survival of the small units that are ethical are higher.

The efforts of the USA, true to its ethical philosophy, have been to ensure that organisations do not cooperate with 'negative economic and social consequences'; their anti-trust laws are intended to ensure this. The Japanese, on the other hand, have been experimenting with efforts to increase cooperation and collaboration among small businesses for 'positive purposes'. The cultural motto of one such experiment, the Yokohama Venture Business Club, is 'Bring a cup of water to take back a cup of water' (Kanai 1995). Kanai describes the efforts of this club to cope with the 'seven paradoxes': self-help v. dependence, the strength of weaker ties, diversity v. homogeneity dilemma, redundancy v. reliability, the greed of professionals v. the help they can give as experts, formal v. informal, expansion v. problem of over-size. The ethical balance the Japanese are attempting in this effort is much beyond market systems and ill-fits American theories. Lunati (1996) also suggests similar ways of cooperation. These can help in ensuring that one can be honest even when one is small.

Self-indulgent Myopia of On-the-spot Moral Rules

Another danger to the ethical decision-making process is the moral standards set to convenience—the on-the-spot moral rules—factors that influence decisions in the conventional marketing theories that believe in maximising profits (Messick and Bazerman 1996).

The Myopia of the Self-righteous

The human mind has an infinite capacity to trick itself.

—*Messick and Bazerman (1996)*

These complex factors tend to generate self-seeming, simplistic, rules, giving a false sense of superiority and self-righteousness. Thus, Price

Waterhouse was publicly condemned as perpetrating itself gender exploitation whereas it had thought of itself as ethically superior. Such situations arise where sychopants are encouraged in organisations and the chief executive turns out to be wearing the emperor's new clothes! Many aggressively moralistic organisations in India, when examined from close quarters, would fail the ethical test. On the other hand, the less self-conscious may pass it.

Social Responsibility that Blesseth

The social responsibility of business is a contentious subject. It must be understood as extending far beyond voluntary and philanthropic activity (Ferrel and Freidrichs 1994), and revolve around ethical rather than legalistic behaviour. Friedman (1962) holds that Ferrel and Freidrichs's definition is useless for practical action; however, at worst, it is a useful reminder. At best, an organisation following this policy may actually end up making more profits (Chapter 2).

> To maximise positive impact on society and to minimise negative impact . . .
>
> —*Ferrel and Freidrichs (1994)*

SUMMARY

This chapter describes recent theories of institutional economics, organisational theory and sociology as springboards to a new ethics of modern organisations. Moving away from a complete subordination of organisations to shareholders, it shows why other stakeholders could have higher ethical rights on organisations. It shows modern organisations as vehicles of enhancement of the ethics of the participating individuals, and different in purport and structure from organisations a hundred years ago. Therefore, it warns against using older theories of organisations to understand the role ethics could play in modern organisations. There is no reason to believe that either the small-scale or large-scale sectors would not normally gain in profits if they follow ethical practices. There is also a warning against ethical self-righteousness and ethical conformism as the usual foibles of many self-proclaimed ethical organisations. This results in their ultimate collapse.

ISSUES TO PONDER OVER

- After reading this chapter would you be inclined to discard Gandhi as an ethical guide?
- Do you believe organisations normally enhance the ethicality of participating individuals?
- Would you consider it possible to avoid prioritising different stakeholders in real-life managements? How is it normally done in your experience?

CASE 7.1 The Parable of the Dark Child of Narhi-La

The events of the three weeks at far-away Narhi-La had a deep significance for Chandra in understanding and resolving the ethical discord he was having with his organisation for the past two years. He was the Export Manager of Mansukhani and Sarkar and Company who were in the business of handlooms and handicrafts. They had exclusive boutiques in several urban centres in India and a few abroad, all making large profits. Their two directors, Mrs Mansukhani and Mrs Sarkar, had close connections with politicians and were therefore able to garner a lot of government support for their company, in the form of subsidies and other benefits. Whereas they projected themselves as great social workers, helping the preservation of ancient crafts and skills of the country, when it came to sharing profits with the primary producers, Chandra felt that they were harsh and unethical. Further, they operated through middlemen, who they knew took big cuts before paying the primary producers.

Mrs Sarkar also had an embarrassing habit of lifting items she liked from the showroom of the middlemen and not ever paying for them. Some of them complained to Chandra, but did not pursue the matter as Mrs Sarkar had powerful politician friends. Chandra often felt like resigning from his job. But his wife always dissuaded him. 'You cannot expect every person in the organisation to have exemplary ethics. As long as they are doing good overall, you should turn a blind eye to their faults,' she said. Chandra was not sure if she said so only to prevent him from taking any disastrous course which would hurt her and their children. It was however true that the company gave him considerable freedom to develop a network of artisans in the deserts of Kutch in Gujarat and in the poverty-stricken Erode district of Tamil Nadu. Mrs Sarkar was invaluable in getting contracts abroad, and the company was free with its finances and could support a large turnover with sufficient credit arrangements. Admittedly, this large number of artisans who manufactured for exports through Mansukhani and Sarkar were much better off than the other artists of the area. A couple of them even managed a free trip abroad with government support and high-profile publicity. Chandra was in the last stages of clinching a long-term contract with an American party. He had sent them samples and a quotation. Before he went abroad to negotiate with them, he thought he should undertake a Himalayan trek, to spiritually recharge himself away from his mundane life at Mansukhani and Sarkar.

The trip had unexpected consequences. The group had a mixed crowd—geographers from Japan, a black American medical technician, a Norwegian journalist, Chandra and Dr Gulati, a paediatrician from Delhi. They were to assemble at Tehridun at Uttarakhand, transported 350 km by jeep to Jyoti Math and than trek to Narhi-La 150 km away. After acclimatisation at Narhi-La they had to go to the Chinese border.

Narhi-La had a scanty population of 30, mostly the aged. The able-bodied had all gone to the plains. Five-year-old Lakhan was one of the few children whose parents had gone to the plains for work, leaving him in the care of his old grandmother. Unusually dark for a child from Narhi-La, he was held in reverence by the villagers as in their mythology the gods when they came to earth were dark. The team members became great friends with Lakhan.

The week's trek along the border was spiritually elevating for all the members of the team. They reflected on the follies of humanity inflicting violence on each other. The spirit of the mountains seemed to help them in communicating with each other: without sound, without words and without language.

Back at Narhi-La they were horrified to find Lakhan in coma due to high fever. Lakhan's grandmother was wailing. The whole village was in panic. The team was rudely awakened from their spiritual euphoria to the realities of the world. It seemed the spiritual centre of their world was now in Narhi-La. Everyone's first inclination was to see Lakhan through his difficult days and leave only after he was well. But each had second thoughts.

How could Dr Gulati miss his sister-in-law's wedding? How could the Japanese miss the conference at Beijing, where they hoped to present an important paper? How could the American leave his wife for so long, when she was battling with the task of looking after his old mother? Chandra had this important meeting in New York which was the fruition of two years' effort to get a good deal for his artisans. The Norwegian had a little more time as he could mail his story a little later. But what could he do sitting there and watching the child die. Chandra found that everyone had devious ways of legitimising their ethical stand of not wanting to go full length in their ethical duty. They were however willing to do their best within their self-imposed constraints.

The Japanese rummaged in their rucksacks and brought out some medicines, luckily good enough for Dr Gulati to revive the child. Dr Gulati remembered he had a friend at Tehridun who was a good paediatrician. The Norwegian said that his wait would be worthwhile if he would carry the child to Tehridun, first on his back to Jyoti Math and thereafter by motor transport. The American remembered he had noted the telephone number of a medical laboratory at Jyoti Math where some help may be available. Chandra would monitor the entire operation by telephone from New York and Bombay, and support it with money. All the team members gave whatever money they could spare. Everyone seemed a little relieved but not entirely free from a feeling of guilt. But the plan worked.

Lakhan was nearly cured when the Norwegian left him at Tehridun in the care of the doctor. Chandra came back after a successful trip from the USA and organised the shipment. He then went to Tehridun, picked up Lakhan and dropped him back to Narhi-La. He felt that the entire episode was a clear answer to the worries he had had with the ethics of Mansukhani and Sarkar.

Analysis for the reader

What do you think was the answer which Chandra found in this episode? (See Chapter 2 on ethicality of groups and the views of Niebuhr and Kautsky.)

CASE 7.2   **Satyakam Foundations**

Satyakam Foundations was often cited as evidence to show that honesty can pay in India. They were best known for the activities of their main subsidiary, Satyakam Housing, which was in the real estate business in Ahmedabad. A respected Gandhian wrote this about Satyakam Housing in a national daily:

'I was attracted by a tidy new set of apartments near Ashram Road, Ahmedabad, which had the builder's signboard—Satyakam. I found all the flats had been sold out. Later, I had to settle for another builder. I asked him if he knew Satyakam. They are honest, he said. This was little different from what a businessman normally says about his competitors . . . Later I saw some bold advertisements of Satyakam—We sold real estate without black money, satisfied all tax requirements, it said. Satyakam's rates are considerably lower than their competitors'. In a notoriously corrupt industry, Satyakam has deemed to take extraordinary risks, and has emerged as the single largest builder in Ahmedabad, without bribes and without passing on escalations to the buyers.'

The Gandhian praised Satyakam for taking risks. The economic journals however perceived passing on the costs of such risks by the management to the shareholders as unethical. Thus when Satyakam came out with a public issue, there were scathing attacks on the 'emptiness' of its claims of ethicality. The journals felt that it was a cover-up for inefficiency. Therefore, Satyakam had problems in getting the issue fully subscribed. But they persisted in their mission and ultimately the shares were selling in the secondary market at a modest premium. Much later, Satyakam proclaimed that in an annual general meeting, one of their prominent shareholders silenced the protests against moderate dividends by saying that they should be proud to be members of an honest company.

Philosophy of nobility and compassion

Ramdas Shah, the Chief Executive of Satyakam, spoke and wrote about his philosophy extensively. It is therefore possible to see the links between his beliefs and his actions. In one of his letters, he says, 'I have been deeply impressed by Ayn Rand's concept of the virtue of selfishness . . . it initiated my process of real self-development and discover the image of human potential . . . arrogance is inevitable for the emergence of leadership, but humility is inevitable for the positive functioning of leadership . . . Ayn Rand had failed to recognise that leadership qualities must be tempered with the quality of compassion.'

Consequently at a practical operational level, Shah believed in the great leadership potential of modern organisations for doing good to society. He also believed in instilling, even enforcing, plain living and high thinking on his executives. As the chief executive of a prosperous large company, he could afford luxuries and perquisites but he chose a modest salary and used only public transport for travelling on work. Satyakam attracted several highly talented persons for employment in spite of their very modest salaries, much lower than the market rates.

As a practical articulation of Satyakam's mission of compassion, they said that their corporate priorities had made them first take to housing and thereafter to energy management. They said that in the absence of any other better plan, they wished to go along with the priorities the government had been laying down in the recent past. They felt the direction of the Indian law was positive and they would endeavour to be one step ahead of the law in ethicality. They believed that the combination of nobility with compassion would surely not countenance acts of corruption, and that in the face of such nobility, they evoked a spontaneous admiration in the erring, corrupt officials who never dared to ask them for bribes.

Response to ethical probing

Ramdas Shah and his band of executives were so inspired by the grand vision of their ethical destiny that they were impatient with any efforts at ethical probing. 'Try to understand us first with sufficient study before raising irrelevant questions,' was one of their usual statements. A few instances of the issues raised with them by some and their first reactions are given here:

• On being asked if it would have been proper for Satyakam to finance itself with loans instead of shares, Shah brushed it aside as of no consequence. The question was an attempt to put in ethical perspective the criticism of the economic journalists mentioned earlier. A loan would have shifted the risks more fully to the management, as interest would have to be paid irrespective of profits, whereas shares would accrue no dividend if there were no profits.

• When asked if the image of ethicality was a unique selling proposition in the housing industry and could be a good marketing strategy, Shah saw the question as an example of the cynicism of modern management schools which would pursue ethics only as a means to make profits and not for its own sake. And yet in the ads for their engineering firm, the honesty act had been played down and only the technical qualities and high thinking of its executives was emphasised.

• On being asked if there was democratic discussion among the executives of the company, they saucily turned the question around by asking the meaning of democracy. They saw democracy essentially as the opportunity to choose the leader, than one of prolonged dysfunctional debate.

• On being asked why they employed workers through contractors instead of directly, they said the contractor had better vibes with them. When further asked if this is an indication of some alienation, they said that the question was misconceived and did not recognise that Satyakam had made a large number of them permanent and given the best perks to its workers. They would still not squarely face the fact of differential treatment from their executives.

• They believed in selection of their executives through family connections rather than open recruitment, which is the more universally accepted ethical norm. They would also have fast-track and slow-track careers for the executives.

When asked about the effect of both the practices on the morale of the executives, they said that this was accepted.

• They believed that they should not distinguish between the personal and official lives of executives, and therefore took the responsibility of correcting imbalances in either of them. Did this give the executives a feeling of oppressive interference? They said they did not believe it did.

• They believed that homogeneity was important in the company and that dissent should be hived off. Some time ago, 20 of their senior executives suddenly left all in one go. The company responded by giving high publicity to the executives who stayed back, with a striking advertisement with photographs of each one.

Analyses for the reader

1. Would you like to work for Satyakam?
2. If you were Shah would you like to diversify into other industries? If yes, to which one and why?

8

THE KINDLY GARDENER
Practical Aspects of
Human Resource Management

The Analogy of the Gardener

Human resource management attempts to integrate the long-term policy and planning of an organisation with the development of its human resources. As opposed to crisis management, it provides ample opportunity to consider ethical issues carefully. It includes personnel management, industrial relations, and most importantly, management planning and control. Having discussed the ethical duty of managements to their most critical stakeholders, let us look at operational insights into the concept of human resource management as based more on 'caring' than on 'justice' (Gilligan 1982).

Mahesh (1993) believes that organisations should treat their employees as a gardener would his plants to enable them to achieve their greatest self-fulfilment within the constraints of their genotypes. Says he, 'Corporations have funds at their disposal, and are used to taking quick decisions and following them through implementation, have well-defined power structure to support what is considered useful for their profitability and longevity and are today acutely aware of the fact that their existence depends on attracting, training and retaining a critical mass of self-actualising people.'

We must however note that the ethics seen in this vision is one of duties and not rights. Mahesh's vision is conditioned by the personnel practices in the Tata group.

The Ugly Face of Reality

Mahesh's idyllic vision ignores the reality of conflicts and power struggles described by Ramaswamy (1984) and Pande and Pathak (1996). The model of the employer–employee relationship developed by Mahesh is sustainable on strong feelings of empathy across the organisation. This is possible, if at all, only if there is homogeneity in the population, which may be missing in India. The composition of the managerial classes is strongly skewed in favour of the traditional upper classes of the past (Dutta 1997: 175). Typically, an aggressively ethical organisation as in Case 7.2 addressed itself primarily to the officer class. It saw industrial relations in a different light. While it maintained a correct ethicality, the relations with the workers did not exhibit the warm glow of concern. The alienation of the managerial classes contrasted with the rhetoric of political leadership which courted the working class with egalitarianism. But the reality is depressingly different. Let us look at two real-life examples to see what this could mean in actual managerial practice.

EXAMPLE 8.1   Textile Engineering Company

The firm's practices are as detailed by one of the personnel officers. The company carefully scans the legal decisions and lists the offences in which dismissals will not be overturned by the courts. It is seen that violence inside the factory never gets any sympathy.

It marks its victim and asks a confidante to pick up a fist-fight with him. An inquiry is ordered. The confidante turns approver. The witnesses are cooked up. The marked man is found guilty and sacked. The state labour department is 'kept happy'. Sounds like a typical Indian movie but is nevertheless true to life.

(Source: Summarised from Ramaswamy 1984: 72)

EXAMPLE 8.2   The Simpson Group

This account is from the Sarkaria Commission Report. The Simpson Group had a perfectly happy industrial climate with an active trade union leader who looked after the workers. When the DMK party came to power, the new Chief Minister wanted this union leader out of the way. The company, out of a selfish desire to keep on the right side of the government, got rid of the old leader. That was the beginning of the end of good industrial relations and of the long period of trust between the management and labour.

(Source: Summarised from Ramaswamy 1984: 61)

This depressing reality notwithstanding, we continue to see the merits in Mahesh's approach at the same time retaining the concept of rights. The fragility of the concept of duties in the teeth of the conflict endemic in India between the castes and classes can be seen in Case 8.2. Giving up the concept of rights could be suicidal.

Organisational Codes as a Training Guide

Carrying forward Stevenson's (1987) analogy of Dr Jekyll the angel and Mr Hyde the devil, let us see if it is possible for an organisation to encourage its

EXHIBIT 8.1   The Caux Principles

1. Equity between stakeholders
2. Support for innovations and justice
3. Beyond letter of law towards spirit of trust
4. Inter-firm cooperation and not increase of competition
5. Multinational trade beyond isolation towards a world community
6. Respect environment beyond protection towards enhancement
7. Avoid illicit profit and work towards peace

employees to behave with its external parties as Mr Hyde and in its internal working as Dr Jekyll. This may be functionally required in a situation where an organisation bases its external dealings only on market systems, and by extension on profits, at the same time expecting its employees to internally maintain bonhomie and ethical social skills. This is surely a tall order and requires the manifestation of a split personality. Some organisations have unsuccessfully attempted to trigger this behavioural response by a system of reward and penalty. That is why many of them have now formalised ethical codes that attempt to avoid any expectation of unrealistic extremes in behaviour. Several well-run companies have adopted formal codes of ethics for their internal and external working. Harris (1989) reports a ten-fold increase in the number of codes in the last 30 years. In a recent declaration, a group of businessmen have spelt out seven principles for such a code. Called the Caux Principles (XLRI 1994) and based on the earlier Minnesota Principles from the USA, they attempt to project the ethical image all the way through.

Hosmer (1987) explains the gap between pious resolves and practical applications. Ethical codes are statements of the norms and beliefs of an organisation, generally proposed, discussed, and defined by the senior executives, and then published and distributed to all the members. It is easier to describe the norms as a series of negative statements, a list of things a person should not do rather than the things a person should do. However well designed these norms are, they do not always work. Further, no norm, if explicitly stated, can avoid offending some employees, customers, suppliers, distributors, stockholders or even some section of the general public.

The basic difficulty with codes of ethics is that they do not establish priorities among the various norms. The priorities are the true values of a firm. For instance, if one division of a firm is faced with declining sales and profits, it has the option to reduce middle-management employment and cut overhead costs—the classic downsizing decision. But while the code of ethics advocates respect for employees it also includes 'fair' profits. What is fair in this instance? The code of ethics obviously does not specify.

In Chapter 6 the reader was asked to ponder over whether the codes of professional councils would on occasions conflict with organisational goals. This is another dimension of Hosmer's problem. Hosmer feels that ethical dilemmas are conflicts between economic and social performances, with the latter being expressed as obligations to employees, customers, suppliers, distributors and the general public. Ethical codes can express a general sense of the obligation senior management feels towards those groups, but the codes cannot help a middle- or lower-level manager choose between the groups, or between economic and social performance. Hosmer's ideas see organisational ethics only as a 'calculus of calculations'. There is more to organisational ethics than this, as we have discussed through the course of this book. Many of the problems mentioned by Hosmer can be taken care of by the codes that emerge from participatory processes. These processes themselves could change the ethical climate of an organisation. Process and product are inextricably intertwined (Kitson and Campbell 1996: 130).

The Head Knows not What the Feet Do

Hosmer despairs at the inability to convert ethical vision of organisational leaders to operational rule for the managers. Assuming that the reality of ethical development is represented by Hosmer's vision of unidirectional ethical controls, with which we do not agree, it would be useful to know how Hosmer has tackled this problem. He treats ethical controls as extensions and natural analogues to other management techniques that cover strategic and operational controls. He quickly surveys them and concludes that they are quite complex in nature.

The most obvious problem with management controls is 'information inductance'—the biased behaviour of the affected departments in giving data and information due to their apprehensions and fears of how top management will use it. If this is true of economic performance, reports on ethical performance would be more liable to be distorted by information inductance. He then goes on to suggest remedies for this. These remedies are the same as in management control systems (systems audit, internal audit, etc.) but would have a greater value in ethical audit.

The essential features of these audits are that they are conducted by a set of independent persons who are not involved in the operations. They are expected to be free from bias and also possess a fresh vision. In a one-way process of controls, these audits are precautions against attempts by the bottom to 'beat the system' and by the top to 'fix the blame'. In a two-way system of controls this cat-and-mouse game would not occur. Proponents of rational management control systems at Harvard (Simons 1995) now recognise the role of ethics and beliefs in internal controls. 'Think of them as the Yang of Chinese philosophy—the sun, the warmth and the light', says Simons, a philosophy not new to Indian thinkers. The essence of these controls is in continuous dialogue and not in mechanical reports.

Ethical failures abound in companies claiming to be ethical fanatics: General Electric, Johnson & Johnson, etc. These have been traced to the failure of the top executives to communicate their meaning to the line-managers or to a system of reward and penalty at odds with ethical princi-ples. Much in Indian methods would help ethical controls. Simons (1995) now recognises that these controls are more effective. But to reiterate, codes are not useless instruments; they just have to be supplemented by other supports.

The Corporate Scapegoat

The previous section discussed the problem of the top management attemp-ting to generate and enforce ethics at the operational level. Recent cases in India have shown that sometimes when a breach of ethics occurs, there is a shifting of blame between the top management and the operational level. If the breach of ethics takes the form of breach of law, this mutual mud-slinging is done in public. We can see that the issue is not of an ethical top trying to keep an unethical bottom under control, but the top itself being under the shadow of unethicality and attempting to make a scapegoat of the bottom.

In the recent case of the Indian Tobacco Company, the blame is being tossed among the foreign directors of the firms, the nominated directors of the Indian financial institutions (who are usually expected to have the mandate of the nation to maintain ethical purity), the top executives and the operating executives at the junior level.

Some of the accused had taken a radical stand that breaking foreign exchange regulations was *ipso facto* not unethical. Their positions could have been credible if they had in the process not feathered their own nests. Here again, harping on 'systemic unethicality' and passing on the blame to others could have a backlash and the Indian remedies discussed earlier need to be considered. The processes of the Evidence Act and the Criminal Procedure Code can make a mockery of the more creative ways of imple-menting ethical development. Lest one is misunderstood, the substitutes suggested are not the ways of Kautilya or Manu but those of Patanjali, Gautama Buddha, the *Kural* and the *Bhagavad Gita* as was described in Chapter 5.

Raj Rishi or Rasputin

The concept of an ethical ombudsman is a deep-rooted feature of the Indian normative ethics and can be described as the *raj rishi* (a sage who is also a king) or the *raj guru* (a sage who is also the teacher to the king) concept. Vasishtha and Bhishma were *raj gurus*; Kautilya is a more recent and turbulent example. This ancient tradition is used extensively in Indian organisations. It is also prevalent in the West (Hosmer 1987). This provides for an orderly person, not in a direct line function, whose dispassionate advice is sought in ethical disputes.

> The usage of good men and desire born out of due deliberation are the sources of Dharma.
>
> —*Yajnavalkya, 1st Century BC*
> *(Gajendragadkar 1993: 425)*

He is usually past the age of active work and is no threat to anyone. But a system which depends solely on this advice would soon get unstable and the *raj guru* may turn out to be a power-broker, a Rasputin who plagued the court of the Russian emperor.

Symbolic Gestures as Ethical Aids

Indian organisations usually make social welfare programmes synonymous with ethical behaviour. Several Indian companies have adopted villages or communities. The tax laws allow these expenditures as permissible deductions from their income for tax purposes. Where do such gestures figure in the discussions we have had so far? Friedman (1970) savagely attacks these as unnecessary hypocritical facades. We had earlier said (Chapter 6) that the concept of social responsibility of business is much more than the triviality of voluntaryism or contributions to charity. Admitting these as trivial compared to the loftier goal of 'maximising social benefits' (Ferrel and Freidrichs 1994), these symbolic gestures do have a value for organisations. Friedman appears to have missed the point.

Companies who run social welfare programmes feel that these induce an ethicality in the minds of their employees (usually senior managers) that makes them more effective. Aguilar (1994) describes vividly why 'a person who read to the blind in the night would not cheat on his expense account the next day'. Several Indian companies have reported similar impacts.

Right Way to Recruit, Promote and Part with Employees

We will now touch upon the ethics of personnel policies in respect of recruitment, promotions and disciplinary action, training and counselling.

Haydock (1996) believes that ethical recruitment should have the following features. Advertisements should contain full details and accurately reflect the realities of the job. No candidate should be called unless he or she

The Kindly Gardener **149**

satisfies the minimum criterion. Candidates should not be asked personal questions which have no relevance to the job. The reasons for the selection should be publicly announced. The referee's comments should be made public. Interestingly, Haydock gives special consideration for the aged in recruitment. Discrimination against the aged is considered unethical. This has

Ethics of Caring

We deal with alternate (feminine) morality of care as opposed to a (masculine) morality of justice.

—*Gilligan (1993)*

a 'situational and contextual' relevance in England where the elderly were retrenched due to 'structural adjustments'. This has a special relevance today for India as well (see Chapter 11).

EXAMPLE 8.3 **Arun and His Bottle of Hair Dye**

Arun Sengupta, Financial Controller of the multinational Bengal Silkington, had just turned 50 when he got the boot. Silkington had stuck to the old technology of making plate glass when sheet glass had taken over and so had to wind up. Arun had two daughters of marriageable age and could not afford to be without a job. He was told that because of his age it would be difficult for him to get a good job. So when he applied to Hindustan Coal for the position of Deputy General Manager, he omitted to mention his date of birth. On his wife's advice, he dyed his hair for the interview. He was brilliant and highly qualified, and the MD of Hindustan Coal offered him the job across the table lest he miss out on such talent. Arun joined immediately.

As the formalities were later being completed, his age came to light. The MD was furious. He had an unwritten understanding that no one above 40 should be recruited. 'They are useless,' he said. He had however not mentioned this in the advertisement or in the interview. 'Oh God! At your age and with your experience to be so unethical!', he screamed.

Who was unethical—Arun or the MD?

Some of the norms for ethical recruitment can be contested; there can also be strong 'ethical relativism'. Thus, the Indian Constitution requires all recruitment to government jobs to give equal opportunity to every citizen. This is what Haydock (1996) also advocated. But this constitutional provision does not apply to the private sector. In their case, giving preference to employees' children could be an ethical practice. In a country with serious unemployment problems this would be considered fair practice. The Tatas follow this practice, as did a large number of coal mine companies before they were nationalised. When Coal India, the biggest public sector employer in India, discontinued this practice to be more ethical, they were contrarily accused of being unethical!

The ethicality of promotional policies in India has been discussed by Chakraborty (1995a: 209), who believes that discretionary promotions based on performance would tend to become unethical. By implication, he supports promotion by seniority. Many organisations in India have also felt similarly in spite of a strong pull towards 'rewards by results'. The Japanese success in sobering the promotion polices is an eye-opener. They show the other angle of the ethics of promotions, that it can be a reward for loyalty and that results would ultimately emerge out of loyalty and experience. The affirmative implications of reservations for certain castes and classes and for the disabled are explosive ethical issues having several layers of conflict. The laws of affirmative action are still not applicable to the private sector in India, unlike in the USA. In India, ethical organisations have to say, 'We are better than the law'. In the USA, they have to say, 'We do not bypass the law, we follow it in spirit'.

Nosey Parkerism

Preserving the right to privacy is an ethic to be valued. However, managements can breach this right by using methods that may be harsh, cruel or uncivil, e.g., use of lie-detectors, employment of detectives against the employees, etc. Even if there were benign versions of this infringement, there could still be ethical issues as in Example 8.4, typical of the paternalistic approach that comes naturally to many Indian organisations.

EXAMPLE 8.4   Bala's Plastic Belt

Bala was one of the most competent architects in the company. But of late he had been moody and consequently his work suffered. Dr Nath, GM Personnel, tried to find out the cause from him, but drew a blank. He then took the unusual step of asking his neighbours. They had a story to tell. The moment Bala came home, whatever be the time, his wife and mother lay in wait for him to complain bitterly about one another. Loud arguments followed, usually ending in Bala taking out his plastic belt and giving both his wife and mother a whacking with it. Bala was a posthumous child and his mother had gone through considerable hardship to bring him up and educate him at one of the most well-known institutions in the country. His wife was a Ph.D. in chemistry but his mother would not allow her to work. Dr Nath persuaded Bala's mother to stay separately in a flat which he helped Bala to acquire in the same building. It worked. The separation helped to ease the tension. Dr Nath talked about this with great pride as evidence of the ethicality of his company's HRM. Do you agree with Dr Nath that it was his duty as the GM Personnel to intervene?

Lazy Acceptance of Class and Caste Conflict

There has been an increasing acceptance in India, in recent times, of the concept that class and caste conflict cannot be avoided and it is best that everyone fight it all out. This philosophy is ultimately proving dysfunctional. A laid-back approach to class and caste conflicts as being inevitable negates any attempt to establish ethicality. Admittedly, an ostrich-like refusal to accept the existence of conflict is not helpful either (Beteille 1996). There has to be a balance between the two approaches. It is more than necessary to go back to the roots of Indian history and pick up again the strands that enable reconciliation and mutual consideration. It is obvious that neither the Sanskritised values nor those based on orthodox left thinking are of any real help in resolving these conflicts. Agitationist movements, some of which are financed by external agencies or egged on by irresponsible persons vulgarly labelling themselves 'pluralists', only make matters worse.

Proof of the Ethical Pudding

Industrial and labour laws with the best of intentions could nevertheless lead to a miserable state of affairs. The goal of ethicality in human resource management cannot, any more than in any other field, be reduced to a formula. Adherence to industrial and labour laws in itself is no proof of ethicality. Thus personnel managers highly educated in law are not the ultimate means for ensuring ethicality in the human resource function. They need sensitising in the wider areas of learning and experience.

Out of Rights Come Duties

The conflict between rights and duties becomes more apparent in human resource management. We should by now be able to see that these concepts are not necessarily opposed to each other. The concept of rights should enable us to crystallise ethical thinking on duties and give it a sense of direction. It is somewhat unfashionable to question the ethics of rights. But those who stridently support it in populist platforms admit in private that this has caused more harm than good. One of the important functions of a human resource manager is to effectively weld the two ethical concepts.

SUMMARY

This chapter operationalises the concepts presented in Chapter 7. The philosophy of human resource management should be one of care rather than of justice. An analogy of a kindly gardener is invoked. The process of developing organisational codes is described, whose impact is likely to be greater when evolved participatorily. Organisational codes are not magic wands. They may run counter to the normally understood systems of rewards and penalties based on economic performance. But these differences need not be exaggerated. The ethics in recruitment and promotion policies, and the impact of mergers and acquisitions on personnel policies are discussed as is the play of cultural relativism between India and the West.

ISSUES TO PONDER OVER

- Reflect if you are comfortable in the company of persons from a much lower economic status than yours. Does this background affect your behaviour towards them?

- Reflect as to whether you have at any time pushed the company to adopt policies that are basically personally beneficial to you.

- Have you ever felt that your employer was intruding on your privacy?

CASE 8.1   Excellent Pesticides

Arvind Vasawa's resignation of ethical protest

Bhimabhai Desai (Vice President Personnel, HRD and Administration) of Excellent Pesticides was discussing (November '93) the letter of resignation of Arvind Vasawa (31) with Surendra Patel (Vice President Operation Technology, and Research and Development). Surendra was keen that Bhimabhai should dissuade Arvind from resigning; he was relying on Arvind's scientific talent to help him to fulfil his promise to the Managing Director to develop some new bio-organic fertilisers. Bhimabhai was worried that his company should not be shamed by a resignation that sounded like an 'ethical protest'. The company had won the year's national award for 'Fair and Ethical Business Practices'.

The resignation letter read as follows:

'I am fed up with the hypocrisy in your organisation. Krishna's monthly philosophic lectures on the 'seven sheaths of the *Taitreya Upanishad*' are painful. They make no sense to me even if they make the old man chuckle irritatingly with the pride of understanding the 'inner secrets of existence'. The weekly meditation sessions he arranges do not enthuse me any more. And yet if I do not attend, his withering look makes me grit my teeth. As a board director he is an influential person. But as a retired officer he has no responsibilities whatsoever. He makes us waste our time. I am told your company values him because as Personnel Manager seven years ago, he introduced daily prayer sessions in the beginning of each shift and got a well-known religious order to brainwash the workers to accept wage and productivity settlements. These enabled you to go from losses to 40 per cent on shareholders' funds (400 per cent on shareholders' equity).

'You talk about ethics but your products are priced with 15 per cent mark up on costs whereas the industry's average is only five per cent. Who pays for this—the farmers, my people in the villages?

'You talk about environment but you do not mind earning profits from chemical pesticides that your own publicity brochures describe as hazardous chemicals.

'I cannot work in this atmosphere of hypocrisy.'

They both decided that they should talk to a few others who were likely to know what provoked this outburst.

What his friend Gandhi had to say

Pravin Gandhi said that he was a close friend of Arvind. He felt that Arvind's decision was provoked by the fact of his doctoral thesis being rejected by the University of Gujarat. His work had been in the use of bio-organic fertilisers. Whereas his product had been a commercial success, his examiners found that his theoretical explanation of the results was not satisfactory. They were not willing to accept the empirical results of successful use in the farms of the company as these could be biased.

He further said that Arvind was allergic to Krishna as he felt that he hobnobbed with the Shankaracharya crowd who were strongly inimical to scheduled castes like himself.

He said that Arvind was in fact quite proud of Excellent Pesticides. While presenting his research proposal to the Department of Scientific and Industrial Research he began with the statement: 'My company is known for its honesty and would not agree to bribe anyone just to get a project through.' Arvind did not understand that Excellent Pesticides had never needed to say this openly as it was in anycase understood by all as their philosophy. The Department of Science and Technology had taken offence at the insinuation and refused to fund the project.

Meanwhile his admission to a US university which Excellent Pesticides had agreed to fund was also rejected as he had very poor marks in his postgraduate degree.

He had an offer for the post of a clerk in a nationalised bank. It paid well and he said he would bid goodbye to the field of science and technology where he had proved to be no good.

The observations of Dr Jaswala, Manager, Research & Development

Dr Jaswala said that Arvind was somewhat different from his other assistants. The latter worked as a team and flowered under the open system that Surendra Patel encouraged. Many of their suggestions had in fact resulted in cost reductions and improvement of safety standards.

Dr Jaswala said that he was also not with Krishna in much of his metaphysics, but his enunciation of the *Bhagavad Gita's* concept of detachment had personally helped him to concentrate more on his work.

He said that it was no accident that in the last seven years the company had repeatedly won national awards for export and import substitution. Their turnover rose from Rs 380 million to over Rs 2,500 million. Moreover, they were the first in the pesticides industry to get the ISO 9000, an acid test for ethical conduct.

But he felt that Arvind was an outstanding scientist and the company could not afford to lose him.

The views of Rajan Menon, Personnel Manager

Rajan Menon said that Arvind's prejudice against Krishna prevented him from recognising that the daily prayer sessions were not compulsory and yet the attendance of the workers was 95 per cent, and that of the supervisory staff was

100 per cent; the managerial cadre attended only 50 per cent of the time. This was despite the fact that 20 per cent of the workers were Muslims and another 20 per cent Christians, while most of the prayers were Hindu *bhajans*.

Rajan also said that another powerful system introduced by Krishna was one of open review of all work by groups. All promotions were group decisions. Recruitments were also fair and equitable with an accepted criterion of giving preference to the local village tribals. But otherwise the working strength had representatives from all over the country.

Arvind was not very comfortable with this open system. He felt that it led to conformism and would not be able to recognise major breakthroughs, though it would encourage small improvements.

Arvind should at least have appreciated Krishna's idea of having a common canteen where everyone from the MD to the unskilled worker shared the same table and meal!

The views of Gobind Parikh, Manager, Safety Engineering

Gobind said that knowing the hazardous nature of the products, special prizes were offered to encourage safety improvements. The factory had won the safety award continuously for the past seven years.

Discussion with the Managing Director

The Managing Director, Madhav Patel, said that Arvind's point was not without some substance. His father who had pioneered research in the field had first concentrated on ensuring the success of the Swadeshi movement under Gandhi's directions. The environmental issues had dawned on him only in the last five years, and he felt that they should go in for more bio-fertilisers and bio-pesticides, but this could be done only gradually. As a strategy he had therefore invested a sizeable part of the profits in a subsidiary investment company which in turn invested it in long-term securities. 'I believe it is the correct ethical policy to price our products with a high margin and use the profits for diversification. Meanwhile, we are spending a lot of money on educating the farmers to use the pesticides carefully. I have repeatedly taken our shareholders in confidence in all these matters and they have happily agreed with me. That is why our Rs 10 share is now selling at Rs 630.'

(The facts of the case are from an organisation highly respected for its ethical values. See Acknowledgement.)

Analyses for the reader

1. Would you say that the case shows a typical Indian slant to ethics? Discuss thoroughly.
2. Do you think on the basis of the facts of the case you would prima facie agree that the company deserved the Ethics Award?
3. Depending on your answer what would be your suggestion to Bhimabhai Desai for handling Arvind Vasawa?
4. Can you relate the pattern of attendance at the *bhajan* sessions to Kohlbergh's ethical levels (refer Chapter 5)? Does it mean that religious

prayers are useful devices only up to Stage 4 and suited to those whose intellectual powers can reach no further?

5. Do these incidents say anything about ethics of individuation (refer Chapter 5) as a desideratum for scientists?

CASE 8.2   Kalu's Folly

Kalu had several follies, all of them as transparent as his personality. But the greatest was his ear-shattering loud voice. As Kalu would enter the office building, Chandra could hear him on the third floor.

Kalu was a peon in a central government department at Jaipur in Rajasthan, part of the outfit of a constitutional dignitary stationed at Delhi. He had special protection under the Indian Constitution. The position was held at that time by an urbane and sophisticated member of the Indian Civil Service, Mr Anil Kumar Tagore. Kalu's ways were an antithesis to the style of Tagore. Kalu was a hefty six-footer, and looked like a black statue carved in ebony. His huge fiery moustache was a contrast to Tagore's delicate pince-nez. Chandra was a young probationer who had just joined the service. Chandra's boss and the head of the department at Jaipur was Mr Rangachari, a devoutly religious person steeped in traditional Indian values.

That was the time when the Central Government employees were poised to go on a nation-wide strike. The main ploy of the strikers was to use public services such as the railways to disrupt life. The lines were divided sharply between the elitist officers and the 'large mass of mediocrity dreaming of reaching for the unattainable stars' (akash kusum as Anil Kumar Tagore put it in his native Bengali). Rangachari had lectured to the officers at Jaipur, 'If only Panditji had not got it all wrong from the Fabians and the Russians, and tempted the people with these false concepts of rights, the elite would have done their duty by them without all these threats. He has ruined our people.' Now is the chance, they all said, to teach them a lesson. Tension was mounting as the midnight launch of the strike drew closer. The spearhead of the strikers were the railway workers. If the Railway strike succeeded it was possible the government would fall. All the officers were asked to stay back for the night so that the staff did not create any havoc.

During the day, Chandra was puzzled when Rangachari asked him if he felt any of the staff was a problem. Chandra reflected a little and mentioned Kalu's name. Kalu had a habit of bursting into his room twice a day and guffawing at the nervousness of the young officers in tackling the troublesome public. Rani Chabra, his section officer, once came crying to him complaining that Kalu had teased her. While he was around, her whole section would crowd around him cracking jokes. The angrier she got with Kalu the more boisterous he became.

At the appointed midnight hour, the shrill whistle of a railway locoengine announced the failure of the railways strike to take off. Rangachari was jubilant. But for the staff there was no jubilation.

Rangachari served dismissal orders issued by Tagore to five members of the staff. Kalu was one of them. Chandra did not know the circumstances of the other four but he was worried that he may have unwittingly caused harm to Kalu. 'It is your recommendation,' said Rangachari, confirming his worst fears. 'But I did not intend that. I only suggested counselling,' said Chandra.

'Some damage to innocent persons is inevitable in a dharma yudha. The correct signals of authority must be sent out as Kautilya advises in his Artha-shastra,' said Rangachari.

However, he was taken aback when Chandra rang up Tagore. But the results were the same. Tagore told Chandra that 'good administration means that an order once given cannot be withdrawn'. On the other hand, Chandra was accused of being an irresponsible and weak-minded administrator.

Chandra asked the union secretary whether he could help Kalu's cause. 'Not with this devastating failure of the strike and the constitutional protection available to Tagore,' he said. Chandra understood why they had not dared to issue the dismissals before they knew the strike had failed.

Chandra had little hesitation in flinging his resignation at Rangachari with a threat that he was going to make a public announcement the next day. As he went home, he told his wife of this decision. She had already heard of it from Mrs Rangachari who had come to console her.

Chandra stayed at home the next day. But something seemed to have happened at the Delhi office the previous afternoon. Kalu rushed home with the good news. The dismissals had been withdrawn. He placed his turban at Chandra's feet. Between sobs he said, 'You have saved me, my maibap [mother and father].' As a crowd gathered, an embarrassed Chandra pushed Kalu away.

Analyses for the reader

1. Was Chandra a weak or an effective administrator?
2. If the concept of rights (including the right to strike) was removed from India's ethical and legal directory would the elite classes be likely to do their duty to the poor and oppressed better? Would their plight improve or deteriorate?

(Use essentially only the arguments flowing from the case.)

9

LISTENING TO THE INNER VOICE
Problems in Whistle-blowing

Whistle-blowers of Varied Hues

What is whistle-blowing? It may be defined as an attempt by an employee or a former employee of an organisation to disclose what he proclaims to be a wrongdoing in or by that organisation. When he reports such a misdemeanour to someone within the organisation the whistle-blowing is 'internal'. If he reports it to an outsider it is 'external'. If the matter concerns some harm done to the whistle-blower it is 'personal'. If it is at the behest of others it is 'impersonal'. If it is done by a former employee it is 'alumni'. When the identity of the whistle-blower is revealed, it is 'open', when it is not revealed it is 'anonymous'. The organisation may be public or private; it could also be a body of professionals (James 1993).

From this definition one may note that the entire field of whistle-blowing is one of conflict of ethics. The conflict is between the right to privacy on the one hand and the ethics of trust on the other. Both are nurtured values. One would have expected law to have resolved this conflict amicably. Contrarily the need for whistle-blowing arises precisely because law is unable to settle this satisfactorily.

Whistle-blowing Applauded

The three arguments that support whistle-blowing on the basis of absolute morality could be:

1. The whistle-blower has moral motives; if not, he is being unethical.
2. The whistle-blower acts in accordance with his responsibilities for avoiding or exposing moral violations.
3. The whistle-blower has tried all existing internal procedures and has failed to get the moral error corrected, and has to go to Kohlbergh's sixth stage (refer discussions in Chapter 5).

In this sixth stage of moral development if you witness a wrongdoing in your organisation that would adversely affect, say, a customer, you would have to put yourself in the position of the chief executive to see if you would have countenanced your subordinate who is disloyal to you because he was more loyal to your customer. If you think you would have, then you should go by your moral conscience and blow the whistle as a morally correct thing to do in pursuance of the sixth stage of Kohlbergh's moral development.

Five other arguments based on consequences to society could be:

1. The whistle-blower perceives that the violation can lead to serious danger.
2. The whistle-blower has enough evidence.
3. The whistle-blower's action has a reasonable chance of success.
4. Organisations will come to grief if they do not ensure that whistle-blowers bring out the unsavoury features of the organisation for remedy.
5. It reduces the cost of monitoring implementation of law (see Chapters 4 and 12 for Becker's economics of penalties).

Whistle-blowing Decried

A typical condemnation comes from James Roche, the former President of General Motors:

> Some critics are now busy eroding another support of free enterprise—the loyalty of a management team, with its unifying values and cooperation. Some of the enemies of business now encourage an employee to be disloyal to the enterprise. They want to create suspicion and disharmony and pry into the proprietary interests of the business. This may be whistle-blowing ... but it is another tactic for spreading disunity ... Whistle-blowing is not courageous and not deserving of gratitude and protection; it is corrosive and impermissible.

Duska (1990) disagrees with this approach and says, 'Isn't it time to stop viewing corporate machinations as games. The activities not only affect the players but everyone ... the appeal to loyalty though understandable is misleading; in the moral sphere competition is not the prevailing virtue ... Whistle-blowing is not only permissible but expected when [a] company is harming society. The issue is not one of disloyalty to the company, but of whether the whistle-blower has an obligation to society and if blowing the whistle will bring retaliation.'

Who Protects the Whistle-blower

It is now accepted that there is very little protection provided to the whistle-blower by laws anywhere in the world. There is a tremendous pressure from consumer movements to amend the law in order to give such protection. Several studies have shown that most whistle-blowers come to total grief; they are sacked, demoted and socially ostracised 'as men who let down their comrades' (Glazer and Glazer 1989). In the USA, as in India, the whistle-blowers among the civil servants have better protection. They attract much greater public attention and sympathy, while whistle-blowers in the private sector have a tragic fate.

In the USA, there appears to be a major change in the offing to protect the whistle-blowers (Near and Micelli 1995). Some of the practical advantages of whistle-blowing to society have been dealt with in Chapter 11. It makes monitoring and surveillance cheaper. Conversely, whistle-blowing ensures that legal penalties need not be that severe, as the threat that any breach of law is likely to be caught would be deterrent enough. In spite of this, whistle-blowers are by and large an unhappy and miserable lot who usually end their lives tragically. The two Indian cases at the end of this chapter amply illustrate this.

Usual Subjects for Whistle-blowing

Ralph Nader, the great pioneer in consumer movements, lists areas for whistle-blowing (Nader *et al.* 1972).

1. Defective vehicles marketed to unsuspecting customers
2. Waste of government funds by private contractors
3. Industrial dumping of pollutants
4. Discrimination by age, race or sex
5. Misusing pension funds
6. Deceptive advertising
7. Companies and campaign contribution
8. Adulteration
9. Government power used for private gain
10. Non-enforcement of pesticide laws
11. Corruption
12. Suppression of occupational diseases
13. Monopolist price-rigging

Items 7, 9 and 11 are the more common causes in India. More recent writings have strongly supported whistle-blowing against sexual harassment (Dandekar 1993).

Markets as Substitutes for Whistle-blowing

Whistle-blowing would not be required if the free market systems had a way of punishing the wrongdoer, that is, if the products of a polluting company are boycotted in the market, or the state subsidies are withdrawn, or the monopolists' products with high prices are shunned by the consumer. But as mentioned in Chapter 3, the magic of markets can work only if information is freely available. Since this is suppressed, the value of the whistle-blower consists precisely in supplying this ethical link—the information.

Prevention is Better than Cure

Most civilised societies have several institutional mechanisms that attempt to reduce the need for whistle-blowing, such as the concept of democratic discourse (discussed in Chapter 1) and the safeguards of law (see Chapter 4). In India, there have been valiant but unsuccessful efforts to radically modify and liberalise the Official Secrets Act. It would seem that it makes even the noblest of us disloyal backbiters. Interestingly, Chawla (1992: 2), Mother Teresa's biographer, narrates some anecdotes to show that Mother Teresa does not support whistle-blowing; obviously of moral persuasion, she is willing to concede that tale-bearing and informing on a thief is morally repugnant, even if stealing itself is also morally repugnant. Support to whistle-blowers as heroic individuals who should be encouraged had been the prevalent mood of the US academic community (Near and Micelli in Burton and Near 1995) till some time ago. But after the laws for protecting whistle-blowers are going apace, the same academicians are having second thoughts (Near and Micelli 1995). Are they throwing away the benefits of privacy and autonomy? However, they seem to get hopelessly divided if the stakes involved are perceived to be very high, such as in national defence. Suspected spies in the USA get the electric chair far too quickly and easily for the moral conscience of many.

Fails When it Most Needs to Succeed

Research in the USA on whistle-blowing is in turmoil, unsure of the consequences of the newer laws protecting whistle-blowing (Near and Micelli 1995). Approaching the problem entirely as an exercise in understanding the consequences, Near and Micelli hypothesise 12 propositions for future research. Their admittedly unproven hypotheses in a simplified understanding is that whistle-blowing is least likely to lead to positive consequences when the organisation is highly unethical, as at that stage it is less transparent and sensitive to warnings. As it gets exposed it gets more defensive and wilier in covering up its tracks. Thus, the more the absolute moral reason for blowing the whistle, the less it is likely to pass the test of consequential benefits of whistle-blowing! Things gets worse after the whistle is blown. This message of despair is significant. It would perhaps be more desirable that the need for whistle-blowing be removed. Prevention of wrongdoing is better than its doubtful cure through whistle-blowing.

Some Tips for Success

On the assumption that whistle-blowing is morally and legally to be supported, the potential whistle-blower should begin by asking the following questions (Nader *et al.* 1972):

1. Is my knowledge complete?
2. How is public interest affected?
3. How far can I go inside the organisation?
4. Will I be violating my employment contract?
5. Will I be violating any ethical rules affecting external parties?
6. What is the best way to blow—anonymously, overtly, by resignation or in some other way?
7. What will be the likely response from inside and outside the organisation?
8. What can be achieved by whistle-blowing?

Nader's writings blatantly prescribe the strategies on how to use the answers to the above questions to successfully blow the whistle. The five tips given are:

1. Identify precisely not only the objectionable activity but also the public interest or interests that is or are threatened and the magnitude of the harm that will result from non-disclosure.
2. Verify accuracy of your knowledge of the situation.
3. Identify ethical standards as well as laws and regulations that support your decision to blow the whistle.
4. Develop a plan of action; consider the personal costs and the likely response of allies and antagonists within and outside the organisation.
5. Select an appropriate outside contact.

We will discuss some typical and well-known examples of whistle-blowing in an attempt to understand the context in which it was done. The examples are from the proceedings of a conference on whistle-blowing (Nader *et al.* 1972).

EXAMPLE 9.1   **Dr Jacquelline Verret**

Dr Jacquelline Verret (JV) was a scientist in the Food and Drug Administration (FDA) of America. She was working on the sugar substitute cyclamates. She found that chick embryo injected with cyclamates developed cancer, and called a press conference to release this information. As a consequence, a national television network sought her interview. She informed her superiors of the TV interview and assured them that it would not be conducted to cause panic.

Nevertheless, the FDA accused her of being unethical as the correct procedure would have been to publish her work in a scientific journal and subject herself to peer review. They felt that research on chicks did not necessarily mean that the results would be the same for human beings.

JV replied that publications in scientific journals take too much time and there was an urgent need to take action. FDA could not fire her as meanwhile a public outcry ensued, nor could they cut her budget as she had built up a reputation. But JV admitted that the press had unfortunately used panicky language. Nevertheless, it was the moral duty of scientists to keep the public informed without creating any panic.

Analysis for the reader

Can we see this in terms of only absolute ethics or also in terms of its consequences? If we think over the consequences, we have to realistically assess *(a)* the pressures that could be building on the FDA by companies making cyclamates and those producing competing products, and *(b)* the asymmetry of information among the users, scientists and producers.

EXAMPLE 9.2   **Dr Gofman and Dr Tomplin**

Dr Gofman and Dr Tomplin (G & T), nuclear scientists at the Atomic Energy Commission (AEC), leaked to the press the dangers of atomic pollution in nuclear power plants. Consequently, they were hounded by the AEC with savage cuts in their budgets. The more they were attacked, the more vehement their cry became. So much so that they turned hysterical and many doubted their sanity. But G & T went on. 'Where the future of the human species is at stake, your voice must be loud enough, incisive enough to be heard well.' Objective observers felt the G & T were not always balanced and scientific. But G & T said that this was by design; they had to be heard.

Analysis for the reader

In a democracy where we believe in democratic discourse as an ethical value, how do we balance the enormous complexity of the factors involved in such decisions, and the time and energy available to the people to come to sound judgements? How do they delegate it to credible and ethical people to give them a balanced judgement? Is whistle-blowing one of the more feasible methods to ensure democratic decision-making?

EXAMPLE 9.3   **Edward Gregory and the Chevrolet Exhaust System**

Edward Gregory (EG) was an inspection engineer at General Motors. He found that the design of the exhaust system was unsafe as it could lead to the formation of carbon monoxide. A series of accidents that could be attributed to this leakage confirmed his findings. He was willing to testify publicly. When the consumer movement picked up the gauntlet, EG was pushed to an innocuous position in the company. But the public outcry became violent. EG had to be reinstated to his position and he continued to perform his inspection function without fear or favour. General Motors had to recall seven million Chevrolet cars with the defective exhaust system!

Analysis for the reader

What is the lesson a whistle-blower can learn from EG?

SUMMARY

Whistle-blowing as a concept is examined by absolute moral standards and by its consequences. Development of public institutions and laws to avoid the need for whistle-blowing is considered important. Currently academicians are in support of whistle-blowing as socially desirable and are less concerned with developing public institutions and laws which could reduce the need for whistle-blowing. Whistle-blowing in defence establishments is much more of an ethical dilemma. After describing the conditions under which whistle-blowing becomes morally justified, the tips for successful whistle-blowing are discussed.

ISSUES TO PONDER OVER

- If you were to make a law to discriminate a genuine whistle-blower from a mere muckraker or informer or stool pigeon, how would you suggest the law be framed?
- Would you justify an anonymous letter from a student to the director of an educational institute complaining of cheating by the other students?
- Would you justify an anonymous letter in the same situation as in the previous question, if it were a case of sexual delinquency or harassment?
- Have you ever listened to a tale-bearer? Did you encourage him or not? Why?
- Do you think the system of internal audit is institutionalised whistle-blowing and therefore has all its ethical problems?

CASE 9.1   **Ernest Fitzgerald and Dr Subba Rao**

Ernest Fitzgerald (EF) in the USA and Dr Subba Rao (SR) in India were both examples of vendetta against brilliant mavericks who did not fit into the conservative, conformist and secretive defence and atomic energy set-ups.

EF, a cost accountant, reported to the senatorial committee against his department for having exceeded the sanctioned budget for a project—the C5A Transport Plane Project. An ex-employee of a private agency, he had been inspired to do this by the American Code of Ethics of Civil Servants which read as follows: 'Any person in Government should put loyalty to the highest moral principles and to the country above loyalty to persons, party or Government department . . . Expose corruption wherever discovered.' He mentioned that the cause of this increase was not innocent; it was linked to large-scale migration of senior defence officers to employment with the contractor.

He had tried to warn his superiors, but they would not recognise the issue. When they realised that he would testify before the US Senate Committee, they built up a case to get rid of him even if it meant bending the rules. They tried to establish that EF had a conflict of interests on account of his previous employment, but failed to prove it. They tried to prove a case of moral lapses, but had to give this up too. Finally, they abolished his post and covered themselves technically in 'parting company with him'. This final order was passed personally by President Nixon. In an internal note which was subsequently reported in the Supreme Court of America, the officials had recommended to the President that 'we should let him bleed . . . Fitzgerald is no doubt a top-notch cost expert, but he must be given low marks in loyalty; and after all loyalty is the name of the game.' It was obvious that the case was one of disciplinary action and not of abolition of post.

EF's herculean and historic efforts to get the President of the United States of America to come down on his knees and take him back in service were ultimately thwarted by the orders of the Supreme Court. Fitzgerald pursued his case against Nixon even after he was no longer President. In a historic judgement (*Richard Nixon v. A. Ernest Fitzgerald, 24 June 1982*), the Supreme Court upheld the right of the President to claim personal immunity against legal suits by a close margin of 5:4. EF got several offers to work in 'investigative' jobs which gave him minimum sustenance but 'good' jobs became out of bounds for him.

SR, a scientist in the Indian defence establishment, was a specialist in the use of computers for mathematical designing. In 1976, he was assigned a project for making a nuclear submarine which involved a collaboration between the Navy and the Bhabha Atomic Research Centre (BARC) under the Department of Atomic Energy of the Government of India. This project had been under development from 1971 and had reached a stage of maturity according to BARC.

Six months after SR had been working on the project, he thought it had a faulty design. His seniors, on the other hand, had got enormous funding commitments from the government on the basis of their own design. SR alleged that BARC ridiculed his ideas as coming from one who had only six months' work experience in the field. Since he had access to the highest quarters, his criticism was accepted. Meanwhile, SR prepared his own designs, but BARC tried their best to shoot it down. They prepared a second design ignoring his. Once again, SR blew the whistle and the highest political level took notice of it. BARC had to concede to his criticism on a point on which BARC were supposed to be the experts and SR would at best be considered an intelligent amateur.

Meanwhile the political leadership in the country changed. According to SR, BARC avenged their humiliation. Disgusted, he resigned and wished to migrate to America from where he had received good offers. But he was 'caught with defence secrets while leaving the country' and was arrested for espionage. SR claimed that these were nothing more than his Ph.D. thesis which did not contain classified information. He was imprisoned for 20 months. During this period, the support of his wife saw him through and the Supreme Court ultimately exonerated him. SR alleged that some of the most famous defence scientists of India had ranged against him. He accused them of conniving with the police. One of the illustrious scientists accused of harassing him was well known for his philosophic and ethical public discourses. SR said that the scientist had earlier admitted to him that he was a specialist in the field of nuclear science which had little to do with engineering. Therefore he had little to comment on his designs.

The case writer was told in confidence by a close friend of this illustrious scientist that SR's insinuation against the scientist was totally ill-founded and not based on facts. He said that the delayed process of justice was part of the ills of the police and judicial system of the country. He admitted that SR was probably a victim of petty politics and jealousies but was in no way 'a victim of a heroic attempt to avoid waste of national resources in a bad submarine design'.

It was intriguing why such a prominent and avowedly ethical senior scientist whom SR had apparently misunderstood did not endeavour to rescue SR out of this situation. The law provided enough scope of withdrawal of a case by prosecution or the complainant. It is still not known to the public whether SR's allegations of victimisation as a result of his exposè were true or not. The case in draft was acknowledged to me by the concerned scientist in October 1995; the response is still awaited. Was there any other weightier ethical consideration that has held back his comments? There could be.

In 1995, SR wrote two articles in the Madras daily *The Hindu*. He wrote: 'Those at the helm of affairs of the Department of Atomic Energy have damaged national interests and managed to escape scrutiny under the veil of secrecy ... For too long the Department has been guided by men with limited vision and confused priorities. It is time it is reoriented and restructured lest the country should pay a heavy price.'

The article also had rejoinders. The BARC chief (not the eminent nuclear scientist) reiterated that he had only 'permitted to prosecute' and that his sympathies were with Dr Subba Rao, reaffirming the line conveyed to the case writer and mentioned earlier in the case. 'Let the law take its own course' was apparently the line taken by the BARC chief.

Both the USA and India had a powerful constitutional authority, the Auditor General, to report on the 'propriety and regularity' of government expenditure. Both the constitutional dignitaries had developed some conventions on how far they would *(a)* reveal government secrets in their reports, and *(b)* comment on the wisdom of an expenditure which is primarily discretionary or involves technical judgement. But when an Auditor General is politically inclined, he or she bends this convention to suit that purpose. This happened more often in India than in the USA; it happened in the Bofor's case concerning Rajiv Gandhi, and in the case of defence facilities producing coffee percolators concerning Krishna Menon.

(The case is based entirely on newspaper reports and the material supplied to the author by the United States Information Service on the court battles of Ernest Fitzgerald. Even though the case is located in defence establishments, it has important lessons on the psychology of whistle-blowers.)

Analysis for the reader

1.   Is the case on the same moral footing for both EF and SR?
2.   Does SR's case show that if indeed there was a problem in the submarine design, the Indian system could benefit from a whistle-blower?
3.   What would be your ethical valuation (even with the limited information in the case) of the illustrious scientist and the BARC chief?
4.   If you were EF or SR would you behave the way they did?

CASE 9.2   **The Voids of Gold**

Subedar Major (Retd) Hukum Singh of Dhanbad, Bihar, had never been seen smiling before. But that Diwali, he was boisterous and guffawing with exuberant mirth. Besides Chandra, no one knew the reason.

Chandra and a few other top officers had been chosen by the minister to take over the coking coal mines in lightning action, before the owners of the mines could shift their assets. The Presidential Ordinance for taking over the coking coal mines hit Dhanbad with the morning news bulletin. Dhanbad was the city of wealth as the Hindi meaning of its name suggests: wealth not for the coal-mine worker nor even for the nation, but definitely for the owners and their small band of loyal top officers and the nefarious criminal gangs that the system spewed.

The takeover task force briefly addressed the top officers of the erstwhile private sector. Their services with the mines were terminated by law. They would be screened and those with track records of dishonesty would not be offered employment with the new public sector. The rest would be absorbed in the new set-up. This news spread rapidly in Dhanbad. When Hukum Singh heard of it, he was elated. He felt that his long period of anguish was over. 'Honesty will now rule Dhanbad,' he thought. No longer would he have to surreptitiously meet the senior officers of the Coal Board and complain against his own company, his *annadata* (giver of daily bread).

Hukum Singh had retired from the army and had sought post-retirement employment near his son's place of work. Ramanuja Iyengar had been impressed with his religious attitude, and had offered Hukum Singh the job of his confidential assistant. Iyengar, the Financial Controller of Watson Coal Company Ltd, had also got this appointment cleared by Edgar Watson, the Chairman in England; the company was still a foreign one with 51 per cent foreign shares. Hukum had started his new job with hope and happiness. But his earlier expectations had been belied. Edgar and Iyengar had told him that they hoped, with his help, to rid the company of all corrupt officers. He had therefore gone hammer and tongs at the sand deals.

Sand was transported to the mine site by contractors either from the riverbed 10 km away or from the Coal Board Ropeway sand dunes which were 1 km away. These were stowed into underground voids created by mining out high quality coking coal which was a scarce resource for the nation. This stowing enabled the mines to recover nearly 100 per cent of the in situ quantity of coal. The Coal Board, a body of the Government of India, was set up to ensure conservation and for this purpose they levied a flat charge on all coal mined. They used the funds to subsidise mines with high quality coal which needed to stow sand. They reimbursed the transportation cost of sand from their sand dunes. If the sand was not available there, they supported the higher costs of its longer transportation from the riverbed.

The officers of the private sector operating at Dhanbad soon found that it was much easier for them to make profits for their owners by getting this subsidy, and cheat on the corresponding costs to the extent that they may not even stow the mines. Cost reduction by other means was difficult and tortuous. No doubt this way they had to leave pillars of coal inside the mines and lose valuable coal. But the owners were more interested in immediate profits than in the long-term benefits of fully using their resources. Who cares, they said, as tomorrow we may die!

Hukum Singh built up documents to show where Watson's officers had cheated and pocketed part of the expenses billed to the Coal Board. Some portion of it was also used for discharging genuine expenses of the company. Iyengar failed in his attempts to stop them. Edgar was angry with the officers. But the company was in serious financial crisis and Iyengar could hardly find a way out without the subsidies of the Coal Board. Willy-nilly he had to tolerate the other part of the financial arrangements contrived by these officers. In this ambience of permissiveness, looting the company in several ways had also to be tolerated. It was rumoured in the coalfields that Edgar and Iyengar had met the minister in private and told him that it was time they nationalised the coking coal mines as they found it impossible to maintain honesty and keep the company financially sound. Watson had huge arrears of provident fund to pay to the Coal Mines Provident Fund, most of it representing deductions from the wages of the workmen.

The officers were angry with Hukum Singh and Iyengar, and would have got rid of them but Edgar with his British sense of justice drew the line against it. This uneasy situation prevailed for some time. Hukum Singh now tried another method. He had heard about a new senior officer of the Coal Board, Satyen Bose, who was an exceptionally honest person. He used to have secret meetings with Bose and pass on this information. He did not feel safe to let either Iyengar or Edgar know about this. Satyen tried to intervene but he found that every time he asked his officers to investigate, they reported that it was all above board. The void created by extracted coal continued to be one of ill-gotten gold. This process described colourfully as 'slaughter mining' resulted in several disasters. Roads and houses suddenly collapsed in the area. Fires broke out in the mines and spread to the neighbouring areas, destroying valuable national property. Hukum Singh bore the pain of it all with stoic resignation, till the nationalisation took place. The preamble of the legislation specifically pointed out that the prime purpose of nationalisation was to stop this 'slaughter mining'.

Hukum Singh had detailed records to show which officer had used these voids of ill-gotten gold. His tenacious nature led him to document not only the mines of his company but several other mines. His wife Parvinder Kaur complained that the spirits had gotten her husband's head (sar tae bhoot savar ho gaya, as she described in Punjabi). He spent sleepless nights pursuing his mission in life to rid Dhanbad of corruption. This Diwali night he would sleep well, as he had handed over to Chandra a detailed dossier on every corrupt officer of Dhanbad.

Chandra was taken in by this lanky Sikh with a flowing white beard. He showed the dossier to the head of the takeover task force and the minister. The next month saw the process of screening of the officers. The news about Hukum Singh's diary had gone around. Chandra's office was blitzkrieged with telephone calls from mighty names from all over India for safe-berthing of the erstwhile officers of the private sector. Most calls were on behalf of those who figured adversely in Hukum Singh's list. The pulls and pressures enabled many of them to get positions of authority in the new set-up. But some were thrown out and Hukum Singh was the target of their anger. Chandra's efforts to provide a good position for Hukum Singh himself were thwarted by the new norms of educational qualifications. The personnel director of the newly formed public sector did not also wish to risk his reputation by favouring one of the 'most hated persons in the coalfield'. Iyengar got a top position as he was a highly qualified accountant and had known the minister since before the nationalisation. He however had little inclination to now use Hukum Singh as a 'bloodhound'. The ceremonial glory of his new high-sounding designation in the public sector was enough to keep his spirits going.

Soon thereafter, the minister died in an aircrash. The culture that emerged was not particularly keen on conservation. Profit was required as evidence of efficiency. There was a strong move to abolish the Coal Board and merge its operations with the nationalised undertaking. Satyen Bose in one of his last public statements before retirement said that socialised mines were no guarantee for better conservation. An independent organisation could have better chances to ensure this. He was publicly dubbed as a confused reactionary. The investigatory powers of the Coal Board were slowly reduced. Satyen Bose retired a sad man.

The sand gangsters restarted their business with renewed vigour but with a closer nexus with political parties than ever before. Subedar Major (Retd) Hukum Singh did not however stop maintaining his diary. He felt it would be useful some day or the other. Parvinder reconciled herself to his 'mad' ways. 'He is shortly going to retire anyway and I hope that he can at last make peace with himself. In the public sector we can at least be sure we will not be sacked or murdered; our salaries are also assured,' she said.

(This case is based on real-life facts barring a few minor additions and alterations to disguise the personalities.)

Analyses for the reader

1. Do you think Hukum Singh was ethical, judging by his intentions or the consequences of his actions?
2. Do you think Hukum Singh should now make peace with himself?
3. It is said that the more the intrinsic need for blowing the whistle, the less likely is it to succeed. Is this borne out by this case?
4. Do the case facts in anyway show that the need for whistle-blowing is different in different economic structures—capitalist, socialist or one of a controlled economy?

10

JUDGE NOT THE GO-GETTER
The Thankless Tasks of Marketing and Purchase

The Ever-suspected Go-between

Marketing and purchase personnel live dangerously and tend to get trapped in the ethical gap discussed in Chapter 2. They tend to become the ethical scapegoats of society while some others adopt a holier than thou attitude. Several situations arising in these functions have been cited in the preceding chapters. This chapter aims at consolidating the understanding, discussing a range of tasks considered extremely ethically vulnerable. The views of the *Mahabharata* that the innate tendency of traders is to be unethical, and the suspicion against traders in the *Arthashastra* is the natural perception of buyers or sellers or vice versa.

There is a second kind of apprehension arising out of the principal–agent relationship (Ross 1973, Eisenhardt 1989). The principal is the organisation and the men who buy or sell for it are its agents. These jobs need considerable delegation of powers and make close monitoring difficult. Such a situation leads to the suspicion that marketing and purchase managers are bound to cheat the organisation to a lesser or greater degree.

Let us therefore approach the subject with some sympathy for the eternal scapegoats whom society is quick to blame but needs nevertheless. Such a balanced perspective of a neutral arbitrator also emerges from Weber (1995). Marketing and purchase managers, precisely for the reason that they are the 'go-between', are more considerate to society as compared to production personnel.

The Tasks Considered

The executives in these areas would typically deal with the subject under different heads:

- A. *The marketing and sales function*
    1. gathering market information

2. product decisions
3. pricing decisions
4. advertisement decisions
5. sales decisions
6. distribution decisions

B. *The purchase function*

These functions are sometimes clubbed under the heading 'commercial operations'.

Like Cleopatra of Infinite Variety

In Chapter 4 we described the overlaps and the uncommon elements between law and ethics. We noted that several ethical principles evolved in these functional areas have been converted to laws. Even as these laws give a standardised approach to ethics, the understanding of these is possible only through a variety of examples that bring about a subtle interplay of law and ethics. We will therefore look at various examples that will benefit the reader provided he or she ponders over the issues and discusses them with others.

The three main ethical approaches to the seller–purchaser relationship are (Valesquez 1982):

1. the contract view
2. the due-care view
3. the strict-liability view

The first view is developed in the Contract Act, Sale of Goods Act, MRTP and Consumer Protection Act. Under the Contract Act and Sale of Goods Act, the buyer and seller must willingly enter into the contract. There should be an offer, an acceptance and a consideration. There should be no misrepresentation, but a full disclosure, of facts. However, the earlier fall-back position was caveat emptor; the buyer should beware.

The major problem in this arrangement is the asymmetry of information. The seller who is usually closer to the manufacturer always knows more about the product than the buyer. Also, in a long chain of buyers and sellers, the ethical responsibilities of the earlier sellers get extinguished. The MRTP and Consumer Protection Acts give relief to the purchaser from

The Ancient PFA Act

Penalty for describing an article of low quality as of higher quality: eight times the value.

—*Arthashastra, 4.215*

the strict application of the principle of caveat emptor. The Consumer Protection Act protects the purchaser from his prior ignorance of the nature of the product sold. It is an effective means of enforcing the performance of the contract by the seller and providing damages for non-performance. It however applies only to purchases for consumption and does not cover commercial purchases for profit-making activities.

The second view is that at every stage, the seller should take 'due care'—the concept of caveat emptor is replaced by a weak caveat venditor, or the seller beware. The several judicial decisions under the unwritten laws of tort have supported this ethical principle. The famous case of Donogue v. Stevenson in England started this trend. A user who has no contractual relationship with the seller can also sue him for damages in case there is a loss due to bad quality. There are several other legislations in India on the quality of the products: The Seeds Act, Prevention of Food Adulterations Act, Standard Weights Act, etc., where all the sellers in the chain are accountable.

The third principle is somewhat drastic. The producer may have taken reasonable care, but if the product causes damage, the producer has to compensate even if the person suffering the damage had no contract with the producer. This is the extreme case of caveat venditor. It has some support from the judicial pronouncements under the laws of tort, e.g., the Ryland v. Fletcher case mentioned in the Bhopal gas tragedy case in Chapter 3. The economic theory behind this is that if the producer is made to pay for any damage even if he could not have reasonably anticipated it, he will be doubly conscious. His extra costs would be shared by all his customers who will thereby share the risk. The resources

> **The New PFA Act**
>
> If any person who manufactures or sells or imports adulterated food . . . can be punished with imprisonment upto two years.
>
> —*Prevention of Food Adulteration Act, Section 16*

> One thing mixed with another should not be sold.
>
> —*Manusmriti, 8.203*

will be allocated more rationally and the end result would be the greatest good for the greatest number. In India, the laws of tort are poorly developed and it would be necessary for the sellers to be ethically in 'advance of the law'. The laws in ancient India as seen in the *Arthashastra* and *Manusmriti* were quite close to the concept of caveat venditor, just as the modern Prevention of Food Adulteration Act.

In our endeavour to concentrate primarily on those areas of ethics that are not fully captured by law, we will use an illustration to clarify the three approaches. The cases are entirely fictional, synthesised from several well-known judgements of Indian and foreign courts of law.

EXAMPLE 10.1   Swaraj Home Appliances

Stage 1

Swaraj Home Appliances, a well-known producer of home electric products, developed an electric coffee pot. They had to rush the product into the market as a multinational was scheduled to release the same product in India. They had reason to believe that their product was superior to the competitor's as the design was tested for voltage fluctuation and rough handling in Indian homes. An ISI certification was also obtained. As later events showed, the tests did not fully replicate the typical conditions in Indian homes.

The electric pot was released with great fanfare. Television advertisements claimed that it was rugged and could withstand rough handling. The pot was distributed through wholesalers who in turn sold it to the retailers. A one-year warranty was provided to the ultimate consumer if supported by adequate evidence of purchase from the authorised dealer.

The electric pot was also slated for export. Before this was done, it had to be tested with greater thoroughness by the research division of Swaraj. The internal tests showed that if the pots were dropped twice from a height of one foot or once from a height of two feet, 20 per cent could start leaking under full steam. If the user was holding it at that time, it would scald him on any part of the body which was in the path of the outgoing jet of steam. Market researchers estimated that an average of 30 per cent of Indian homes would drop the pot from a height of one foot at least twice in one year or from two feet once in a year. The R&D department found ways of correcting this defect with better quality components, but this would substantially increase the costs. These costs plus minimum profits were now close to the competitor's prices. Their product was still superior to that of the competitor or so Swaraj liked to think.

Swaraj decided that in terms of the first approach, they would replace all defective pots if received within a year, because if they did not do this, they were likely to be hauled up in a consumer court and compelled to 'perform' and face damages. They could even be punished for cheating under the Penal Code. They also decided that in case anyone claimed damages for injuries, they would be able to prove it was due to mishandling—this position could be supported by their in-house research findings, and could sustain them even in the consumer courts; anyway there was no harm in sticking to this position. Since they were a famous name in the field of home appliances, there would be little chance of their reputation getting affected.

Stage 2

If Swaraj took the second approach, they would advertise in all the newspapers likely to be read by the users of the pot, asking them to return these to the dealers for replacement at the additional costs of the new parts. They could explain the low but distinct probability of six per cent of the old pots developing a defect. They could do so partly because of their belief that if Indian courts chose to follow the American pattern, they may slap unbearable damages and partly because this would enhance their reputation as an ethical company.

Stage 3

Let us assume that, as it usually happens, users did not respond and only two per cent of the pots sold were returned in the two months after the advertisement.

None of these were leaking. Swaraj could then choose not to take the third approach, and not make any further effort to reach the users. This approach may possibly be quite safe from the legal point of view. But should they act in this manner in violation of absolute ethical standards? Would a user of the pot who had missed the advertisement and whose child had got grievously hurt forgive Swaraj? Is there any chance of some activist court in India taking an adverse stand against Swaraj? Would this ruin Swaraj?

The reader may consider other options that could be consistent with their ethical approach and not likely to be too damaging to Swaraj in the short and long run. But even if it were damaging, should they follow the third approach for reasons of ethics and not of profit?

Rights and Wrongs in Information-gathering

An essential prerequisite for effective marketing is accurate and timely market information. This can be gathered by the personnel working in marketing organisations or obtained from marketing consultants. There are important ethical issues which could arise for marketing consultants or the in-house personnel in collecting, analysing and interpreting information. Further, marketing organisations could question the ethicality of the way such information is used. The ethicality could relate to the respondents, the clients who would be the guinea pigs in the resultant marketing strategy, and lastly, the competitors.

The basic ethics of information-gathering is rooted in the ethics of privacy as also in the ethics of not using human beings as the means and not as the ends in themselves. The latter arises from the ethic that we should not do to others what we would not like others to do to us.

Chonko (1995) lists the following issues:

Ethics towards respondents

Respondent anonymity, avoiding stress to the interviewees, prior knowledge that one is using special equipment to record the interview, full information to the respondents on why the interviews are being conducted. Not using deception or coercion, selling disguised as research, being embarrassing and offensive.

Ethics towards competitors

Misrepresentation, influence peddling, surveillance of competitors through measures such as planting electronic bugs in their office, intelligence obtained even though not solicited.

Ethics of market researchers towards users of marketing information

Intellectual integrity and limitations of the data gathered.

These issues would be clarified by the following examples. Most of these are generalised accounts of common situations in information-gathering in India.

EXAMPLE 10.2 Murarka Market Research Consultants

Murarka hires Arun Menon, a fresh MBA, and puts him in charge of a major market consultancy contract. The consultancy was obtained by them on the assurance that it would be supervised by the senior partners of the firm. But Arun realised that he would be functioning more or less unsupervised as the partners had other international commitments. Arun is a novice and knows next to nothing. Should he tell the clients about this?

EXAMPLE 10.3 Ramnath Puri

Ramnath Puri conducted a market research in 1993 which showed that an encyclopaedia of Indian mythology had good sales potential. This was the favourite idea of Giri Iyer, the Marketing Vice President of a book publishing company. But, Akhilesh Tiwari the Managing Director was stonewalling the project. In 1995 Tiwari left the company and Giri Iyer took over as the MD. He now wishes to revive the project and also give Puri a promotion. But Puri meanwhile has found that the idea of putting an encyclopaedia on the Internet has been gaining ground. In five years, printed encyclopaedias would become obsolete. Puri is aware that Iyer would be deeply disappointed on learning this and his own promotion would be at stake. What should he do?

EXAMPLE 10.4 Suraj Televisions

Krishnan of Suraj Televisions is asked by his boss to conduct a survey that would prove that a 20 per cent increase in the subscription rates is justified. How should Krishnan respond?

EXAMPLE 10.5 The Ultraviolet Ink

Usha, an executive in a firm of market research consultants, is assigned a massive postal market research of 30,000 respondents. The client has been assured of a thorough job. Her boss Ram Saxena tells her this can be done only if she personally cross-checks with the respondents. This would require the names and addresses of the respondents to be recorded on the response sheets. But the client has said that as the product is for personal use, the respondents should be informed that their names would not be recorded. Saxena suggests that the names should be recorded in ultraviolet ink and decoded at the office. Usha is told that if the project goes through, both she and Ram would get a promotion. Should Usha agree to this?

EXAMPLE 10.6 **The Magic Flute**

Anirudh, a sales officer of Sangeetha Music Company, received a surprise gift on his birthday from one of his best dealers. It was a cassette recording yet to be released by a competitor, Gan Bharati, whose representative had absent-mindedly left it behind with the dealer who had been consulted in confidence. New releases are usually made during Durga Puja which was two months away. The singer was a newcomer, Sajan Kumar, and the unknown composer had used the flute in a most original and charming way.

Sangeetha was one of the biggest music companies in India. Anirudh felt that if they released a number sung by their star artist Ranjan Kumar using similar musical motifs, they were bound to beat their competitors hollow. He was also sure that the Copyright Act would not be violated. The criteria, developed by the famous Indian composer Naushad and accepted by the industry, prescribed the maximum number of similar bars of musical phrases permitted in the new composition as compared to the old one. Should Anirudh pass on the cassette with the magic flute to his company?

The cautions in product development

The crux of the ethics in product decisions arise out of the fact that the producer or seller usually knows much more about the product than the buyer. Therefore he has to take extra precautions not to breach the trust the buyer has reposed in him. Product decisions can typically follow the reiterative models we have described in Chapter 2.

Ethical issues arise in product decisions in seven stages (Chonko 1995):

1. When the idea is first mooted

Free discussions from the legal safety point of view are scotched in the name of providing free scope for a creative atmosphere. There is a trade-off between the atmosphere to be created for 'individuation' (see Chapter 5) and ethical democratic discourse (Chapters 1 and 2).

2. Screening of product designs

Only the profitability criteria, and not the safety and welfare criteria, are usually applied till the in-company investments are too high to be turned down. There is a bias in favour of products on which considerable money has already been spent.

3. Product development and evaluation

There is little attention paid to the way consumers will actually use the products, and consequently to the risk to their welfare.

4. Marketing strategy

What are the product's unique selling points to be emphasised? Should the company be honest about its weak points? How are the packaging and labels to depict the product? Does the product enhance the welfare of the buyers or should one concentrate only on the immediate profits?

5. Test marketing

Is it a correct sample to judge its misuse, etc. ?

6. Introducing in the market

Should we watch out for and be aware of the risks?

7. Product decline stage

Do we persist in pushing a product by devious means once a better product is available in the market?

The following examples based on the author's generalised experience and on newspaper reports clarify the issues.

EXAMPLE 10.7   The Water Purifier

Abdul Rashid sells aqua purifiers. His company uses personal selling. In the selling process, the salespersons use the certificates of experience of their numerous earlier purchasers. These certificates truthfully indicate that the incidence of stomach upsets reduced considerably in all the members of the family, particularly the old, with the use of the purifier. A recent paper in a medical journal has however come out with a finding that the chemical they used for purification could be carcinogenic; the correlations were low (+0.25) but not insignificant. Should Abdul reveal this information to the intending purchasers?

EXAMPLE 10.8   Gita Garment Exports

Gita Garment Exports had a flourishing business exporting garments to the USA. Suddenly, the US administration banned the imports because they found that the garments, made of synthetic material, could cause dermatitis, a skin disease. Faced with this debacle, Gita Exports explored other markets and found that several African countries may like to import this product. The profits would be lower but the company would avert financial disaster. Should they export to Africa without confirming that there would be no risk of dermatitis?

EXAMPLE 10.9   The Kimayana Story

New Wave Publishers claimed that they were a most ethical company which propagated free speech and expression of views. They were excited by a script titled 'Kimayana' received from Mast Singh. It was a full-blown account of an old palm-leaf rendition of the story of the *Ramayana* in which Ram and Sita were brother and sister, and their relationship incestuous. The publishers felt that this had tremendous potential in the West which was looking for new variants of 'scholarly pornography'. Mast Singh was a widely read writer whose writings thrived on the thrill of new twists to old stories. Should New Wave release the book in India and abroad?

EXAMPLE 10.10   **Ramco's Overstrong Axle**

Ramco was reviewing its new 10-tonner truck model. The axle strength was designed to be slightly overstrong for this load. The launching advertisements had flashed across the media. Just a day before they were to release the truck in the market, Jethmalani the Vice President proudly showed it off to Buta Singh his ex-driver who now ran a trucking service. Buta Singh asked if the axle was okay. Jethmalani said that it was designed for 12 tons. But Buta Singh said that this would prove a disaster and lead to serious road accidents as the trucks are usually loaded up to 18 tons by fitting sideboards. Jethmalani smiled smugly and said that the company could not be held responsible for such foolishness. If he had to design the axle for 18 tons, the costs would go up by Rs 20,000. 'Why should I do something which the law does not require of me? Moreover, Arjun Arcland will release their trucks sooner than we can replace the axles,' he said. Do you agree with Jethmalani?

The Law Lays Down Much of the Ethics of Pricing

A naive understanding of the ethics of proper pricing would be that it is just an exercise in working the elasticity of demand to price, and fixing the price in such a manner that the organisation can maximise its own profits. This approach would appeal to those who are convinced of the ethical superiority of market systems—(see Chapter 3). As markets are free only in theory, ethics in pricing becomes important. Much of the ethics in pricing have been incorporated in law. These cover the Monopolies and Restrictive Trade Practices Act, Essential Commodities Act and Industrial Regulations Act (provisions of price control). Another useful monitoring mechanism for ensuring reasonable prices is the Cost Audit Rules issued under the Indian Companies Act. This enables the government to obtain information on the cost of production in a company. This provision is unique in the world; no other country has a similar legislation.

Section 2 (i) of the MRTP Act defines monopolistic pricing practices which can be curtailed by government intervention. This can be done if the prices are much higher than the costs in a monopolistic situation. Section 33 of the Act covering restrictive trade practices contains several sub-sections wherein instances of predatory pricing, resale price maintenance, cartel pricing and discriminatory pricing are to be reported to the MRTP Commission. Section 36A of the MRTP Act refers to 'deceptive bargain prices'. The MRTP Commission or the consumer courts can issue cease and desist orders against such pricing practices. The Essential Commodities Act and the price control mechanisms enable the government to fix controlled prices for those essential commodities that are in short supply.

Ethical organisations may prefer not to play a cat and mouse game with the law, and would by themselves follow pricing practices that are in consonance with the spirit of the law. They can, but are unlikely to, stretch the law in their favour by literal interpretations (see Chapter 4).

The following examples clarify the spirit behind the law.

EXAMPLE 10.11 Hyderabad Asbestos

Hyderabad Asbestos had two pricing practices which were investigated by the MRTP Commission (RTPE 1987 decided on 26 December 1980). The first involved very high variations in pricing between different order sizes. The second was that they sold below cost to the public sector and the government (predatory pricing) due to excessive competition. The Commission allowed it to continue. As for discriminatory pricing, they instructed the company to follow uniform pricing with suitable discounts based on cost savings subject to the size of the orders.

EXAMPLE 10.12 Carborundum Universal

Carborundum Universal had four price slabs. The MRTP Commission (RTPE 28 of 1974 decided on 21 November 1975) advised them to have only three slabs, with the difference between each slab to be not more than one per cent.

EXAMPLE 10.13 Philips India

Philips India used to give the 'recommended price' in their price lists. This gave the impression that the product should not be sold below that price. The MRTP Commission (RTP 5 of 1978 decided on 26 September 1979) directed that the price lists should show the maximum retail price and the dealers should have the freedom to charge less.

EXAMPLE 10.14 *The Statesman*

The Statesman was offering concessional rates for advertisements published in all its issues. The MRTP Commission (RTP 53 of 1974 decided on 2 April 1976) decided that there should be separate rates for the Calcutta and Delhi editions, and the combined rates should not be less than 92.5 per cent of the individual rates.

EXAMPLE 10.15 Ghee Manufacturers' Association

The Ghee Manufacturers' Association used to direct its members to sell their ghee at uniform prices. The MRTP Commission (RTPE 23 of 1976 decided on 14 February 1977) directed that it should not give such directions; this amounted to a cartel.

EXAMPLE 10.16 **Snowline Clothiers**

Snowline Clothiers advertised an unusually high discount of 50 per cent. The MRTP Commission (UTP 13 of 1984 decided on 2 May 1986) ordered the following guidelines for the future:

1. The period of discount should not be less than ten days and should be mentioned in the advertisement.
2. The normal price of each category should be mentioned.
3. The quantity of the articles for the maximum and minimum discount should be mentioned.

Interestingly, some of the famous cases of whistle-blowing (see Chapter 9) in the USA are internal evidences which enable the government agencies to catch the companies indulging in unethical pricing practices.

Advertising Not a Free-for-All

A well-known book on advertising (Littlefield and Kirkpatrick 1970) defines advertisement as a 'means of communication of information to persuade buyers so as to maximise profits'. An ethicist may however replace the word 'profits' by the expression 'the greatest good of the greatest number'. The ethics of advertising more complex than this simplistic definition. This industry has an astronomically high annual turnover around the world. Its ethics needs to be understood carefully by any business manager.

Symmetry of information between the buyer and seller is an essential prerequisite for the ethicality of market systems. This symmetry cannot be even dreamt of without a cost-effective means of communicating the information. Advertisements are one such medium. They are often cheaper than other means of communication. But they should not be used for manipulation and deception, nor should they result in reducing or eliminating competition by unfair means, or have unintended and adverse side effects on those who see or hear the advertisement and who are otherwise in no way connected with the transaction of purchase or sale. They should not take away resources from more socially useful purposes, e.g., during a cholera epidemic, television advertisements of holiday resorts in Switzerland should not get precedence over public messages that help prevent cholera.

Having agreed on these criteria one can ask the following questions, with the corresponding possible answers.

1. Can the criteria be achieved without a legal framework to guide advertisements ? The answer is 'No'.
2. Can the criteria be achieved only with the backing of law but without self-regulatory councils of advertising professionals ? The answer is 'No'.

3. Can this be achieved with the aid of law and of professional associations but without the backing of the ethics of individual organisations? Not in a free market system.

4. Would bad advertising ethics adversely affect profitability? Yes, particularly in the long run. One cannot fool all the people all the time.

5. Will ethical advertising make all advertising too factual and boring, and kill the joy of life and adventure? Most emphatically 'No'.

Coming to the specifics of the ethics of advertising, Hymen *et al.* (1994) cover the following issues:

1. Does it misinform?
2. Does it mislead?
3. Does it make false promises?
4. Does it criticise other products—truthfully or otherwise?
5. Does it create socially undesirable demands?
6. Does it cause socially undesirable action by the target audience?
7. Does it try to influence target groups who are not mature enough to understand and discriminate, e.g., children?
8. Is it in any way offensive to good taste?
9. Is it using money power to blackball fair competition?
10. Does it lower the dignity of women?
11. Does it revel in intimate physical details which good taste should leave alone?
12. Does it defame any person or class of persons?
13. Does it build a stereotype which results in some class of persons having a disadvantage in normal social relationship.
14. Does it manipulate the viewer by subliminal suggestions or emotional blackmail by wrongly, unreasonably, irrationally invoking basic and hidden fears of death and injury, or visions and fantasies?

A verdict on all of these can rely in some measure on the legal processes—criminal or civil law—available in the country. For the general issues of public offences, the Indian Penal Code is the basic law. Defamation and libel are covered by the laws of tort. But by and large the issues are nebulous and contentious. Therefore it is felt that advertisers should exercise self-control through their own councils (see Chapter 6). Decisions would then be more flexible and adaptable to current social thinking. Lastly, the right and wrong in advertising can hardly be dictated by a few law-makers, a coterie of professional advertisers, without understanding what the general public think about them. The consequences of advertisements are conditioned less by the intentions of the advertisers than the mindsets of the responding public. As was mentioned by a judge in the well-known case of *Lady Chatterley's Lover*, the test of whether a particular publication is obscene or unethical depends on its consequence on the behaviour of its readers. Arya and Rao (1995) have reported that most readers can laugh away an advertisement and can see through a 'puff' or a joke, and it would be ridiculous to get into their literal analysis to determine if they are ethical or not. Some advertisements may be ineffective or infructuous if they carry a joke too far or inappropriately stress on sexual themes; they may not turn out to be unethical as they may not be taken seriously by the public and therefore their impact may be negligible.

The following examples from well-known sources would clarify the issues.

EXAMPLE 10.17   **The AIDS Advertisement**

A television advertisement shows a lecherous *mama* (uncle) telling his *bhanja* (nephew) that he better use condoms when he goes with his numerous girl-friends. 'Do not risk AIDS. It is incurable,' he says. The advertisement is telecast at prime time when children are watching television along with their parents. Can you think of a way to improve the advertisement ethically?

EXAMPLE 10.18   **The Grim Mother-in-Law**

A *masala* (spices) advertisement shows the mother-in-law menacingly standing in front of her trembling daughter-in-law who is trying to pick up the right ingredients for cooking. She makes the inevitable mistake, to the glee of her mother-in-law. If only she had chosen this *masala* powder, she would have got it all right—so goes the advertisement. Can mothers-in-law object to this stereo-typing?

EXAMPLE 10.19   **The Song of the Sister-in-Law**

An advertisement shows a petulant young man being cajoled by three women: his mother, sister-in-law and wife. Comes the new *masala* powder and he bursts forth with a hit song on his sister-in-law. Is this advertisement demeaning to women?

EXAMPLE 10.20   **Chelsea Jeans**

The Chelsea Jeans campaign featured two women, one thrusting her knee between the other's legs, the copy reading, 'F*** off, leave us alone'. Would you consider it an ethical ad?

EXAMPLE 10.21   **The Detergent Advertisement**

A company marketing detergents advertised on television its competitor's product as being too soft and easily removable from the cake by the gentlest pressure of a finger. Was it ethical by absolute standards or consequentially?

EXAMPLE 10.22 **Fair and Lovely**

Hindustan Lever advertise their fairness cream 'Fair and Lovely' by claiming that its regular use makes the skin fair and lovely. Is this an exploitation of the weakness Indians have for being fair-skinned? Is the ad ethical?

The Harsh World of Selling

This section of the chapter basically deals with the ethical problems of managing a salesforce. In Chapter 8 we had discussed the difficulty in converting codes of ethics to operational practices by the executives. It is nowhere more difficult to do this than in sales administration. The salesforce is in touch with the fierce competitive markets and profitability depends critically on sales. Therefore, penalties and rewards tend to depend on sales performance. Most often the signals to the salespersons are that results matter, not ethics. The combining of these apparently contradictory goals of organisations is subtle but not impossible. Codes of conduct are never really wasted on the staff, say Vasquez-Paraga and Kara (1995) who researched in Turkey in an ambience familiar to Indian managers, that of religious sanctions against unethicality.

Robertson and Anderson (1993), in an article provocatively titled 'Does the opportunity make a thief? How control systems influence [an] industrial salesperson's behavior', say:

> The study has assessed salesperson responses to a set of vig-
> nettes involving ethical issue in sales. Some behavior is more
> tolerated than others. Acceptance of a behavior is not totally
> dependent on conformity with an ethical principle but also on
> the perception of how it fits with prevailing industry practice,
> perceptions of the likely behavior leading to outcomes and cal-
> culations of the profits and costs of these outcomes.
>
> Particular attention must be paid to the circumstances which
> provide opportunities for unethical behaviour[:] if employees
> [are] working in autonomous decentralised setting, extra efforts
> to instill the importance of ethics is to be undertaken. If the
> competition is severe, the corporate emphasis on ethics is nece-
> ssary to counteract the effects of competition. If a firm's tran-
> sactions tend to be major ones, in which the employees perceive
> their careers to be on the line, then clearly it is vital the message
> must get through that unethical behavior will not [be] tolerated.

The observation may appear to be a trivial truism. But the underlying philosophy is important. Sales executives tend to be guided by their professional demands for bending ethics. Institutional support for encouraging ethical behaviour is more useful than a punitive or reformatory approach. Marketing personnel are the unfortunate victims of the ethics gap—most of the strain of the consequences of systemic unethicality tends to fall on them. Elsewhere, Hunt and Vittel (1993) say that if ethicality is measured and the data is interpreted to allow for the factor on whom the consequences of the 'ethics gap is falling', sales and marketing personnel may be as ethical as other groups are. This however needs to be reinforced organisationally (Hunt and Vasqeuz-Paraga 1993).

The following examples further clarify the issues.

EXAMPLE 10.23 Govind Nath

Govind Nath, a fresh MBA from the Badami Institute of Management, was recruited by a well-known company which had come to the Institute for campus recruitment for the first time. The company's President Mani Krishnaswamy had heard of the Institute's course on ethics and was keen to get a band of younger managers who would stand by ethics. Govind had expected to start his career with the glamorous task of preparing grand marketing strategies. Instead, he was thrown into the field competing with 'crooks' as he called them, trying to sell the company's whisky. He was given a tough target for the first year. On the last day of the year when he was desperately trying to inch across, he met his immediate boss George Mascahrenes, an old-timer of the company, who told him that he could give him a tip that would enable him to cross the magic figure, provided Govind paid him Rs 10,000. This was 50 per cent of the bonus Govind would get if he could achieve the annual target. Should he agree to George's proposal?

EXAMPLE 10.24 Rakesh Taimini's Travel Bill

Young Rakesh Taimini bragged to his newly married wife Urmila that his company was extremely happy with him and provided him lavish benefits. On his next business trip, he took Urmila along to demonstrate this. At the hotel he arranged for the hotel to give him a single room at Rs 1,500 per day without showing either double occupancy or his wife's name in the bill. The hotel agreed to this arrangement. He billed the company at this rate. The company rules did not permit reimbursement of the spouse's lodging charges. The news that Urmila had stayed with him reached the President. He called up Rakesh to explain, who said that he had not caused any extra expense to the company and that he had not seen any service rule that prohibits the wife from accompanying an executive. Do you think that Rakesh had been ethical?

EXAMPLE 10.25   **Deepak Ghosh and the Campaign Sale**

Deepak's company had a special campaign sale in March 1995. Knowing this, Deepak held back the sales figures of January and February, and included these in the March figures so that he could get the bonus on the campaign sale. Since the campaign sale provided a special discount for the dealer, overall the company lost in the bargain. Had Deepak been ethical?

EXAMPLE 10.26   **Sudip Karnad's False Promise of Delivery**

Sudip Karnad had a hard time meeting his yearly target by 31 December 1995. On the 29th, he had one customer who was directly in need of the material. He was willing to accept a sale provided the delivery was made by 10 January. Sudip included this order in his report to the headquarters. An advance of 10 per cent was obtained from the customer with the order. He however knew that the company's delivery policy is 30 days from the order reaching the factory. He hoped to somehow manage to deliver on time. Was he being ethical?

EXAMPLE 10.27   **Rajesh Menon's Gift**

This was Rajesh Menon's first job at HIPRO, a company which prided itself on its ethical standards. Rajesh had been inducted to this philosophy. Their sales targets were tight. At the year end, the only way he could meet the target was by gifting a clock to the purchase manager of the buying company. He decided to buy the gift from his own pocket as he was terrified of not being confirmed if he did not fulfil the target. Was he being ethical?

EXAMPLE 10.28   **The Special Computers of HIPRO**

Ram Kumar, a sales executive, had the best record for sales in HIPRO. He was very good at demonstrating his company's computers. He waxed eloquent on their ethics and their record of being the first computer company to get the ISO 9000. But he did not tell the clients that spare parts of their computers were non-standard and available only with them. Their systems also did not match others in the field. Consequently, other service companies could not carry out their repair jobs. HIPRO's own service department had therefore a monopoly. Were Ram Kumar and HIPRO ethically upright?

The Several Subterfuges of Distribution Management

The ethics of distribution are varied but concern themselves with the following typical issues: tied-in sales: minimum order quantity; territorial restrictions, grey and black markets; playing one distribution channel against another, keeping everyone guessing; and enforcing exclusive dealership.

Most of these are extensively covered by the legal machinery of the MRTP Act. Many situations border on ethics and just about past muster with the MRTP Commission, as is seen in the following examples.

EXAMPLE 10.29 Territorial Restrictions on Hindustan Lever

The dealership contracts at Hindustan Lever (HLL) contained restrictions on the dealers selling outside their territories. HLL was encouraged to insert this restriction as the Supreme Court in a earlier case allowed such restrictions to TELCO. The MRTP struck HLL down (RTPE 1 of 1974 decided in July 1975). HLL appealed to the Supreme Court but the court upheld the decision of the MRTP Commission (Appeal Number 650). They clarified that the territorial restrictions for TELCO enabled better servicing of their machines and could not be extended to consumer articles like soaps and detergents.

EXAMPLE 10.30 Industrial Components and Services (ICS)

ICS had a minimum order stipulation of 2,500 industrial piston rings, 2,500 industrial pistons and 250 individual piston rings. Their case came up before the MRTP Commission (RTPE 75 of 1976 decided in July 1977), leading to withdrawal of the condition of minimum order.

EXAMPLE 10.31 Hero Honda

Hero Honda required their buyers to buy from them a set of accessories, 25 litres of petrol and an insurance policy. MRTP Commission struck this down (RTPE 53 of 1986).

EXAMPLE 10.32 India Cements

India Cements had stipulated that their dealers in cement should not have the dealership of any other cement company. The case came up before the MRTP Commission (RTP 48 of 1985 decided in 1986). The Commission upheld the condition on the understanding that there was a danger of different cement bags getting mixed up in the dealer's godowns.

Purchasers as Ethical Arbitrators

What is common between marketing and purchasing, both boundary-spanning departments, as also why organisations have an underlying suspicion of purchase managers has been discussed in Chapter 7. Wood (1996) cites evidence to show that many of them do indeed indulge in

Giving a Dog a Bad Name

Bribery is rampant among [purchasing] professionals and not much is done to stop combat the evil.

—*Narayanam (1992: 25–26)*

corruption. But Wood suspects that this finding may have a major problem of 'ethical relativism'. He believes, for example, that accepting gifts may be usual among purchase managers. But it is likely that they would not be influenced by these gifts. In that case, purely consequentially, it would not be really unethical. They will be unethical for deontological reasons as they would not like to be bribe-givers if they can help it (see Chapter 6 for an exposition of the code of ethics for purchasers).

It will be useful for every purchase executive to apply the following checklist suggested by Dobbler *et al.* (1984):

1. Is this action acceptable to everyone in the organisation?
2. Is this action compatible with the firm's responsibilities to its customers, suppliers and stockholders?
3. What would happen if all the buyers and suppliers behave this way?
4. If I were in the other person's position, how would I feel?

They also warn the ethical purchase executives of situations where there may be a conflict of interests. The Indian Companies Act also has strict provisions for explicit disclosure in all cases where purchases are made by an organisation from another organisation in which the executives of the first organisation have substantial interests. Some organisations prohibit purchases that involve conflict of interests. Some others may tolerate it provided there is total transparency and democratic discussion.

> **The Lonely Struggle**
>
> A profession cannot be created by resolution ... they require years of self-denial, when success by base means is scorned ... when no results bring honour ...
>
> —*National Association of Purchase Managers Standards of Conduct (1959)*

It is however a known fact that an ethical purchase manager usually has to wait a long time to be rewarded for his honesty. Two typical examples of ethics of purchase managers are given, both factually faithful to the original happenings, with some minor modifications.

EXAMPLE 10.33   **Sangeeta's Cost Reduction Drive**

Sangeeta, a company manufacturing consumer electronic products, found its market dwindling. Wishing to reduce its prices, it undertook a major cost-reduction drive. It came up with the idea of a new design for part X. Chandra, the GM Purchase, was given the task of negotiating the price with the vendor, within a ceiling proposed to Chandra. They wanted Chandra to also firm up the price. The part involved development of a costly mould by the vendor. Chandra painted a rosy picture of the firm's future production plans which he knew were not true. He also told the vendor that several others were eager to supply the parts to them. In fact, because of their poor track record of payments, suppliers were dropping off. Lastly, Chandra offered the vendor a price much higher than his current costs as encouragement, provided he held his prices. Chandra knew through inside sources that the raw material prices for the parts were to increase sharply six months from now. He did not share this information with the vendor. This way he succeeded in clinching the deal with the supplier. Once the moulds were made, Chandra knew that the vendor was in his clutches, unless he cheated him by supplying the design to the competitor. Was Chandra being ethical and/or wise?

EXAMPLE 10.34 **The Grand Party**

Sidhartha Ghosh was General Manager, Purchase of a large mining company. One of his major deals was to negotiate the import of specialised equipment which would assist in modernising operations. Ghosh belonged to a well-known aristocratic family of Calcutta and was known to be honest; his detractors described him as not 'practical', but he had been handpicked by his chairman. Ghosh had been educated at the same foreign university. That, along with his family background, was good enough reason for the chairman to trust him.

Several companies from all over the world were competing for this purchase. The choice was dependent more on technical analysis than on commercial terms. One of the American firms proposed to have a technical appraisal session for the officers of the company. The draft invitation for the programme as also the list of invitees was claimed to have been informally cleared by the chairman. Ghosh had not been told about this by his chairman but that was hardly surprising. The chairman had a weakness for alcohol and loved watching cabarets. He believed however that he was extremely honest and was not influenced by the sellers in any way.

The invitees were the chairman and all the functional directors on the board (finance, marketing, personnel, operations, technical) along with their spouses, and their own company's PRO, technical head and marketing head. The programme schedule was:

7:00 p.m. Welcome address
7:15 p.m. Light Indian music
7:40 p.m. A technical presentation on the products
8:10 p.m. Cocktails accompanied by Egyptian belly dance
9:30 p.m. Dinner
10:30 p.m. Games with gifts as prizes

Should Ghosh proceed to process the invitation?

SUMMARY

The chapter provides the theoretical framework for analysing the ethical aspects in marketing, sales and purchase. As these vulnerable areas can be understood only contextually, 34 situational and legal examples are given to clarify the concepts and bring the discussions closer to the Indian reality.

ISSUES TO PONDER OVER

- There are four situations described below:
  1. A restaurant sells buffet-type meals to passengers on a railway station.
  2. A company sells a heart–lung machine to a hospital.
  3. A beauty saloon sells haircuts.
  4. An educational institution markets its MBA course.

  Which of the views of ethics—the contract view, the due-care view or the strict-liability view—would be most appropriate for them?

- All advertisements that are critical of competition should be banned. Do you agree?

- Who should decide (a) how much information should be provided by the manufacturer, (b) how good products should be, and (c) how truthful advertisements should be? The government or manufacturers or consumer groups? The free market? Explain your views.

- Does this chapter lay the responsibility of ethics in a sales organisation at the top or at the grassroots which has maximum interface with customers? Why?

- Do you agree that the consequences of systemic unethicality cause an ethical gap for the sales personnel much more than for housewives and MBAs? Give examples from your experience.

- Do you agree that a purchase manager also has a duty to his vendors even if there was a conflict with the interests of his employer? Why?

- Should a purchase manager ban all purchases from firms which have his close relations in key positions?

CASE 11.1 Madhulika Bose

Madhulika Bose was an MBA. She had specialised in marketing and market research. She joined Mudrika. Her referee, her ex-professor of ethics, was asked for a confidential report by Mudrika before she joined the firm. The report said, 'Madhulika is a competent market researcher with a good understanding of statistics and the statistical computer packages to analyse data. She has varied interests in life and had to be counselled often during her stay at the institute to concentrate on fewer things so that she does not cut corners. Guided properly, she can work reasonably hard. She has a soaring ambition for a bright career.'

Her first assignment on market research involved working with part-time field investigators whom she had to train. Soon after training them she told her immediate boss Ajay Dixit that they seemed to be very poorly paid for their work and that their travelling allowances were hardly enough to look after their basic needs. She felt that they were likely to avoid travelling and fudge their response sheets. They would need too much supervision which would be very costly. Ajay ridiculed her line of thinking and said that the rates were competitive and not less than what others paid.

When the response sheets started coming in, Madhulika found that many of them seemed to have similar answers. She told Ajay that she would like to supervise and recheck some of them by reinterviewing the respondents. Ajay had a look at the response sheets and said that this was not unnatural and could be quite representative of the population. He did not agree to her undertaking the tour to cross-check the response sheets.

A little later, she was surprised by a call from the Managing Director Ram Ambani who said that the clients wanted the report a fortnight earlier and that if she accepted the challenge she could get a promotion and could directly report to him. Madhulika said she would accept the challenge. She requested for a generous travel budget. Ram acceded to this request.

As she proceeded with her work, she realised that meeting the deadline was going to be difficult with the slow progress. She decided on a whirlwind tour to personally interview the respondents. Even then she found time overtaking her. She felt that the first sample of respondents she had interviewed herself confirmed Ajay Dixit's theory that the population was homogeneous. She argued with Ajay that the sample size could be reduced without any risk of coming to the wrong conclusions. Ajay, without referring to Ram, said that the client had specified a minimum sample size and so she could not change it.

Madhulika in a panic just cooked up the data for a large number of respondents. She satisfied herself that the clients would not be misled with wrong results. Ajay guessed the evidence of this fudging and reported it to Ram. 'Here is what your favourite has done,' he said with a sneer.

A furious Ram called up Madhulika. He knew that there was no time to cross-check and prove Ajay's accusation. But Madhulika confessed before he could verify anything. But she said that statistically she was satisfied that no harm had been done and the client would get a sound and reliable report and in time. But Ram felt that his company would be in serious trouble if this were known outside. Moreover, his father the chairman was a moralist and would not tolerate this slip-up of moral behaviour.

(This case has been discussed with some of the top market research organisations in the country and they confirm that the situation is a realistic one.)

Analyses for the reader

1. What do you think Madhulika should have done as a good professional?
2. Should Ram Ambani sack her?

CASE 11.2   Uhuru Dudhs

Uhuru wa watumwa uhuru dudhs was the hoarding of the Indian company selling baby milkfood in an African country. It touched the emotional African chord of nationalism and India's solidarity with the African cause. It meant 'Freedom for the Slaves Freedom Indian Milk'. It showed the picture of a bouncing little dark baby laughing and kicking its legs. Milk flowed from its mouth in an exact imitation of the brand of a Swiss multinational with a fair baby. This was reproduced in the packaging too. African mothers, yearning for healthy babies like those of the whites, found the advertisement irresistible.

Uhuru Dudhs was a product of the protocol signed some time ago by the Indian Government with the democratically elected African Government. Under this agreement, Indian milk powder was to be exported to that country, packed there and marketed under the brand name of 'Uhuru Dudhs'. To make that country self-sufficient in milk in 10 years, 30 per cent of the profits were to be ploughed back to dairy development programmes. After 10 years, milk imports were to be discontinued and Uhuru Dudhs would use indigenous milk.

Uhuru Dudhs beat all the other multinationals by their superb marketing and a marginal price advantage. The use of baby milk powder rapidly increased. The dairy development also went apace. But a tragedy lay ahead. The incidence of infant diarrhoea rose rapidly. There was little doubt that it most affected the users of Uhuru Dudhs. The competitors tried to use it to their advantage. But no matter what they tried they could not prove that the Indian product was defective or unhygienic by itself.

A little investigation by a voluntary agency, Mzimu, ironically with strong Indian participation, showed that the incidence was invariably because the mothers did not sterilise the milk bottles after use. They also used impure water for washing the bottles. The agency's social workers felt that African mothers would be much better off if they breastfed their babies, and that the hoardings and packaging of Uhuru Dudhs were misleading. They also felt that it would not be possible to ensure the hygiene, and that the product should be withdrawn from the market. Uhuru Dudhs accepted the defect in their hoardings and illustrations on the packages, and said that they would change them in line with the advertising and packaging in India. They would advise the mothers that breast milk is the most hygienic for babies. But they felt that it was totally wrong to blame them for the lack of hygiene. That was the function of the governments and voluntary agencies like Mzimu.

Mzimu would have nothing of this. They brought a counter slogan to Uhuru which proclaimed *Simu ya kifo dudh* (Death Call is the Indian Milk). They argued that African mothers could not understand the complex ideas in the advertisements and the right thing to do was to ban it. 'We have tried every method to persuade the mothers to be hygienic in cleaning the bottles. But how can they when there is no clean water available anywhere,' they said. They however admitted that in some cases external milk may be useful for babies whose mothers were sick or unable to feed them. On balance they felt that this argument could not be used for a generalised permission in support of baby milk food.

The African Government was in a quandary. Its entire dairy development programme was jeopardised. On the advice of the MD of Uhuru Dudhs, they hired a famous sociologist to advise them on the habits of African mothers. His report said, 'The issue is not so simple. Nutritional status is embedded in socio-cultural and biophysical systems. Changes in food use and diet are related to changes in the social, political, economic, technical, religious and environmental factors ... to deal with the infant formula a complex system of interventions is required.' Both the MD and the Government were dismayed by this pedantic report. Mzimu continued their protest and counter-campaign.

The MD held a board meeting. The marketing director felt that in view of Mzimu's recommendations the milk could be distributed through doctors. This could be a blessing in disguise. The publicity costs would be reduced. He was sure that his salespersons could persuade the doctors to prescribe the milk powder in desirable cases. 'There will be a drop in sales but the profitability will not be reduced correspondingly as publicity costs would be reduced.' The MD said he was not sure if it was the right thing to do. He read out the provisions of the Indian law on the subject (see below). The marketing director felt that the analogy of Indian laws could not be applied to Africa. He requested the MD not to bring these provisions to the notice of Mzimu or the African Government. The MD put forward the marketing director's idea of distribution through doctors to the Government who in turn consulted Mzimu.

Mzimu was however suspicious of this arrangement. They were aware of the inducements the foreign drug companies offered the local doctors to push their drugs. 'Why don't you develop new products and market them to adults?,' they said. The MD knew the margins were far less and the task much tougher.

Extracts from The Indian Infant Milk Substitute Act

Section 8   No person shall use any healthcare system for the purpose of promoting the use or sale of infant milk substitutes.

Section 9   No person who sells infant milk substitutes shall offer or give any financial inducements or gifts to a health worker or any member of his family. Where any contribution is made to the health worker, he shall disclose the same to the institution to which such health worker is attached.

(The case is fictional but is derived from that of a well-known multinational in the dairy industry. Its understanding of the attitude of several Indian businessmen who have industries in Africa is based on the general accounts available in published literature.)

Analyses for the reader

1. What should the MD of Uhuru Dudhs do now?
2. Are there any lessons to be learnt from these case facts?

11

THE EVIL GODDESS WHO TEMPTS
Growing Ethical Pitfalls in High Finance

Where Wealth Accumulates and Men Decay

In keeping with the ethics inventoried in Chapter 1 and the practices of Islamic economics (see Chapter 2), it is obvious that productionist ethics ought to be the norm of the day.

Diametrically opposed to this view are those of the neo-classical economists who contend that 'high finance', in conjunction with free markets, allocate resources to activities which would give the best benefit to society (Lunati 1996). Before we debate on this, let us briefly indicate the meaning of high finance as used in this chapter. These have been described as of four types: *(a)* bank operations, *(b)* stock market operations—primary or secondary, *(c)* versions of the former through derivatives and international swapping transactions, and speculative dealing in money markets in debentures and government securities, and *(d)* mergers and acquisitions. We have limited the scope of the subject to enable us to contain it in one chapter.

The Productionist Ethics

Producing goods and services which enhance the lives of others is good. Spending one's life in speculative purchase and sale of financial claims is bad.

—*Dore (1993)*

How do we evaluate the ethicality of high finance. The ethical purists would say that to seek out only its economic consequences would be incorrect and irrelevant. That would push people to gross forms of greed, unethical according to the refined values spelt out in Chapter 1.

Another school of thought would look for consequences of the greatest good for the greatest number, and may find high finance wanting, diverting the attention of the prime players in industry from long- to short-term gains. This is bad for society in the long run (Chandra 1995, Lunati 1996).

Most people agree that high finance has had many undesirable consequences on society. But like the gun lobbyists of the USA, they would place the blame on the wickedness of man and not on the instrument. We need to work on this wickedness rather than question the instrument.

The Analogy of the Gun Lobby

Guns do not kill people. People do.

—The slogan of the Gun Lobby of the USA

In India, the forces for and against high finance are predictable, following the pattern mentioned in Chapter 4. The left and ultra traditionalists are against it just as they are for more extensive laws. But the new right conservatives are for it just as they are for minimal laws.

Why High Finance Tempts More

The most glaring breakdowns of ethical norms in the world today are undoubtedly in the area often described as high finance. The subject commands considerable awe and reverence; for some it is the evil that tempts. This is precisely the reason that prompted John Shad, President of the Securities Exchange Commission of the USA, to donate US$ 20 million of his personal savings to Harvard University for ethical education (Piper *et al.* 1993). Why is there such an ethical vulnerability in this area and what can we do about it?

The special ethical features of high finance are:

- The basic rewards in this field are not from improving real productivity but in speculative forecasting.
- The focus in the management at organisations is not on effective governance, but as sources of income to fulfil 'naked greed'. There is no incentive to develop permanent and long-standing trust relationships. There is only an unquenchable thirst for profits.
- Decisions are always highly risky and tantamount to gambling.
- The transactions are easily hidden from the public eye and there is no transparency.
- The systems are such that the rewards for risk-taking go to one set of persons whereas the costs are likely to be foisted on other groups.
- The rewards are astronomical and therefore tempt the unscrupulous risk-takers.
- Internal controls are weakened for several reasons, the most important one being the mystique of the subject and the fact that it is not well understood by the generality of management.

Let us see how this happens under the four types of transactions detailed earlier.

The Universal Scamming Propensities of Banks

Recent times have seen a spate of banking scams all over the world, both in developed as well as developing countries. The great Indian Bank scam—still vivid in public memory as the Harshad Mehta case—sent shock waves through the economy, from which it has still to recover completely. This leads us to wonder whether there is anything inherent in banks that makes them prone to scams.

Banks play a crucial role in the economy of a country. They are the intermediary financial organisations channelising surplus funds to productive use. Because of the economies of scale, their transaction costs are much lower than those of individual investors were they to seek individual users of funds. The whole arrangement deals with enormous information which makes comprehension difficult for individuals. Governments, to make sure that the financial institutions do not breach the trust of the investor, prescribe several regulations on the investments (see Chapter 4). These regulations vary from country to country. In the USA and India, banks cannot invest in speculative investments. A certain proportion of their investments have to be made in no-risk investments.

The banking regulations also require standards of public disclosure of information. The ethical role of the accountants and auditors to ensure this was discussed in Chapter 6. The standards of disclosure also vary across countries. Indian law has about the worst record in the number of disclosures.

Before we describe the different views on 'why' scams happen, let us briefly state 'how' they happened.

The massive BCCI scam of the UK took place as moneys were lent to drug traffickers and highly disreputable characters who ultimately failed financially (Beaty and Gwynne 1993). BCCI was able to bribe its way through some of the most highly placed personnel including those of the World Bank. A firm of world-renowned auditors repeatedly overlooked serious inadequacies in the bank's accounts which were in no way fair; this was known only in retrospect.

In the Barrings scam, a young English executive speculated and gambled in derivatives. In the Daiwa case, a young Japanese executive desiring to make money for his bank invested in what he thought were stable debt instruments. But the prices fell. In the Indian Bank scam, an unscrupulous operator forged documents and created fake transactions which seemed to satisfy the banking regulations, took the money from the banks for temporary periods and paid them handsome returns till the overheated market of his creation collapsed.

This is 'how' the scams occurred; the question is 'why' do they take place. Every time a major crisis of the type described about took place, the *pundits* were quick to explain it all away. Typically, the Indian Bank securities scam was glibly ascribed to inadequate control systems and an unwise interference by the government in the market mechanisms. Barua and Varma (1993), felt that the problem arose primarily because the system artificially interfered with the operations of a free market system. Whereas government securities had very low rates of returns, the interest rates prevailing in the market were high. The administrative mechanisms foisted on the system by the government hoped to keep the transactions in low-yield government securities protected by a Chinese wall, surrounded by a vast sea of high returns. The inevitable leakage across this wall represented the events of the scams. The Barrings debacle happened because the British aristocracy were not as smart and educated mathematically as the American whiz-kids. They just could not handle the derivative trades, the stuff of Ph.D.s and computers as developed by Meryll Lynch, Morgan Stanley, Salomon Bros or Godlam Sachs ('The Barrings' Case', *Time*, 13 March 1995). The Daiwa Bank failure occurred as a result of the Japanese Ministry of Finance holding all the powers, perhaps following the secret ways of the ancient Samurai ('Bust', *Newsweek*, 10 March 1995). The BCCI scam was not just a financial scandal—it was all about gun running and drug trafficking, bribing through all control systems in the USA, the World Bank and several Asian and Arab countries (Moscow and Mattingly in Beaty and Gwynne 1993). According to Beaty and Gwynne (1993), the BCCI scam was also attributable to thwarting of the hopes and aspirations of the underdeveloped world by the domineering West. However, others feel that all scams are due to the failure of the internal control systems. How can we improve on the internal controls provided by the world's most renowned auditors? And yet, both in the Barrings and BCCI cases, obviously fraudulent accounts were certified by these very auditors for several years in a row.

The Indian securities scam is analysed in great detail by Chakraborty (1995a: 148), at the end of which he comes to the conclusion that 'adoption of [an] alien ethical model' was one of the root causes of the scam. But what is the Indian model that would have motivated the banking system? One of the main perpetrators of the Indian Bank scam was first interrogated even as he was in the portals of the hallowed Palani temple, wrapped up in the truly Indian model of religion! And we know that the evil genius of BCCI Agha Hasan Abedi was a deeply religious Sufi mystic who genuinely believed that all his activities were for the benefit of mankind and on behalf of God (Beaty and Gwynne 1993: 142).

A composite set of reasons, as mentioned earlier in the chapter, were no doubt responsible not singly but jointly. The ease with which systems could be beaten as also the clumsiness of the controls were undoubtedly the major reasons. But they were compounded by the basic failure of the ethical fibre (Sekhar 1996b). This ethical fibre is not necessarily always present in the behaviour of the traditionalists and absent in the modernists. The background information on the Indian Bank scam illustrates this. The first thing of course is that most of the banks were running in losses. The up-to-date profits (losses in brackets) in rupees million at the end of 1993 were as follows: Allahabad Bank (1,060), Bank of Baroda 80, Bank of Maharashtra (3,310), Canara Bank 260, Central Bank (3,830), Andhra Bank (1,410), Bank of India (3,310), Corporation Bank 40, Indian Overseas Bank (7,530), Punjab National Bank 380, Syndicate Bank (6,710), UCO Bank (4,440), State Bank of India 2,120 (Das Gupta 1993).

The nationalised banks were tied down by the national priorities of distributive justice and directed to lend a prescribed percentage of their resources to the priority sector. The interest rates were also regulated and lower than the market rate. According to most bankers these conditions would not allow them to make profits even with efficient operations. Further, labour rates in banks were six or seven times the national average. Computerisation was also not allowed by the labour settlements which were under the tacit directives of the government. The inadequacies of the disclosure standards in India have already been explained. With this background, if the bank managers were still expected to make profits and their rewards dependent on that, it was only natural that they would compromise and cut ethical corners.

EXAMPLE 11.1   **Syndicate Bank and Canara Bank**

An interesting understanding of the ethics in banking emerges from a comparative study of the ethical philosophies of two banks, Syndicate and Canara. This account is based on Kamath (1991) and Thingalayya and Shenoy (1985). Prior to nationalisation both were private sector banks, working in the same cultural ambience of the Dakshina Kannara district of Karnataka. At the time of nationalisation, 23 per cent of Syndicate Bank's branches were in the rural sector, as against 15 per cent of Canara Bank's. Of the rural branches of Canara Bank, 30 per cent were loss-making. Even though Canara Bank had been ahead of Syndicate Bank in deposits, the gap rapidly closed down between 1970 and 1978. The number of deposits handled by Syndicate Bank per employee was 287 whereas the national average for all banks was 120 (ethics of efficiency). Thus, in spite of a heavy slant towards rural branches where concentration of accounts was low, productivity remained high. Decisions were also decentralised. Syndicate Bank had an extraordinarily innovative Pygmy Deposit Scheme—door-to-door collection of daily deposits from small depositors. In summary, Syndicate Bank followed all the social criteria for banking long before nationalisation and yet maintained its profit line. This was attributed to its highly dedicated managerial cadre most of who had risen from the ranks. Performance was rewarded more in the form of higher responsibilities than higher salaries. Salary increases were by age and seniority rather than by performance.

What are the managers of a highly ruralised bank like Syndicate expected to do when salaries are hiked sharply as it happened after nationalisation? To keep the system from collapsing in public and in the short run, fudging accounts and continuing as long as possible appeared to be the only option. Perhaps it hoped to phase out the understatement of losses every year but in fact this would not or did not work. Meanwhile it could continue to fulfil its social responsibility, albeit now to suit the political purpose of particular politicians. That made the fudging even more compulsive. Doomsday came in 1993 with a disastrous balance sheet that reflected all the past losses.

Canara Bank was a more conventional banker with a stronger concentration on the bottom line. What was it to do in the face of governmental compulsion for greater ruralisation and priority lending at interest rates so low that they did not even cover costs? What else but hope to escape by devious transactions to show results.

One of the most brilliant bankers of the country showed the way. He realised that it would be much more cost-effective to capture the funds of public sector units by deviously compensating the decision-makers under the table. That was quite easy as accountability in those organisations was fuzzy and unclear, with layers of social analysis and administered pricing (absence of the ethics of free markets discussed in Chapter 3). This was the precursor to the great scam. At one stage, Syndicate Bank even appointed experts in this art to the top positions, further drawing it away from its earlier ethical moorings.

We should now pause and ask ourselves if the ethical blame for all this lay with law-makers or the operators who learnt to exploit the loopholes in these rules. Would ethical values arise precisely when one desists from exploiting loopholes? Or should ethicality consist in overhauling the entire banking system on Islamic lines described in Chapter 3? All this could not have happened in that system.

Be that as it may, an analysis of this case gives rise to a very down-to-earth query of what a young person faced with such systemic unethicality should do. Resisting the temptation to moralise, the following practical steps may help. The first effort should be to make the documentation neat, orderly and simple. The critical features should be made available and unnecessary details should be eliminated. Second, if one is using computers, adequate security and back-up must be kept. Third, one must develop routine reports to one's seniors, summarising one's workings. Next, if one finds one's ambition being thwarted by an unscrupulous boss one should not fall into the trap. Fifth, in the banking business one must remember that honesty does ultimately pay. Last, one should share one's information widely and avoid being secretive.

Stoic Acceptance of Manipulation in Stock Markets

Stock markets are the lifeline of high finance. Those who believe in the absolute ethicality of market systems swear by it only under the condition that information is freely available. Insider trading is a total abuse of this ethic. 'To engage in insider trading', says Irvine (1993), 'is, roughly speaking, to buy or sell securities on the basis of privileged information.' Insider trading is considered a mortal sin in the USA. It is however not considered serious in many countries such as Germany or Japan or Belgium (Donaldson 1996). In India, laws against insider trading have not crystallised though it is common knowledge that insider trading is rampant.

There can never be any question of insider trading passing the test of the ethicality of deontology (Chapter 1). No one would like to be a victim of insider trading. Shaw (1993), Irvine (1993), Moore (1993) and Werhane (1993) have however all argued at length that insider trading does not reduce 'the greatest good for the greatest number'. They are however clear that it is a breach of trust and therefore unethical. This line of thinking is intriguing. It can be taken to prove that a thief who burgles a rich man is ethically good as being poor, the happiness it gives him is much more than the unhappiness it will cause the rich man who will not miss the money. It seems that the consequences lie elsewhere; trading of inside information could encourage insiders to suppress information and therefore involve an incorrect allocation of resources seen from the point of view of the population as a whole. Shefrin and Statman (1993) take another approach to assess the consequences. According to them, 'Protection against insider trading fails to offer much protection to naive investors; today, naive investors believe they are safe because insider trading is illegal. Perhaps legalising insider trading would serve naive investors better; at least they would be forewarned.' The height of cynicism, this is a stoic acceptance of the inevitability of unethicality in the stock markets. Let us briefly see Example 11.2, based on White (1993).

EXAMPLE 11.2 **Thomas Hartnett**

Thomas Hartnett, a former employee of General Electric, was accused by the SEC of making US$ 8,472 in the sale of 10 call option contracts for RCA stock. (A call option gives the buyer the right to buy stock at a set price. Each of Hartnett's contracts entitled him to buy 100 shares of RCA stock.) On 6 December 1986, Hartnett learned from one of his colleagues at GE that the company intended to buy RCA. Hartnett asked him to make a copy of a binder that contained the details of GE's proposed offer. Later that day, he ordered the call options from his broker at a cost of US$ 1,805. The takeover was announced on 11 December and, predictably, the price of RCA stock rose. The following day, Hartnett sold the options for a little over US$ 10,000. When accused by the SEC Hartnett agreed to repay his profits and pay a penalty of the same amount.

Analyses for the reader

1. Is there anything unethical in Hartnett's actions? Was anyone hurt? If so, who? Was there a breach of fiduciary responsibility?

2. Remember that Hartnett traded in options, not stock itself. Does this make any difference from an ethical stand?

3. In comparison to the huge amount of money some insiders made, we are dealing here with a relatively small amount. Another individual who traded on inside information about the same takeover made US$ 2 million. Does that make what Hartnett did less serious from an ethical viewpoint? Should they both receive the same punishment? If not, what would be the difference?

4. It could be argued that Hartnett was singled out to serve as an example for other small insiders. One SEC official stated that Hartnett's case 'should disabuse people of the notion that they can trade in a relatively small quantity of stock or options and not be noticed'. If this were part of SEC's motivation in prosecuting Hartnett, how does it affect your assessment of the case or of the penalty?

5. Hartnett's colleague was not charged with wrongdoing by the SEC, but did he do anything morally wrong by divulging the oncoming takeover and acceding to Hartnett's request for a copy of the details of GE's offer? Should he be punished as well?

In summary, we find that there is great ambivalence in the literature on the ethics of inside trading even though we are certain that it is the height of untrustworthy behaviour. This is the paradox of capitalism which has yet to be resolved, and till then, to be suffered.

Derivatives and Money Markets Seduce the Young

Derivatives are new instruments invented by whiz-kids with Ph.D.s in maths and physics, big Wall Street companies like Meryll Lynch, Morgan Stanley, Salomon Bros and Goldam Sachs, aided by computers. The basic features of these new instruments are that there is a 'maker' (option writer) who offers a contract to an 'option holder', that provides for the holder to pay the maker a 'premium' in consideration of an option to be exercised by or on a specified date to buy or sell a specified security at a specified price. If the holder, by or on that specified date, decides not to exercise the option, he loses nothing more than the premium. But the maker would lose if the security being held shifts its price in a direction and in a magnitude not anticipated and provided for in the gamble. The maker will also lose if the holder decides to buy the security which the maker may not possess and which will have to be bought in the market to enable the maker to sell it to the holder. This 'naked option' will obviously result in a loss for the maker as the holder would have otherwise found it beneficial to buy it from the market than from him.

These instruments are far removed from the first-level concepts of primary markets of securities, which enable an entrepreneur to avail of surpluses available with potential investors in a partnership of shared risks and rewards. The instruments in the secondary market enable an investor who does not see eye to eye with the entrepreneur to delink himself and provide an opportunity for someone else who finds the alliance more con-

> Derivatives challenge the slogan of the traditional accounting . . . they allow managers to exploit loopholes in accounting rules.
>
> —*The Economist, 10–16 February 1996*

genial. Speculative stock markets completely lose sight of the entrepreneur and the alliance with him.

Derivatives are the despair of traditional accountants. How do we value them and show them in the balance sheets for a true and fair view? Money markets deal with the conventional instruments of debts, including government treasury bills. They are used for short-term financing. Since the interest rates and prices of these investments fluctuate, they can be used to speculate. The ethical dimensions of the derivatives and money markets is well understood by a quick round-up of the Barrings and Daiwa cases, summarised from various journals.

EXAMPLE 11.3   **The Barrings Case**

Leeson, a young enthusiastic executive of Barrings Bank, was posted in the Singapore branch. He started with the less precarious arbitrage trading, where he made profits by using the difference in the price of security between different stock exchanges. It was just smartness and information-readiness that enabled him to make money. But then he moved over to derivatives. call and put options, straddles, index options and naked options, instruments which could be used less transparently and more dangerously.

Leeson traded in derivatives with precarious stakes. More disastrously, he did not put the loss-making transactions through the account books of Barrings; the day of reckoning could wait till the dealing parties pressed for the related settlement. It was also suspected that on some occasions he misclassified cash transactions deliberately to stow them away under heads where they would not attract attention. Leeson was given the combined responsibility of trading and its accounting in the books. This was atrocious internal control, never done that way anywhere, 'like a school-boy grading his own tests'. It should have been plain to even a casual observer that losses were mounting as London had to send absurdly large funds to Singapore—£900 million—in a very short period to discharge pressing liabilities. Much eartier, in 1992, a Barrings executive had warned against trusting Leeson with so much authority with such little independent check. On 8 February 1994, the treasurer of Barrings, Anthony Hawes, assured a worried Singapore Exchange that Barrings would honour its liabilities. But Peter Barring, the Chairman, woke up to the disaster only after Leeson had fled from Singapore on 28 February. Such was his trust in Leeson or alienation from reality or connivance with the scam, depending upon what one would infer from his unusual behaviour. Barrings' losses were more than its capital and there was no way it could survive. Several people all over the world including the British royalty who had trusted their money to the bank had to face a financial disaster.

EXAMPLE 11.4 **The Daiwa Case**

Iguchi Toshihide joined Daiwa Bank in 1984. The bank was cash rich. Toshihide assessed that it was perfectly safe for his company to buy and sell bonds and make money in this process. Bonds were fixed interest instruments and therefore were not as volatile as shares. Toshihide was 'a great customer' according to the market as he always appeared to be the loser and therefore made the other parties happy. But he continued to hope that he would make good in deals to come. This did not happen. Meanwhile, since he was also in charge of the back-office accounting, he continually fudged the records. He sold several securities of Daiwa Bank to finance these losses. When the auditors checked his accounts, he produced forged documents to show that the securities were still in his possession. The audits were so perfunctory that they did not insist on the confirmation of the parties who were allegedly holding the money in lieu of these securities.

The Federal Agencies checking Daiwa's accounts pointed out the serious deficiency in internal controls inasmuch as Toshihide was operating as well accounting for the transactions (just as Leeson was allowed to do in the Barrings case). Things came to a head when they launched an investigation. Just before the investigation was to commence, Toshihide wrote a confessional to his bosses. 'Just because he spoke Japanese we should not have trusted him so much,' said the top management of the bank (Levinson and Meyer 1995). This was a gross understatement as the transactions had been going on for more than 10 years, since 1984. Toshihide had never taken leave at any time during this period. The final losses amounted to US$ 1.10 million.

There was no evidence that Toshihide had personally gained by these transactions or had intended to make a fast buck. It seemed to be all a 'derailed and false sense of duty to his employer'. But he apparently enjoyed the trust his employers had placed in him as also the access it gave him to exalted circles.

Some public discourse on banks and stock markets, and the risks involved followed these two cases. Public concern had been increasing even before the collapse of Barrings. Many thinkers had been seriously considering if even the interest in normal banking operations was ethically right as it attempted to earn the rewards without sharing the risks. But at the other extreme, investment banking could extend to exposing one's constituents (shareholders and depositors), who may not have agreed to share in the risks if they had known about the consequences of their quest for unlimited rewards. Moreover, was investment banking an exercise of risk–reward trade-off in socially useful investments? Or was it a pure gamble which had no link at all with the socially and ethically desirable activities intended for genuine fulfilment of human needs and wants?

The thinkers inclined towards socialism were not kindly disposed towards derivatives and money markets. They straightaway rejected banks using stock markets to bolster their earnings. The more pragmatic still felt that banks with large moneys at their disposal given in trust, should have no or extremely limited right to speculate. The concept of caveat emptor has been ethically thrown out in the case of marketing of goods and services. Why should it persist in banking? This thinking has suggested three remedies that have emerged only after some soul-searching following the Barring debacle (*The Economist*, 22–28 July 1995).

First, banks must be categorised into two types, those that will not be allowed to speculate and those that will be. The returns of the former will be less than those of the latter and the public can choose. Second, those who will be allowed to speculate must make explicit disclosure. Third, there must be stronger monitoring and control by the government and government-controlled regulatory boards, covering both financial policies and regulations. But unfortunately this would entail social costs. A recent study by a London business school estimated that the direct annual cost to the government in administering its regulations even in the present scenario was GB £ 90 million in the UK and US$ 795 million in the USA, in addition to the costs incurred by the banks themselves. This would go up considerably if the controls were tightened.

In Japan the Daiwa debacle has triggered a movement to break up the Ministry of Finance of the Japanese Government (Hirsh 1995) and to separate the executive and regulatory functions from the monitoring functions. It was felt that lack of transparency due to the concentration of power in the Japanese system had led to the Daiwa situation. In India, the Securities Law Amendment Act (Act No. 9 of 1995) has paved the way for reintroduction of option trading in stock exchanges, prohibited by the earlier law. This follows the economic philosophy now adopted. The implication for investment bankers is not yet known. The question we need to ask ourselves is: what were the causes of ethical failure in all such cases? Was it inadequate analytical training? Was it the system? Was it cultural failure and if so, what was common between Leeson and Toshihide, one from England and the other from Japan? The answer perhaps is a combination of all.

The Other Sides of Mergers and Acquisitions

It is commonly believed that India, once free of the MRTP Act, will go headlong towards companies merging or acquiring other companies. It is well understood that these mergers and acquisitions have an ethical side, some of which has been incorporated into laws. Many others have not. Davies (1996) includes mergers and acquisitions as important ethical issues in strategic management.

The ethics of mergers and acquisitions have six basic issues:

1. manipulations of markets and share purchase transactions
2. processes of valuation of companies and their share prices
3. unfair consequences for the shareholders
4. unfair consequences for the genuine innovators as against those who have never grown even a blade of grass
5. unfair consequences for the consumers and society
6. unfair consequences for the employees

The legal processes required under the Indian Company Law and the regulations of the SEBI have several safeguards in respect of the first two. Jensen (1993) has produced fairly reliable evidence to show that in the US mergers and acquisitions have by and large produced synergies which have only helped the shareholders, consumers and society. This leaves out the classes listed in items four and six. Conclusive analysis for Indian companies is not yet available. Sharma (1994), analysing the data from 1979 to 1990, concludes that nothing can be said about the economics of mergers as these had been few and far between and hamstrung by the restrictions in the MRTP.

The Industrial Disputes Act has several protections in India in regard to the sixth item, at least in respect of workers if not the managerial staff. The Supreme Court in a landmark judgement had upheld the rights of the workers even under the Company Law (*National Textiles Corporation* v. *P.R. Ramakrishnan, 1993*), breaking the earlier legal interpretation that shareholders, creditors and the state are the three main stakeholders who should be consulted for reconstruction and reorganisation of companies.

The recent judgement of the Bombay High Court in the TOMCO case is less helpful and seems to have imbibed the philosophy of the day regarding exit policies. Werhane (1993) and Newton (1993) are devas-tatingly critical of the lack of ethics in regard to employees and entrepreneurs in the USA. The socially destructive features of the market systems on entrepreneurs was discussed in Chapter 3 (Herbig and Golden 1992, Foong and Oliga 1992). With fewer options in India, the impact is likely to be more severe. Quite contrarily, many have felt that the settlements in mergers and acquisitions are taking unduly long and affecting the country's development. The ethics of it all therefore needs to be very much on the agenda of an Indian manager. Case 11.1 will further explain this.

SUMMARY

The chapter deals with high finance in the areas of banking, share markets, derivatives, money markets, and mergers and acquisitions. It discusses the basic issue of ethicality of the instruments used in these areas. If we have to accept them as an inevitable part of our lives, the need for internal controls to ensure that the system does not make us unethical is discussed. It notes that in India, mergers and acquisitions are likely to be more extensive in the future. It emphasises the need for equity to the employees and the original innovators. Through all this runs the thread of adequate ethical sensitisation of managers.

ISSUES TO PONDER OVER

- Would you consider the great Indian Bank scam a failure of control systems or an ethical failure?
- Should India try to tighten its law on insider trading?
- What do you think is ethically the best way to handle the employment problems due to mergers—consultative or autocratic?

CASE 11.1 The TOMCO–HLL Merger

The merger of the Tata Oil Mill Co Ltd (TOMCO) and Hindustan Lever Ltd (HLL) in 1994 was a major event in the history of Indian industry. The merger itself as well as its terms were disputed in the Supreme Court of India (Case number 110) by labour unions, consumer associations and some affected shareholders. Many of the issues raised had ethical overtones. The scheme was however confirmed without any changes by the highest court of the land on 24 October 1994. But that still did not settle all the legal problems of the merger. The Reserve Bank of India objected to one part of the scheme concerning the settlement of the amounts due to HLL from Unilever of the UK. As on 11 September 1995, the Bombay High Court had only passed interim orders. The Court reconfirmed all other parts of the scheme, but ordered Unilever to pay to HLL in foreign exchange the disputed and enhanced amount worked out by the Reserve Bank in their plaint. They advised that it be kept under suspense (23 November 1994). The merger had thus taken effect. The ethical evaluation of the merger had different meanings for the different stakeholders of TOMCO and HLL; these stakeholders included the consumers and public at large. The process of ethical evaluation would involve the intentions of the different actors, real and perceived, as well as the consequences.

Intentions of the managements of HLL and TOMCO

The likely intentions of HLL and TOMCO as seen by Pai (1995) are summarised as follows: 'HLL was a market leader in soaps and detergents with fifteen lakh outlets. TOMCO was second in line with ten lakh outlets; it had some significantly successful brands like Hamam and TOMCO as well as 25 per cent of the national shelf space in retail outlets. The third was Godrej with 8,00,000 outlets. Since TOMCO was running at losses there was a definite possibility of its folding up. When Procter & Gamble decided to join hands with Godrej, there was every possibility of the vacuum created by TOMCO being filled in by the combined might of Procter & Gamble and Godrej. But it would have taken at least Rs 50 million and three years' time for them to do it. HLL on the other hand could ensure that TOMCO facilities all over the country could be efficiently used if they ran it directly as part of their company. HLL's own facilities were running to full capacity whereas TOMCO's were working below capacity. They were also located in the South where HLL had poor representation; this could save them transport costs. The TOMCO brands had penetrated the less-affluent sections of the market much better than HLL products. They could therefore offer an effective competition to Nirma and other small manufacturers. With their merger, the market share of the combine would become 75 per cent. The TOMCO management on their part found it too much of a problem to hold on; apparently they did not see any possibility of TOMCO reviving on its own steam.'

The perception of the shareholders and the Supreme Court's acceptance

The perception of the management need not always coincide with that of the shareholders, who are the prime stakeholders. Unilever, HLL's foreign principals, held 51 per cent of the shares. The distribution of TOMCO shares was:

22 per cent: The Tata Group
41 per cent: Indian financial institutions owned by the government
37 per cent: The general public

Their perceptions could be inferred by the fact that 90 per cent of the shareholding power of both companies agreed that in the merger, the Rs 10 share of their respective companies would be valued in the ratio of two shares of HLL to 15 shares of TOMCO. This condition of clearance of a merger scheme by 90 per cent of the shareholders was required under Section 391–394 of the Companies Act. A small minority of TOMCO shareholders however objected to this ratio as being unfair to them. After their appeal was rejected by the Bombay High Court they appealed to the Supreme Court.

The dispute of the shareholders revolved around the fairness of the criteria chosen by the valuers which was subsequently reconfirmed by two of the country's top experts. The experts had examined the valuation using three criteria:

1. comparison of book value of assets per share
2. market prices on date
3. present value of future cashflows of the two companies individually if the merger did not take place

The first criterion gave TOMCO shares a higher value than HLL's. The second gave the ratio to be adopted as 2:15. The last criterion gave a disastrously low value for TOMCO shares based on the past few years' performance, further adjusted downwards for unusual profits coming from exports to Russia which were not likely to be repeated.

The experts chose the second criterion. The Supreme Court, not wishing to get into the details, agreed that this was fair and dismissed the appeal. Their main argument was that if it had really been unfair, 90 per cent of the shareholders would not have passed it. Exhibit 11.1 details the financial data summarised by the Supreme Court in its judgement.

Three students of the T.A. Pai Management Institute (TAPMI) (Banerjee *et al.* 1995), in a prize-winning paper presented in a national seminar, made a computation which used another criterion not considered by the experts at all. The criterion was not furthered by any of the litigants either and therefore was not available to the Supreme Court for consideration. This was based on the share of the future synergy of the merger between the shareholders of the two companies. Their computation is given in Exhibit 11.2. Their results were vastly different from those of the Supreme Court judgement.

The scheme which had been passed by 90 per cent of the shareholders had one more feature which indicated the mood, expectation and faith of the shareholders. The scheme provided that after amalgamating with TOMCO, Unilever should still have a majority in the company and for this they should be allotted fresh shares not at the market price which was Rs 375 but at Rs 105; this was worked out on the basis of the RBI norms. As required by the Companies Act, this preferential allotment was also passed by a special resolution by the shareholders under the powers given to them under Section 81 of the Companies Act. This unequal treatment favouring the foreign principals was apparently on their understanding that it would enable HLL to get the latest technology and attract good managerial attention from Unilever. Subsequent to the application made earlier by them on 3 June 1994, the norms of the RBI changed and as per the new norms the price should have been Rs 700 per share. HLL held that it had applied long ago to RBI, but had received no reply, and in the meanwhile the whole scheme had been accepted by all parties as a package. This included Unilever's favoured participation, which may not be forthcoming at the higher price. The Bombay High Court is yet to give its final verdict on whether this part of the merger should stand.

The perception of the labour

HLL had stormy industrial relations with its employees at Sewri, Bombay. Their bargaining position with the labour had to be maintained by getting their products manufactured by other parties. The HLL labour felt that the takeover would further weaken their bargaining position. The TOMCO labour felt that they would be axed as a direct consequence of the synergy. The Company Law under Section 394 required that the continuity of employment and protection of service conditions should not be lost through the merger. This clause was incorporated in the scheme. But the law did not provide for assurance of continuance of employment for all time to come.

HLL was known to be a tough employer and maintained dossiers on all its employees; thus incriminating evidence, if any, against every employee was meticulously kept and could be used as a threat at any time. The employees did not as yet ask specifically for a commitment from HLL–TOMCO on a share of the future synergy. On the other hand, they were afraid that the whole concept of synergy was based on the premise that they would be declared redundant and thrown out of employment at some stage or the other. The Supreme Court dismissed all their apprehensions as irrelevant as these could be handled under the labour laws and not as a dispute of the merger (April 1996).

Perceptions of the consumers

Their perception was that this would increase monopoly and adversely affect their interests. With the scrapping of the portions of the MRTP Act dealing with monopoly, the Supreme Court had little hesitation in dismissing the consumer petitions as unreasonable and inconsistent with current public policy.

What happened after the merger

TOMCO executives were given titles and designations far inferior to those they had had prior to the merger. HLL also offered to ex-TOMCO offices a Voluntary Retirement Plan never extensively discussed with the labour unions. They gave very short notice to the workers to exercise their options. There were no schemes for retraining the retrenched staff for new work. This was a culture shock to TOMCO employees who were used to the paternalistic style of their earlier employers.

The retrenchment of the staff is going ahead full steam and several TOMCO executives have left the company. Executives at the top and middle levels who left TOMCO told the case-writer that HLL was not attitudinally inclined to encourage and support anything that belonged to TOMCO, be it people, systems or even products. Many felt out of place in the new set-up. It was particularly hard on senior officers past their prime; the long years of devotion to TOMCO had yielded little reward for them from its successor HLL. Their bargaining power in the market was also low. These were undoubtedly only perceptions. One can be sure of the intentions only in the future. But it raises the issue if synergy expected from the merger would ever be realised at all and second, if any part of it would be passed on to the employees or society at large. On this revolved the ethicality of the merger.

(The case is mostly from published material; a few incidents reported are from personal knowledge.)

Analyses for the reader

1.   Do you think the ethical basis of Exhibit 11.2 is superior to the one actually accepted by the court? Why?
2.   Was it likely that the settlement was accepted by the TOMCO shareholders because they had no other option? If so, is it ethically satisfactory?
3.   Was the presence of Nirma a happy ethical antidote to HLL as it provided competition? Has this been lost by the merger?
4.   Are there any indications to show that HLL has adopted a less than paternalistic and sympathetic approach to the ex-employees of TOMCO? Should HLL share the value of its future synergies with its current employees?

EXHIBIT 11.1   TOMCO–HLL Data Presented to the Supreme Court

	1992		1991		1990	
	HLL	TOMCO	HLL	TOMCO	HLL	TOMCO
Earning per share (Rs)	7.03	0.30	5.77	0.50	6.29	5.19
Dividends (%)	42	–	38	12	42	20
Assets/Share	23.80	29.15	20.75	29.25	27.30	36.17

Market price in 1993 was Rs 375 for HLL and Rs 52.50 for TOMCO.

EXHIBIT 11.2   The Valuation of TOMCO–HLL by Sharing the Value of Future Synergy Discounted for Time

Basis of sharing synergy effect HLL : TOMCO	Ratio of share exchange value HLL : TOMCO
1 : 1	1 : 0.87
3 : 1	1 : 1.157
4 : 1	1 : 1.190

12

AL-AMIN, THE TRUSTWORTHY
Consequences of Corruption

The Clinical Meaning of Corruption

Corruption, a worldwide phenomenon, is as old as the ancient Greek and Indian civilisations. In the perception of some Indian managers, coping with corruption is the single largest component of business ethics. That is a somewhat lopsided way of looking at business ethics. Nevertheless, corruption is one of the major issues in business ethics.

It is possible to define corruption precisely and clinically under the 'agency theory'. This theory is currently a popular framework for academic analysis of ethics; it combines law and organisational theory (see Chapters 4 and 7). There are other ways of defining corruption. Some restrict it to government transactions (Pavarala 1996, Werner 1983) or rely on the Prevention of Corruption Act which is applicable to a very limited set of persons. Corruption is also sometimes taken to mean all unethical acts (Pavarala 1996, Werner 1983). Since we propose to use the analytical methods developed in Chapters 4 and 7, the agency theory has been chosen as the appropriate framework.

An agent, in contract acts universally, is one who is entrusted work and delegated responsibility by a principal in return for consideration. He has to deal with the outside world on behalf of the principal. The principal and the agents have an agency contract. The actions of the agents are binding on the principal. In this framework, let us say A is the principal and B is his agent who deals with C in that capacity. C could settle with B that B could keep part of the consideration which is legitimately due to A as per the agency contract. In return for this C will get terms more favourable than the ones offered by A. This arrangement between B and C is without A's knowledge and consent. This in essence defines corruption; it could also be described as an act of bribery. This way of seeing corruption as a breach of trust brings it closer to Islamic thinking. Prophet Mohammed who never betrayed the trust of his employer was given the sobriquet Al-Amin, that is, the trustworthy.

A could represent a government of any political or ethical persuasion, or an organisation of any economic character, or a single person. On the other hand, B could be a customs official, a bank, a minister, a police constable, a railway ticket checker, a director on the board of a company, a purchase or personnel or finance or sales manager. C could be a multinational, a poor farmer, a frantic seeker of a railway ticket, etc. A, B and C can therefore take a variety of shapes and forms.

Corruption is thus not exclusive to interfaces with the government. Those inimical to state controls would have us believe that corruption arises from excessive controls by the government and too little of free markets (*Newsweek* 1994). The notion that free market economics is the hot-bed of corruption arises from a belief that there would be no corruption if there were no greed and that market economics induces more greed (Werner 1983: 148). Later in this chapter we will touch upon the possible ways to contain corruption when we attempt to take up a balanced position in this controversy.

Can Corruption Ever be Right

It is the endeavour of this book not to prejudge any issue but to encourage the reader to make his or her own ethical choice. Therefore, we will examine the issue of corruption *de novo* from the basic criteria developed in Chapter 1. If we do this, the judgement on corruption will emerge under two sets of logics, the first arising from conscience and the second from the philosophy of the greatest good for the greatest number.

A. The test of conscience

1. Bribe-taking would be unethical as one would not like that others' agent should claim bribes from you.
2. Bribe-giving would be unethical as one would not like one's own agent to take bribes and betray one's trust.
3. Bribe-giving may not be unethical if one felt that if one were in the position of the principal of the agent whom one is bribing, one would exonerate the bribe if the circumstance was extenuating. The agent could be an extortionist exploiter and the principal may not be aware of the circumstances under which one is bribing the agent. This is reminiscent of the situation wherein Kohlbergh (1981) felt that thieving was ethically correct (see Chapter 4).

B. The test of the greatest good for the greatest number

1. Taking bribes is unethical as this will result in loss of trust, uncertain transactions, and escalated costs in business. Long-time and sustained business relationship will not be possible and no one will make long-term investments or do research and development. Some degree of certainty of

future benefits will be expected. Everyone in society will consequently suffer.

2. Giving bribes is unethical as in this process bribe-takers will be encouraged and all the evil consequences of the previous condition will apply here too.

3. Giving bribes is ethical as bribes are really indicative of prices in the market system and resources will be consequently correctly allocated consistent with people's free choice (Werner 1983).

4. Giving bribes is ethical when there is a systemic pratice all around and a single individual can do nothing about it. Consequently, if one gives a bribe and ensures that at least incrementally the sum total of happiness is increased or unhappiness is decreased, it is ethical.

Drucker (1985: 237–45) argues that in the well-known bribery case in Japan, the bribe-giver Lockheed Company would be exonerated under condition A3—one of extortion. At the same time, if the company pleaded under condition B3 or B4, it would amount to double-think, hypocrisy and a practice of casuistry which is reprehensible. But Dutta (1997: 106–8), mentions that Indian business houses are usually willing to bribe under the argument of B4. In Chapter 4, we have said that some law-breaking is found justifiable by the business classes. However, Sekhar (1995) found that corruption was not considered ethical per se, but its alienation from the state led the business class to think of breaking laws as a necessary evil. It is possible that this alienation in India is owed to the traditional hostility of the state of traders as described in Chapter 3.

Let us examine some common cases of corruption to look at the issues involved holistically. Take the case of smuggling involving the bribing of customs officials. In this the government is the principal A, the customs official its agent B and the smuggler the outsider C. If a ban on imports was imposed in order to protect the domestic capitalist who enjoyed a monopoly and was making super-profits, smuggling would then provide the consumer another option, maybe even a better deal. The customs official's personal benefit is minimal vis-à-vis the larger benefits accruing to the consumer at large. On the other hand, if the domestic industry were a nascent one, then smuggling might cause irreparable damage to indigenous industries. If the goods smuggled in were life-saving drugs as is sometimes the case, the answer becomes blurred. One could lay the blame on the unethicality of banning the desirable import and not the venal sin of corruption. The current economic policy proclaims to have corrected this unethicality.

Let us next see the recent India *hawala* scam. It involved two stages, the first where false invoicing resulted in creating the pool of *hawala* money, and the second when it was allegedly used as bribe. It may have resulted in an undesirable economic decision for the nation. In both account, moneys which should have belonged to the government had been passed on to individuals. It is only when we feel that the social value of the money is greater when it is with the government than with individuals that there is a loss to society. The money could have been used for better infrastructural development in the country or for poverty alleviation, whereas in the hands of those who partook in the scam it would just get frittered away in conspicuous consumption. One may say that it resulted in a net economic loss, with long-term damage to the nation.

Take a third case of a public sector like the railways which tends to overbook its capacity and therefore has a leeway for corruption in allotting wagons. The consequences are shown in Figure 12.1. If the wagons were in full supply, the market rate of the railway tariff would have been say P1. If wagons were in short supply, the market rate increases to P2, but the rate fixed by the railways is actually much lower at P3 because they feel that the transport is required for foodgrains, an essential commodity. The outsider who gets in touch with the railway officer (the agent of the railways who are the principals) would be willing to pay the difference between P2 and P3 as bribe. If this happened the surpluses, instead of going to the poor through transport subsidies or to the railways, would go to an individual (the agent). The chances are that the railway official would use it for his children's higher education!

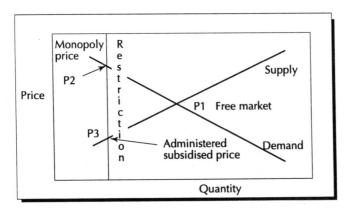

FIGURE 12.1 **Scope for Corruption**
(Source: Sekhar 1996b)

Take another situation where a murderer bribes the police and gets away. In this case the government is the principal and the policeman is the agent. The society at large would lose much but the policeman would gain something.

A fifth situation is that of ministers (being agents of the government) seeking a cut to permit an investment by a multinational. The latter may find it unaffordable and may not want to continue investments. Or if they do invest they would get it back through the prices they charge the consumers. They would do so if they are assured of a monopoly. This is not uncommon even in China. The nation would also lose if the most efficient company is not chosen.

In a sixth situation, typically in the well-known Barrings case in Singapore, the directors were willing to take risks and allow loose control over the dealings by one of their employees as he was able to 'bribe' them with high bonuses. The rewards were there for the directors who were expected to treat the company as their trust. The risk failed and the ultimate sufferers were the trusting shareholders. There was a net loss to society. Further, risk and reward were unfairly distributed ethically. Those who took the risks, namely the errant employee and the directors, did not bear the losses. The arguments in the Barrings case could be extended to corruption in any organisation. But unlike in government inefficiency, corruption in private organisations is more likely to be followed by the death of the company. But the timelag may be quite long, and corrupt organisations may take a long time to collapse.

Let us look at some other real-life situations in India. A village *karnam* (an agent of the government) can take illegal money from the villagers in return for which he provides an effective database for land records. This can enable the villagers to function in a more orderly fashion. In this case corruption may actually increase social value and this would come under the condition of B3 discussed earlier. This argument would hold for the bribe-giver. The moot point however is whether the *karnam* who is an extortionist is ethical in demanding a bribe. Is he more ethical than another who is neither an extortionist nor willing to keep proper land records? This would be covered by the condition of B3.

In the seventh situation, a police constable takes extra money from his beat and effectively preserves law and order. He is actually increasing social value compared to a constable who does not take bribes and also does not ensure law and order. This would be similar to the previous situation. One can argue that the policeman is getting his salary from the government and his taking bribes to do his job is absolutely unethical. One can ask if it would be better for society that those who are angered by his asking for a bribe kill him, the net effect of which will be that there would be no more policemen. Or, if the government cannot afford a higher salary, what is wrong in market systems supplementing the income to match market prices. Such was the argument of the 'functionalist school' much criticised by many (Werner 1983: 148).

A railway ticket collector provides railway reservation to those in dire need provided they grease his palms. The railways' normal rules are not flexible enough to respond similarly to the needs of passengers in acute distress. The bribe is just an articulation of the market-driven price of a ticket, and a harsh ethical judgement on the bribe-giver would certainly be misplaced from the angle of economic consequences. It may also pass the test of ethicality under both A3 and B3.

In summary, if our judgement against corruption depends on our assessment of loss due to breach of trust, it would come under the B group of arguments. The normal understanding is that corruption results in all-round losses. But strangely, reports of Transparency International (Swaminathan 1996) show that the impact of corruption on development is unpredictable. The International Monetary Fund reports that a 30 per cent drop in corruption results in only a four per cent drop in investments (Maoro 1997). Indonesia, Taiwan and Hong Kong are very corrupt but have developed fast. Is it in spite of or because of it, is a moot question.

Lest the reader get the impression that corruption is being condoned, we hasten to add that corruption is not a purely economic matter. If we thought so we would be very myopic. The damage to the quality of life in a corrupt society is far more than can be justified by clever arguments and sophistry. It can eat into the vitals of the soul of a nation. Whatever be the economic logic of corruption, it would most certainly be socially damaging and insulting to human dignity.

These are not naive impractical thoughts. The Alacrity Foundation of Tamil Nadu totally eschewed corruption and gave self-fulfilment to every employee in the organisation.

Transparency International

In the backdrop of some of the arguments in the previous paragraphs, an international organisation with the prime purpose of combating corruption has been formed in Berlin. This is known as Transparency International. It proposes to hold together all organisations dealing with underdeveloped countries to ensure that they do not lose out due to corruption. Thus its interest is to persuade underdeveloped countries to control corruption so that mutually beneficial relationships could be formed with Western entrepreneurs. The somewhat cynical angle of self-interest of Western entrepreneurs and the academia who see it all from their point of view is evident from their preference for corruption in command economies rather than corruption in decentralised economies (*Newsweek* 1994). Thus if they have to settle for corruption, they would prefer China to Russia or India, as corruption in the former can be managed without too much loss of profits.

If the media reports and the pronouncements of the Transparency International are to be believed, corruption is overwhelmingly present worldwide, be it die-hard capitalist countries such as the USA, Japan, Korea, France, Belgium, Germany, Spain, Italy and England, or socialist countries such as China, or countries attempting to deregulate such as Russia, or developing countries in Asia, Africa and Latin America. The prevalence of corruption is a historical problem. Plato and Aristotle had complained bitterly of corruption in ancient Greece. Kautilya had recognised corruption as a major problem. Quite possibly, the perception of the explosive nature of the current phenomenon could be due to four factors:

1. The scale of monetary operations is increasing rapidly and the spillage from this could be correspondingly higher.
2. The expectations of good governance have increased with democratic processes being more pronounced in modern times.
3. The greed or envy of those who cannot partake in the spoils of corruption is getting more pronounced.
4. The press is much more free now to pursue investigations.

Contrary to the expectations of the school of functionalist economists (Werner 1983), corruption has not died down but only enlarged in advanced capitalist countries. This concern of Transparency International is now reiterated by the World Bank as a precondition for receiving aid.

Indian Perceptions of Corruption

Some Western thinkers feel that the Indian attitude towards corruption is conditioned by its historical feudal traditions. This is also reaffirmed by some Indian writers (Jain 1995: 402). Feudal landlords were used to getting gifts from the citizens (called *nazrana* in the north). It became a part of the mind-set. Thereafter, even if any law, say the Indian Penal Code, forbade corruption it could not take root and therefore became irrelevant. This is a plausible explanation (Werner 1983: 151) but is far from the truth in India. The Transparency International also believes so (Swaminathan 1996). Corruption is considered utterly unethical by the Indian people and not accepted as inevitable or necessary. Breach of trust in business is condemned as a bad business policy by Indian ethical writers such as Thiruvalluvar. Corruption has been explicitly condemned in the Indian legal tradition through the centuries. Kautilya has dealt with it extensively with finesse in his *Arthashastra*.

> **The Importance of Trust in Business**
>
> Agents should consider the principal's moneys as their own and treat it with prudence and care. That is good business.
>
> —*Kural*

It is significant to note that corruption has Draconian punishment only if it involves losses to the state or if the loss to individuals is high. The relative social values of the *Arthashastra* can be understood if we juxtapose the punishments for corruption against the punishments for other crimes.

> **Punishment for Corruption**
>
> Corruption involving revenue of king: Death
> Corruption involving private loss: Death if more than 40 *panas* otherwise mild
> Sex of man with the queen: Death to the man
> Sex of woman with slave: Death to the woman
> Sex by woman outcast with Aryan: Cut off nose and both ears of the woman.
>
> —*Arthashastra*

While the modern Indian law drafted by the British Macaulay also retained this distinction between corruption against the government and against private individuals, and was also concerned with adultery, its relative abhorrence for intercaste adultery was less than that of Kautilya.

Under the current Indian civil law, an abuse of trust in an agency relationship would call for damages being payable to the affected party. Only in rare circumstances would it become a crime under the Indian Penal Code (Section 406). On the other hand, if the principal is the government, it is invariably a crime under the Indian Penal Code (Section 161). Since the betrayal of trust cannot obviously be laid at the door of the giver of bribes, it was not a crime under the law as originally drafted by Lord Macaulay. Only a recent amendment under Section 165A has made the giving of bribes also a crime. Its ethical meaning is significant and will be examined later in the chapter.

Indians are not benumbed by corruption (Sekhar 1995). They are not accustomed or inure to it. An opinion survey done by students of TAPMI covered a cross-section of society, including housewives, senior executives, white-collar workers, blue-collar workers, engineering students, doctors and college students. The problem that emerged is that these concerns are not adequately reflected in political systems. In this context, Niebuhr's (1932) apprehension that individuals get de-ethicalised while forming groups may be recalled (Chapter 2).

Bribe-givers and Bribe-takers

Indians view taking bribes as far worse than giving bribes (Sekhar 1996b). Though a breach of trust by the bribe-taker is involved in any act of bribery, the bribe-giver usually has no option but to pay. Succumbing to extortion may not be unethical (Drucker 1985: 237). The Indian outlook recognises the more powerful position of the bribe-taker in an unequal ethical tussle. When we discuss later the countervailing forces against corruption, we will see that this is a positive feature of the Indian situation.

Differentiating between Big and Small

An issue that inevitably recurs is the varying degrees of unethicality that reflect the acceptance of varying degrees of corruption. It is easy to say that one cannot be ethical by half. But we have to guard against adopting any attitude that could equate a petty thief with a grand larcenist. Jurisprudence recognises differnet penalties for varying degrees of offence. An analogous approach ought to be applicable in ethics too. This could be construed as mild-hearted support for the mildly unethical.

A Faint Heart Never Wins a Fair Lady

Seshan (1995) is anguished not just at the existence of corruption in India but by its extensiveness. Even if it is true, it need not be forbidding to a manager. Even if we understand the frailty of the mildly unethical, the positive response one can get from the boldly ethical must be recognised. The boldly ethical can be a prime minister, a businessman, a manager—anyone who is strong enough to have his way in business. This feature was highlighted by Amol Karnad, the Managing Director of Alacrity Foundation, the well-known ethical builders who demonstrated that ethics can also pay. Karnad feels that 'when we meet officials, our reputation precedes us. Something makes them too shy to press for a bribe. Some phenomenon of osmosis takes place and more often than not we find our going surprisingly smooth' (Sekhar 1995).

> Tell me one aspect in this country which is not steeped in corruption.
>
> —Seshan (1995: 108)

The Leader Sets the Example

> Whatever a great man does, others will do the same: what standards he sets up that is followed by the world.
>
> — Bhagavad Gita, Chapter III, Sloka 21

This spiritual journey has to begin at the top of the organisation or nation. The leaders set the pace is what the *Bhagavad Gita* says. But the top would also cover managers in positions of authority as can be seen in Case 12.1. Pushing all the blame to the Prime Minister of India is only a refuge of the weak.

Several Steps to Clear the Air

To understand the possible ways in which corruption can be contained, we will return once more to the opinion poll conducted by the students of TAPMI (Sekhar 1996b). The survey results show that common opinion in India, untutored in formal ethical analysis, envisages a multipronged cure for corruption. Academicians, on the other hand, tend very often to develop a fixation for their hobby-horses.

Interestingly, while prioritising remedies for corruption, activism tops the list; this recommendation echoes Werner (1983), an expert on corruption studies. The dominant recommendation of the Chicago school of economists (see Chapter 3) is deregulation (*Newsweek* 1994). They believe that market systems are essentially ethical in their outcome. But they have ignored the compulsions of providing remedies against the inequities of the market system and have only partially tackled the problem. As part of the philosophy of a cure-all market system, they suggest that the salaries of the agents should be equal to the market (*Newsweek* 1994). The salaries of top officers are much higher in the private sector than in the civil services. At the same time, the salaries of the junior staff are much lower in the private sector than in the government. If we have to follow the markets, the salaries of the top officials should be considerably enhanced and the salaries of the junior officials reduced. Many would consider this trend as basically unethical. Moreover, empirical evidence does not support the argument that this by itself can contain corruption. There is no limit to greed. The popular ranking for deregulation is medium, unlike that of the Chicago school (*Newsweek* 1994). General opinion would seem to be a more balanced one.

The improvement of law enforcement is also suggested. Becker's (1964) formula of working out the penalty to be provided by law can be applied to corruption in the following manner:

Penalty = (Loss of gross social value by breach of law less private gain by the law-breaker) divided by the probability of being caught

In this context, the one who instigates breaking the law could be the outsider C and the agent who is tempted to accept this could be B. Till recently, no penalty was to be borne by the bribe-giver C even though he could have gained more than the agent. The probability of being caught could be improved by several methods, one of which could be increased surveillance. But this would increase costs and add to 'loss of social value' in the numerator of the Becker formula. This is a vicious circle. We have yet to resolve in practice how Becker's formula should be logically applied in such cases.

The sophistication in this mathematical model does not however match the ingenuity of the culprits in dodging the law and keeping low both the probability of being caught and the penalty. It seems difficult to bridge the gap between law-makers and law-dodgers. It is often suggested in Western literature that the probability of being caught could be considerably increased by encouraging whistle-blowing. Whistle-blowing may be defined as an attempt by an employee or a former employee of an organisation to disclose what he or she considers to be unethical (see Chapter 9).

All these alternatives, including the options from the survey by TAPMI students, are based on the central notion of the selfishness of man. Therefore, the central principle in this brand of ethics is 'checks and balances' so that one person's selfishness is pitted against another's to maintain overall equity. This could be the principle behind the belief that free and fair elections are the key (Seshan 1995). This approach has little faith in education and character building.

This could be viewed by some as a signal of a hopeless feeling that education is beyond redemption. This is however not so. Ethics should also be learnt within the family, as a part of the socialisation process. That seems the best way to stem corruption.

SUMMARY

Though corruption is an important issue, it should not become the sole concern of business ethics. Corruption can be dealt with in a multipronged manner, including activism, free press, better laws and deregulation. The basic cultural training at home and in schools is a more permanent solution. It has been argued that corruption could lead to good consequences for society and could be considered ethical in some situations. But the evidence reveals that corruption introduces too much uncertainty and high transaction costs. It dissuades innovations and long-term planning and therefore is very undesirable. Moreover, it is insulting to human dignity and basic values. These observations are made in an analysis using the currently popular agency theory.

ISSUES TO PONDER OVER

- Explain your stance on the following, classifying it as corrupt and/or unethical.
    1. Bribing the counter clerk in a private cinema house for out-of-turn cinema ticket
    2. Buying a cinema ticket in 'black' directly from the cinema owner who does this to cheat on entertainment tax
    3. Paying capitation fee against formal receipt to a prestigious management institute

- A minister instructs an industrialist to pay Rs 3 crore to an opposition political party to vote in favour of a government motion. No evidence of special favours to the industrialist is available.

- A director of a management institute pays Rs 1 lakh by cheque to a well-known magazine for an article praising the institute to be arranged by them from a well-regarded journalist. Based on several such deals, the manager who organises it gets a hefty commission.

CASE 12.1   Rangamati Iron Ore Mines

Budhadev Bose (BB) and Krishna Kumar Misra (KKM) had been handpicked by the MD of Kalinga Ores (a private sector company) to be the Manager and Asst Manager of Rangamati Mines (RM), one of the mines in the Barbil cluster. The mines had been running at a loss because of recurrent breakdowns in production due to accumulation of stocks, thus blocking space and restricting production. At the same time, production below capacity also contributed to the loss.

BB and KKM were close friends in spite of their totally different temperaments. BB was religious, a scholar of the *Vedas* and a believer in Swami Vivekananda. KKM loved the good things of life and had no respect for any religion, least of all the ritualistic one practised by his family in Darbhanga, North Bihar. He had been an indifferent student till BB became his guide, after which he not only passed but topped the degree and professional mine manager's examinations. He was beholden to BB for this change in his fortunes.

BB and KKM on arriving at RM noticed that the wagons were being underloaded. The loading supervisor Mehto however got the Railway Receipt (Owner's Risk) made out for the full load. 'The customer will pay for the loss. It is no loss to Kalinga Ores,' said Mehto defending his position that he was not breaching the trust of his employer RM. It was true that the purchase orders were worded that way, but this had two consequences. First, surplus and unaccounted ore was available at the mine site and could be sold by truckloads. BB and KKM discovered that this was exactly what was happening. As it took place on the sly, the company was not benefiting from these sales. It lined the pockets of Mehto and his gang, but gave RM a bad reputation causing them to lose custom from the steel plants. How long could the steel plants suffer these losses?

Second, they discovered that there was a perpetual shortage of wagons in the area. It was because the tracks were badly designed and involved too much shunting back and forth along zigzag tracks. The number of wagons that could be pushed into the Barbil system was restricted due to this bottleneck and the wagons had to wait for a long time. This resulted in rationing of wagons by the railway staff for a consideration—an average monthly payment of Rs 10,000 by each of the ten mines in the Barbil group. 'Scarcity is the root source of this corruption,' remarked KKM to BB, who was more inclined to blame this on lack of moral values. BB and KKM stopped both the practices. As a result, matters got worse. The RM wagons were not placed. The crisis continued for a month, with telexes and telegrams piling up from clients' steel plants, and angry comments from the MD. Meanwhile, the neighbouring mine owners in the Barbil group benefited from these short placements of wagons on RM's account. 'The alcoholic selfish rascals can never work for a common cause,' said BB.

BB could bear it no longer and wished to seek a transfer from RM. But the MD would have none of it. 'You solve the Rangamati problem or quit,' said the MD. He was more angry with KKM and asked BB if he would like to get rid of him straightaway. It was BB's turn now to refuse. Through thick and thin, KKM supported BB declaring that he would quit if BB did. 'You are my conscience. With you around I am sure I can solve any problem' was what KKM told BB. BB was intrigued by KKM's supreme confidence in going away to Jamshedpur for the all-India mine cricket meet, as if nothing had happened. KKM was the captain of the team.

The Barbil Club captained by KKM, representing all the 10 mines of the group, won and received the trophy from Mrs Ram Kumar, the wife of the Chief Operating Superintendent of the Railways. She had come all the way from Calcutta. It was a remarkable achievement of teamwork against the Joda Club who had better players. Mr Ram Kumar in turn said he needed help from the Barbil group of mines. Could they not increase their wagon loading, so that his figures became respectable? 'My promotion to the position of General Manager depends on that,' he said. He seemed to be only vaguely aware of the problems in the area. KKM took the opportunity to explain these to Ram Kumar. He also explained the underhand dealings of the junior staff in the mines and the railways. Ram Kumar said that due to a shortage of staff he had not been able to study the problem. Moreover he needed to entrust this work to someone who knew the soil conditions. He was also not sure if he could get a budget allocation from the Railways to undertake track-realignment.

KKM felt lighter after the discussion. He estimated that the changes in the track would cost them only Rs 30 lakh which could be recovered in three months with the resultant extra loading of the Barbil group of mines. He told BB that there was going to be a fairy-tale ending. And that is how it did happen in three months.

(The case closely follows an actual happening which was witnessed by the author.)

Analyses for the reader

1. What could have been KKM's strategy?
2. Summarise your understanding of the causes of corruption and their remedies essentially as derived from the facts of this case.

13

CONTAINING THE NEW DEVIL
Power, Equity and Spirituality
in Environmental Ethics

The Three Facets of Environmental Ethics

The necessity of an agreed code of ethics in dealing with the environment has been thrust on humanity fearful of complete extinction. The ethical issues which it has raised are complex and unique, not tackled earlier in the book. In order to grasp the complexities of the issue, we need to define the words 'environment' and 'environmental pollution', which can enable us to clarify the scope of environmental ethics.

Environmental ethics derived from these definitions would deal with three types of situations:

1. Actions that directly affect the livelihood and quality of human life. These can be dealt with as ethics of conflict resolution.

Meaning of Environment

Environment includes water, air and land, and their inter-relationship with human beings, other living creatures, plants, micro organisms and property.

—*Environment Protection Act, 1986, Section 2a*

Meaning of Pollution

Environmental pollution means any solid, liquid or gaseous substance which may be or tend to be injurious to environment.

—*Environment Protection Act, 1986, Section 2b*

2. Actions that will affect the livelihood and quality of life of the future generations. This is inter-generational in character. Our models of distributive justice and democratic discourse with the affected persons would break down in dealing with this issue. One cannot negotiate and have a social contract with a person who is yet to be born. This would be inter-generational ethics.

3. Actions that affect animals, birds, plants and inanimate objects. Ethics that have so far been only human-centered would also have to be animal-

centred, life-centred, rock-centred and ecologically holistic (Elliot 1993). This is spiritual ethics.

Obviously, environment is something 'external' to oneself, as a person or an organisation. If we pollute only ourselves, we would not be polluting the environment. Environmental ethics revolves around the duty of not polluting the 'external world'.

Living With the New Devil

The magnitude of the problems of environmental pollution are only a recent phenomenon. They are the direct consequence of the uncontrolled greed of human beings. Since market systems aggravate this greed, the very philosophy of markets heralded so ecstatically by Paine (1792) is turning out to be the newborn devil. We had seen in Chapter 3 that the sage vision of Paine also had a savage facet. This is brutally thrust on the environment.

> There is no polite way of saying business has ravaged the world.
>
> — *Paul Hawken (1993)*

The converse, that non-market systems are always environmentally friendly, is also a fallacy. We have only to look at the erstwhile Soviet Union for confirmation; a non-market-driven society, it experienced the worst case of environmental pollution. The problem therefore is not merely of economics but of the human spirit and the power of technology to do things that could not be done earlier. This is what Chakraborty (1995a) says while commending Indian values as he sees them; many would not see the Indian past as kindly as he does. Western thinkers, more often than not, look at environmental ethics as basically human-centred and not nature-centred. The definitions of environment and environmental pollution in Indian law are amenable to be used both as human-centred and nature-centred values.

Is man caught by a new devil hell-bent on destroying humanity? Or is the devil a more sinister creature using man to destroy nature and the universe? Lovelock is of the former view whereas writers like Capra and Pauli (1996) are of the latter view. Indian thinking has been more in line with Capra; in fact he derives his inspiration from Indian thought. Capra and Pauli, quoting the Norwegian philosopher Aern Naess, call the former the 'shallow' ecology and the latter the 'deep' ecology. Those who profess deep ecology are a committed lot even as they may be outrageously self-righteous.

> **The Shallow Ecology**
>
> We don't pose much of a threat to the planet . . . our threat is to our own civilisation and livestock and food crop that accompany it.
>
> —*Lovelock (1996)*

All the three facets of environmental ethics—conflict resolution, intergenerational and spiritual—can be dealt with a disarming consistency by the ancient Indian normative approach of the fulfilment of one's duty to nature. This would, however, wish away the realities of human behaviour. Establishing institutions that can practically cope with the stresses emerging from the 'rights' concept of environmental ethics will require more thought. We will have to rethink if it is ever possible to make them workable without invoking an ethicality also based on duties.

The Deep Ecology

The [West] creates a dissociation between [man] and nature . . . India emphasise[d] the harmony of the individual with the universal.

— *Rabindranath Tagore (1988)*

Development Planning, Markets and Eco-terrorism

The first facet of environmental ethics is the problem of conflict resolution. Conflict of interests arise in modern economic environment in two ways: first, invisibly through the operations of market systems, and second, through development planning by the state, which in theory has a democratic sanction in India. In India, it is this second set of conflicts that usually escalates into open confrontations of 'environmental politics'. The former kills silently, while the latter has eco-terrorists defending the cause of environment and accused of holding up progress.

Let us first discuss the invisible conflicts. Arguments on environmental ethics have in the past usually hovered around the classic problems of the 'tragedy of the commons' (Hardin 1968) and the 'prisoners' dilemma' (Tucker 1955). The prisoners' dilemma describes a hypothetical situation epitomising the difficulties men face to act in a cooperative manner if they are true to the model proposed by pure capitalist theory. The theory visualises two prisoners, A and B, in two different prison cells with no means of exchanging information, each suspicious and mistrustful of the other, just as the model capitalist would be of a fellow capitalist. They do not know that they will be let off if neither confesses and condemned if both do. On the other hand, they are told that the one who confesses will be let off. We can safely assume that both will confess if interrogated separately. They would be better off if neither confessed. This would have been the natural outcome if they had exchanged information between themselves.

People destroying the environment because they feel that someone else will even if they do not, are in a similar situation. If they joined hands, they could together decide not to destroy the environment. The tragedy of the commons is described by an eminent biologist, Hardin (1968). He says, 'Picture a pasture open to all. Each herdsman seeks to maximise his personal gain; he concludes the only sensible course is for him to add another animal to the herd. And another. But this conclusion is reached by each and every herdsman sharing the commons. Herds are increased without limit, resulting in the destruction of the commons. Therein lies the tragedy: Freedom in the commons brings ruin to all.' This in summary means that in a system in which each person looks after his own affairs and has inadequate infor-mation on the other, they would jointly destroy the commons, i.e., the environment, even though it is for their mutual good that this should be protected.

If we persist in the belief that human beings are basically selfish, there could still be several institutional measures or situations where this selfishness itself could make them cooperate (Singh 1994); it is for us to invent such institutions. Thus, in the case of the commons, there could be a law that each herdsman would pay grazing charges to the common pool based on the number of hours their herd spent grazing. Another way would be for the central authority to impose an iron law to establish order and good behaviour; in the long run this would be good for everyone. A third way for government intervention is to support environmental controls with incentives of tax concessions and subsidies. The more carefully they are crafted, the more likely would they by to achieve the intended results (Daly 1996). Lastly, governments can have tradeable permits that contract out environmental tasks by public auction. The lowest bidder gets the job and then bargains with the polluter to pay him a fee for helping to reduce pollution with the least cost to himself. The ethics of free markets are therefore harnessed for public good. This practice is followed in some parts of the USA.

Many of the problems of the 'prisoners' dilemma' and 'tragedy of the commons', according to some, are self-created and imaginary, and under-rate the innate desire of human beings to cooperate (Sekhar 1993, Bardhan 1995). The tribals of old never had this problem not because their productivity was low and their resources limitless as opined by Hardin (1968). The problem arises precisely because of an unduly high regard for the ethicality of market systems with inadequate attention to the other ethical values. Human beings fortunately are not universally greedy. Indian rural development abounds with examples of cooperative principles having overcome greed. The complex task of watershed development, which is full of these problems, has been tackled not by theoretical models but by using age-old concepts of *bhakti* in getting persons of different castes and economic levels to work together and achieve miracles. This was the case in Ralegaon–Sidhi, Maharashtra, where Anna Saheb Hazare, a retired truck driver, achieved the impossible (Pangare and Pangare 1992). Hence the hope.

The second more visible area of conflict is a direct consequence of the concept of rights that has taken root in India. This calls for an activist attack on the hegemonistic assault on the lives of those who had so far remained unprotected. We mentioned the ethical approach of the left in Chapter 4 in highlighting the ethics of the underprivileged. One of the most sordid aspects of India's environmental problems arises not through the market forces in the model of the tragedy of the commons. It arises from the deliberate actions of the state against the 80 million tribals of India. Even as ancient India mostly left them alone, modern India has seen millions of them displaced in the last 50 years of Independence, due to dams and deforestation, with 80 per cent of them living below the poverty line. And yet, the very people who initiated these 'devilish' development were their greatest admirers. Nehru (1989) exclaimed that long after stock exchanges die, their song and dance will survive. But their songs today are full of sorrow and despair.

Beyond the river lo! behold fields green and
beautiful
Me and my beloved singing and hand in
hand
As we go closer, Oh heart! it has vanished
from sight
Has it gone beyond that yonder mountain
Beyond the mountain must be the fields
green and beautiful
Me and my beloved climb the mountain
singing and hand in hand
As we reach the top we stare at the distant
horizon
Where are the fields green and beautiful?

*— Gadkor Porom Re, a Mundari
song from Chhota Nagpur, Bihar*

Some of the recent cases in India cover both types of conflicts. Example 13.1 is from published literature and conversations with some of author's students working in Narmada Andolan. Examples 13.2, 13.3 and 13.4 are from personal acquaintance.

EXAMPLE 13.1   The Narmada Dam

The construction of the dam involved three states: Gujarat, Maharashtra and Madhya Pradesh. It was understood that once completed, it would help in providing water to arid lands, and generate a large quantum of power. But it would also mean destruction of forests and displacement of a large number of tribals. There was also a suspicion that some of the land alongside the canals would get waterlogged. It was stated that smaller sets of irrigation facilities would have created none of these problems. Once the construction commenced, the agitation against it grew stronger. Contrasting technical arguments were exchanged by the contesting parties. The main argument of the agitationists was that the resettlement of the tribals was not worked out and not likely to happen; it involved inter-state movement of populations over long distances. They also said that the contractor's lobby was bribing the politicians to sing to their tune. The leader of the agitationists, Medha Patkar, got international recognition with the 'alternate Nobel Prize'. Her critics however described her as an interested lobbyist who was motivated by her own selfish interest for publicity. The international funding agencies withdrew the funding but the Indian state governments continued with indigenous funding. The problems and issues have remained unresolved for more than a decade now. The project costs have escalated due to the delays. There is little hope for the discerning public to get a disinterested and balanced opinion. Rhetorical speeches continue to be made by the contending parties, with little hope of a democratic dispassionate discourse which was described as an important ethical value in Chapter 1.

EXAMPLE 13.2   **The BRPL Pipeline**

BRPL (name disguised), a petrochemical plant, was set up by one of the biggest business houses in India. It was said that they acquired a lot of land, much in excess of their requirements, at very low prices; their processes were perfectly legal but the farmers from whom the land was acquired were not much aware of their rights in this regard.

The excess land thus acquired was resold at abnormally high prices. BRPL got clearance from all government and pollution control bodies for discharging their effluents into the sea. About the time of their building the pipeline to discharge their effluents, political activity was strong due to the forthcoming elections. One of the contesting parties organised the fishermen to protest against the pipeline as the effluents would destroy the fish. The company had an extremely adverse public image due to its land deals. The fishermen, supported by an opposition political party, went on a rampage even as the company issued public notices to the effect that the effluents were not harmful to the fish. The agitationists became violent and several people were killed.

The company ultimately relented and promised to build an effluent treatment plant. The commissioning of the plant got delayed, with considerable financial loss. This business group had had similar experiences in several of their plants throughout the country. They had apparently not reconciled themselves to the fact that political patronage was under severe strain with democratic, popular movements.

EXAMPLE 13.3   **Gulistan Alcohols**

Gulistan Alcohols (name disguised) manufactured alcohol from sugar molasses. They had an ongoing and persistent problem with the pollution control authorities about their effluents. They paid astronomical sums as bribes but were continually threatened with public interest litigation against them in the High Court and the Supreme Court. Dr Patel, who was a chemical engineer working in Gulistan Alcohols, got sick of it and devised a method to use the effluent for generation of methane which could be used to generate power. He found that the government offered subsidies for pollution-control devices. With this subsidy his anti-pollution process was in fact profitable. What appeared a threat turned out to be an opportunity.

EXAMPLE 13.4   **The Bishnoi Story**

The Bishnois are a tribe living in the heart of the deserts in the Bikaner district of Rajasthan. Though surrounded by desert, their village is lush with vegetation. They have a self-imposed rule that they will never cut trees. The trees yield fruits which give the community a steady income, and also ensure that groundwater is preserved and the wells therefore do not run dry.

As against this, sand dunes in several neighbouring villages are destroying them. The main reason is that the charcoal-makers from Bikaner have been plucking out the shrubs that hold the sand together. The villagers cannot organise a protest by themselves since they are too few to matter and also fragmented into caste groups.

Such examples of both the fruitful and the harmful environmental ethics are innumerable in India. But the negative examples are more in number and their total impact is extremely high. There is worldwide support for activists who are fighting against it. As we mentioned in Chapter 4, such international support is however a double-edged weapon. It may have a hidden agenda not visible or obvious (Sekhar 1997).

> The quantum of solids in the air in micrograms per cum Delhi: 1480, Calcutta: 601, Madras: 306, Bombay: 407, Std: 100. 90 % of water in India polluted and 60% of all diseases water-borne.
>
> —*Narula et al. (1995)*

The lessons from these four cases are:

1. Environmental planning cannot be done without the total involvement of the affected.
2. It needs total transparency.
3. It is not a matter of just technological appraisal. It needs continual technological innovation.

> Mahesh Chandra Mehta, the unstoppable Indian public litigationist chosen as the conservationist hero of the year by Goldman Foundation, San Francisco, 1996.

4. Bureaucratic and legal machinery has its uses but cannot be relied upon totally to support environmental ethics, particularly when the rewards for evasion are high.
5. Activist support and a free press are useful but not if they come too late after an adverse environmental plan has been put through.
6. Local level (and not parliamentary) democracy is logistically useful for ensuring the ethics of distributive justice and democratic discourse.
7. In the long run it would help an organisation to follow environmental ethics rather than dodge it.
8. Taxation and subsidy could sometimes be more cost-effective in pollution control than physical controls by government. Business would welcome this more than physical controls which are more prone to corruption.
9. Destructive competition is a socially created condition that can be corrected to cooperation by cultural changes.
10. International acclaim of Indian activism may have an ethical shadow of doubtful motives.

Tomorrow We Die

The human-centred environmental norms for inter-generational ethics of more recent inspiration are owed to Rawls (1971) who argues that in a situation like this, distributive justice would require that one should pass on to posterity what one wants or inherits from the previous generation. It is an odd social contract with the dead and the unborn.

If we are serious about this, we would have to review many of our project appraisal methods. Thus in project appraisals we apply what is known as the net present value technique, which incorporates the typical Western capitalistic outlook—giving greater importance to present consumption than to future benefits to the unborn. This is the basic reason for environmental degradation.

That a profound change in the theories of financial management is required has hardly been understood by conventional financial analysts of the day.

The Lady of the Forest Will Not Slay

Rawls' approach to inter-generational ethics was a brave effort to bring in a rational logic to the ethics of the environment. Much of our discussions so far used considerable amount of analytical and logical argument, hardly alluding to the sacred. If we extend our personalities to include those of our children and grandchildren, the ethics of environment can be justified rationally. But how do we include the reverence we feel for the deep forests or the mighty mountains? As mentioned in Chapter 1, Indian ethics did cover this reverence. The *Rig Veda* was full of this, as we saw in Chapter 1, when we talked about the ethical value of harmony. Why should we care more for the children of tomorrow than for ourselves? And so, we are back to the supernatural, however much the rationalist may be uncomfortable with it. As Gupta (1996) asks, 'Is there not a place for the sacred?' Indian philosophers thought of the environment with much more deliberate sophistication than as mere tribal totemic intuition. Venkataswaran (1962) refers to the concept of *bhuta yajna* in the *Vishnu Purana*,

> **The Ultimate in Environmental Ethics**
>
> The new vision of deep ecology is consistent with 'perennial philosophy' of spiritual traditions, whether of Christian mystics or of the Buddhists or of the American Indian traditions.
>
> —*Capra and Pauli (1996)*

to say that Indians had a sacred respect for the environment; they attributed the existence of *atma* (soul) to all things animate or inanimate. Chakraborty (1995a: 52) has expanded this thinking in Indian ethos to say how appropriate this concept of *bhuta rin*, i.e., the debt we owe to the environment would be in the present scenario. Quite possibly, texts like the *Vishnu Purana* do owe their primary inspiration to tribal societies which till today have much greater concern for the environment than the modern world.

Lest we be carried away by exaggerated chauvinism, the readers must be reminded of the discussion in Chapter 5 that Indian thinking is vastly variegated and it is possible to pick up other diametrically opposite threads. These values cannot obviously be intellectually derived from the primary principles. But we dare to gradually, and grudgingly, accept them as no less valid.

Capra and Pauli (1996) have seen the decided relevance of such a spiritual approach to business ethics of the environment.

To Strive to Seek and Not to Yield

The role of innovative technology in environmental ethics is crucial to all the features we have delineated. Scientists and technologists, whether driven by law, conscience, profits or sheer resentment of the affected public, have in

Traditional Recycling	Zero-emission Thinking
Recycle paper	Recycle ink and paper
Inefficient (65% deinked)	Efficient (100% deinked)
Toxic sludge	Zero emission
Capital intensive	Low capital
Expensive	Price competitive
Replace one problem with another	Total solution
No net economic effect	New industry

— Adapted from Capra and Pauli (1996)

recent times come out with several innovations that would ultimately increase profits in business. Environmental stewardship that is seen as an opportunity rather than a threat may trigger off another industrial revolution. This would also mean that business should strive to seek and to find. One of the typical challenges facing industry is shown alongside.

Coping with Law, Power and Brutality

Let us finally address the varied approaches business managers have taken in this area and reflect on the desirable future directions.

1. The earliest defensive approach is to find legal and illegal means of bypassing the laws. These could include corruption (discussed in Chapter 12).

2. The second approach is to see the laws as unjust and unfair, and fight against them openly and lobby for change. It is possible that some of the laws are not quite right, and we must concede that this step would be ethically justified sometimes, though not as often as it is made out.

3. The third approach is to just follow the laws and nothing more. This had the approval of the Chicago school of economists of old (see Chapter 3), which now appears to be on the defensive with regard to the environment

(Hoffman 1993). In 1989, it was the right thing to say that it would be totally unethical for business organisations to lobby against environmental legislation, but they were not ethically bound to do anything more than required by the law (Bowie 1990).

4. Being proactive in matters of the environment is the prevalent view of even the hardliners of the Chicago school. Environmental ethics has literally broken into the sanctum sanctorum of the 'business alone' types. Side by side, laws that are based on social benefit–cost analysis have gone apace to compel the polluters to 'internalise' the costs required to restore the original state and/or compensate others who have consequently suffered. The Caux Principles (described in Chapter 7) adopted the world over incorporate the responsibility of business organisations to take a proactive stance with regard to the environment.

5. Ethical organisations may find that they are not able to compete effectively in the market as their competitors are wantonly destroying the environment and saving themselves the corresponding costs. If they go on this way, they may have to close shop. It would be ethically desirable for them then to lobby for strict enforcement all round of better environmental regulations. This should be done through collective effort, discussed earlier in this chapter and in Chapter 6.

6. Vested interests or incorrect perceptions may be thwarting business through eco-terrorism. Effective communication and the ability to negotiate mutually beneficial social contracts helpful to all are then the crux of desirable ethical conduct. Most foreign multinationals in India are ill-equipped to do this, with disastrous consequences. The inadequacy flows both from suspect intentions and clumsy communication.

SUMMARY

The chapter discusses the three facets of environmental ethics: (*a*) conflict resolution within the living, (*b*) inter-generational ethics, and (*c*) spiritual and non-human-centric ethics. The sources of conflicts are traced to aggressive market forces as also state-driven development planning which has done untold damage to the tribals in India. Environmental ethics is more inclined to be intuitional than analytical in inspiration. The chapter finds the ethical beliefs of the tribals and ancient India surprisingly close to modern-day thinking. It sees the tide turning against the belief that business organisations are only concerned with following environmental regulations laid down by the state and nothing beyond. They need to take a proactive and less adverse stand with greater transparency and in partnership with those affected by business activities. Great negotiating and communication skills are also required to work out a truly ethical social contract with the affected; multinationals are known to handle this badly. It is noted that justice to those affected by environmental destruction is often suppressed by violence. The importance of technological innovation is highlighted, as also treating of environmental problems as opportunities rather than as threats.

ISSUES TO PONDER OVER

- Reflect on any of the recent environmental controversies and see if your understanding has improved by using any of the concepts in this chapter.

- What do you think are the factors that prevent people from coming together and solving an environmental problem of common interest?

- Do you feel that in any sector India is overdoing environmental ethics at the cost of development?

- Do you personally feel more assured if you use spiritual reasons for supporting your approach to the environment in modification of straightforward logic of enlightened self-interest?

CASE 13.1 The East Coast Road

Ajit Koulagi, of the Indian National Trust for Art and Cultural Heritage (INTACH), had issued on 18 May 1995 an 'environmental alert' to all his friends and co-workers in Karnataka that they should explore the possibility of obtaining stay orders from the Karnataka High Court against hastily drawn road projects. He recognised the tremendous importance of roads for the country's development, but his organisation felt that the Western experience in road development, which had caused havoc there, should not be followed blindly in India. INTACH believed that a more imaginative way of using roads in conjunction with rail, sea and waterways was much less threatening to the environment. Ajit was an architect concerned with appropriate building technologies and sustainable development.

He was projecting his experiences from the struggle to bring in equity and justice to the East Coast Road Project (ECR). When the case-writer discussed the matter with him on 26 February 1996, INTACH had filed a contempt of court case in the Madras High Court against the Tamil Nadu Government and the Asian Development Bank who had funded the project. On 8 April 1996, the court completely stayed the work, modifying the interim order of December 1995 only to desist from cutting the trees. This was the second time the court had stopped operations, the first being in 1992 which was vacated in April 1994.

The ECR project was a 731 km highway which connected Madras to Kanyakumari. It was projected to:

1. function as the main artery linking the more advanced hinterland, and develop the area industrially and in agriculture
2. spread out urban population from Madras and Pondicherry
3. be strategically close to Sri Lanka and ensure defence preparedness
4. help cyclone relief operations
5. transport coal to thermal stations
6. save fuel costs by Rs 60 lakh
7. ease grain movement from this surplus area

Exhibit 13.1 shows the position of the project on the map of Tamil Nadu, as also INTACH's alternate proposal, which was much shorter and basically

EXHIBIT 13.1   *Alternative Proposal for East Coast Road*

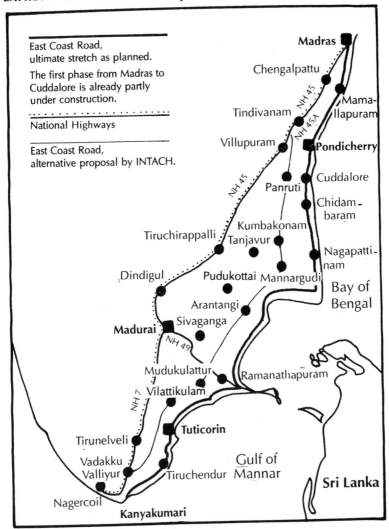

East Coast Road,
ultimate stretch as planned.

The first phase from Madras to
Cuddalore is already partly
under construction.

National Highways

East Coast Road,
alternative proposal by INTACH.

differed from the official plan in that it avoided getting too close to the ecologically fragile sea coast and made much better use of the existing roadways.
They had however not worked out a firm figure of alternate project costs nor a
cost–benefit analysis for the revised project. Intuitively they felt it would be
better than the official project.

The 1988 project report of the ECR was examined on behalf of INTACH by a
team of international experts, Dorriah L. Page and Neil W. Pelkey of P. Squared
Consultants. They found gross errors in the computation of the social cost–
benefit analysis. The maintenance costs of roads as also the air-pollution
damages had been understated, accidents due to fast-moving traffic had been
ignored, and costs of houses that would have to be destroyed had also been

ignored. Even without including environmental and social costs, the return was only 5 to 6 per cent and not 18 to 20 per cent as projected in the report passed by the Asian Development Bank. If social costs were included, the return would be zero. The project could not be expected to pay off its loan. 'The real benefits of the road accrue primarily to the construction company that builds the road,' they said.

The work on the 171 km Madras–Cuddalore section commenced in 1991 and was in full swing by 1992, with funding from the Asian Development Bank. But no environmental assessment had been done, nor had the local people been consulted. This was against the very detailed norms issued by the Ministry of Environment and Forests of the Government of India, which required a two-year advance notice to the affected individuals. The estimated cost of this section of the project was about Rs 95 crore (as on 25 February 1996). Of this, Rs 20 crore had already been spent by 1992. When INTACH appealed to the Madras High Court, the cutting of trees was stayed (December 1992).

The Tamil Nadu Government submitted its Environmental Appraisal Report to the Department of Environment, Government of India, in 1993 and also a counter-affidavit to the High Court. The environmental impact as seen by INTACH differed sharply from the Tamil Nadu Government Report (July 1993). They contented that:

1. The digging of borewells close to the sea would result in salt-water incursions which would ruin agricultural land. If the area was urbanised there would be no other way to get water than through boreholes.
2. Tourist traffic would decrease and not increase if the trees were cut and the beauty of the Coromandel coast would be destroyed.
3. Noise pollution would increase with increased traffic.
4. The road would destroy schools, temples and tanks.
5. The habitat of a wide range of organisms would be destroyed.
6. The project gave no benefits to the local population in terms of employment.
7. The area had no surplus grain to transport.
8. Port development had already been planned which did away with the need for transport of coal by road.

The strategic defence need made no sense to them if the road was anyway going to take so long that the current state of hostilities with the Tamil insurgents from Sri Lanka would have ceased by then. The benefits of increased traffic was taken in the gross, whereas only the net increase, after adjusting the decreased traffic along the old road, should have been considered.

The Government of India cleared the report conditionally after having it examined by an expert committee. Several portions of the project were scrapped and severe restrictions imposed on the cutting of trees. The Tamil Nadu government accepted the conditions and the High Court lifted the stay in April 1994. But again in 1995, INTACH appealed to the court that the conditions had been violated. The court banned the cutting of trees in December 1995, and completely stopped the work in April 1996. The Tamil Nadu Government was preparing its appeal (May 1996). Meanwhile the Asian Development Bank was also now sending its team for a reappraisal (February 1996).

(The material for this case was provided by INTACH in a discussion and acknowledged.)

Analyses for the reader

1. If you were the Chief Engineer of the construction company, would you have made a bid for the work, keeping in mind the Code of Conduct of Engineers?
2. Going by the need to speedily expand infrastructural facilities in India, should organisations such as INTACH be allowed 'to hold the nation to ransom'?
3. Can you think of alternative methods to ensure that ethical decision processes go hand in hand with speedy development?
4. From the limited facts given in the case, prepare a tentative presentation for the inhabitants of the east coast villages.

14

THE BATTLE OF THE SEXES
A Mindset for Gender Balance

Crisis in Gender Ethics

As largely viewed, the basic issue in gender ethics revolves around the right to a minimum standard of living. But gender ethics encompasses more than mere wage levels. Traditionalists would like to believe that today women face problems because of the failure of Indian society to inculcate the ethics of duties as laid down by the ancient scriptures. According to them, Indian women have failed in their duties towards men and the men in turn have failed in their duties towards women. This contrast in understanding gender ethics is the first cause for ideological crisis in dealing with this issue.

The second cause lies in a misunderstanding of the distinction among descriptive (D) ethics which states what is on the ground, normative (N) ethics which a society understands as 'what ought to be' and analytical (A) ethics on the 'why' of an ethical position (see Chapter 1). This accounts for the sharp divide in perceptions in the history of Indian ethics. And so, on occasions like at the Beijing conference, we have two Indians representing alternate views on women's position vis-à-vis men. There is a range of differences in Indian literature on the status of women.

> **Woman as an Equal**
>
> Genius inheres in the soul—it makes no distinction between man and woman.
>
> —*Rajashekhara, 7th Century AD, Kavya Mimansa*

Any attempt to trace the prevailing view to either of these Indian traditions would be a waste of effort since present-day practices have been drawn from both; these have also been influenced by Western feminist writings.

> **Woman as a Dependent**
>
> In childhood a woman should be in her father's control, in youth in her husband's and if he dies in her sons'.
>
> —*Manusmriti, 5.147*

The reality of the sufferings of women in India today is an established fact. Several courses of action are possible in order to alleviate their suffering, and business can contribute meaningfully.

The Primal Mystery

The Western notion of gender ethics concentrates mainly on the issue of discrimination. This understanding of gender ethics means that men and women should be treated as equals. To treat them as different would be unethical. This equality between men and women would then have to be reinforced by laws and regulations.

Organisational policies, therefore, should be similarly fashioned. Any organisation violating this principle should then be punished. Law is only an enabling process. Women must stand up for their rights and take recourse to courts and demonstrations if required.

Another approach to the issue of gender ethics maintains that biological differences between men and women cause psychological differences. These psychological differences should not be allowed to destroy social cohesion. One way of dealing with it is for both men and women to appreciate and cultivate feminine and masculine traits respectively. This understanding would help successfully deal with obstacles in the man–woman working relationship,

> The proletariat can massacre the ruling class . . . but women cannot even dream of exterminating males . . . Male and female stand opposed in primordial Mistein . . . the couple is a fundamental unity of two halves . . . cleavage along sex is impossible.
>
> —*Simone de Beauvoir (Hider 1996)*

that is, their working together as a team (Raj 1996). This is the concept of androgyny. The third approach maintains that men and women are parts of a primal mystery, and therefore indispensable to each other. Thus, efforts have to be made against oppression, not against discrimination (Hider 1996). The sanctification of this primal mystery would form a part of the natural ethical rights of women. Simone de Beauvoir adhered to this notion of primal mystery.

The approach of primal mystery, with due consideration to the second approach, seems to be the most appropriate. The first approach, though intellectually the most acceptable alternative, seems to be doubtful in the result. Gender issues as relevant for business ethics could variously arise in different contexts. These are dealt with in the succeeding paragraphs.

Thwarted Careers

Discrimination in recruitment and career growth affect the self-esteem and self-fulfilment of women. This variety of discrimination is widespread in India, and there are no legal remedies, except when the employer is the state. Article 16 of the Indian Constitution protects women against discrimination in terms of employment by the state (Banerjee 1995). Non-state employers can avoid this Constitutional condition, as we will see in the subsequent example.

EXAMPLE 14.1 **The Hidden Agenda**

Ramaswamy had joined the Institute of Village Development fired by the legendary public image of the idealism of its chairman Philip Mathan. His first assignment was to serve on the student selection board for its two-year management course. As was customary, Philip Mathan briefed the selection board. He said, 'Be careful not to select too many girls. We may have a problem placing them. I myself have never encouraged women to be recruited as executives, unless I am sure that they will never marry and rear children. You know motherhood is emotionally too compelling for them. Women can never be good officers. I need not make a secret of this. We are not a state under the Indian Constitution and have no legal obligations to avoid gender discrimination. I have done more for women than all our feminists; I have given millions of them dignity and self-reliance by marketing what they produce in their homes in the company of their families.'

What should Ramaswamy do? Give up his job? That is what it usually meant, if one opposed Philip Mathan.

Equal Pay for Equal Work

Discrimination in remuneration between men and women is rampant in India. The Equal Remuneration Act is inadequate in its scope for preventing exploitation (see Chapter 4). Thakur (1995) shows that female wage rates are much lower than those of males everywhere in India. Besides, ingenious employers have found several loopholes in the law to circumvent the spirit behind it. She also says that this discrimination cannot be explained away by the logic of supply and demand. It has deep social causes, such as childhood conditioning of women to be docile and less demanding of their rights. Some feel that the differences are also due to biological factors. It is well known that female dogs are more endearing and docile than male ones. Here is an interesting example of this phenomenon.

EXAMPLE 14.2 **The Bruised Egos at Kiriburu**

The labour force at the Kiriburu Mines in Chaibasa District of Bihar was equally divided between men and women. The women were paid about 20 per cent less wages than the men for identical work. The management decided to raise the women's rates. This led to violent riots by the men whose ego was badly bruised. The women were themselves hesitant to accept the raise. They would rather have peace at home. After several rounds of persuasion the conflict was resolved. The workers were mostly tribals and had otherwise very free relationships between men and women. One wonders how a less egalitarian society would have reacted to the situation.

Sexual Harassment at Work

Sexual harassment constitutes any act that reduces women to sex objects, ranging from sexual innuendoes in conversation to rape. In America, sexual harassment is a major problem for which whistle-blowing is often the only remedy (Dandekar 1993). Women in Islamic countries seem to suffer sexual harassment to a less degree (Donaldson 1996). Sexual harassment is not usually a matter of 'desire' but is about 'power'. On occasions, women too play the power game unethically. The ethical administration of this is very tricky as we will see in the following two examples.

EXAMPLE 14.3 The Sadist Boss

Kamala (23), an MBA on her first job, was unfortunate to get Anand Patwardhan (40) as her boss. He was a sadist; he treated the women in the office abominably, much as he treated his wife. No work done by any woman would ever satisfy him. Kamala was advised by her colleague Usha that the only way left for her was to complain to the Managing Director Prem Kumar. Prem Kumar was known to react quickly and effectively to reports of sexual harassment. Kamala got such an opportunity soon enough. Patwardhan asked her to work late (till 10 p.m.). There was nobody in the office besides Patwardhan and Kamala. However, Patwardhan did not make any sexual advances towards Kamala. At the same time if Kamala complained on grounds of sexual harassment he would be unable to give adequate cause for asking her to work late instead of a male assistant. Should Kamala use this opportunity?

EXAMPLE 14.4 The Uncouth Assistant

Madhuri Dubey came from a well-known upper-caste family of Uttar Pradesh. An MBA from a leading Indian institution, she was both brilliant and beautiful. Her Director (Personnel) Gobind Pandey was also a Brahmin, sophisticated and of artistic interests. His wife however was uneducated and orthodox. He had deep family ties and was devoted to his wife. But this did not prevent him from encouraging Madhuri to often drop in to his room and discuss at a 'highly stimulating intellectual level'. Madhuri had one fly in her ointment and that was Dukhan Ram her head clerk. She described him as her 'uncouth assistant'. He belonged to a Scheduled Caste and had got his job on the basis of reservation, as it was a public sector unit and was obligated by Constitutional provisions to provide such reservation.

There was little love lost between Dukhan and Madhuri. While Dukhan was always curt with Madhuri she was always out to find faults with his work. An occasion presented itself when Dukhan summarised a case erroneously. Having got a chance, she shouted at him. But Dukhan was not one to let her go; he retaliated. Madhuri, who had been trying to get rid of her uncouth assistant, got an opportunity to do so. She taped Dukhan's verbal retaliation and took it to the

Managing Director Gokul Varma and said that she was being harassed because she was a woman. Gokul, who was known to have a glad eye, called Gobind and asked him to dismiss Dukhan. Gobind, an ethical officer, informed Gokul of the procedural requirements for dismissal. Gokul waved this objection and told him that it was Govind's job to fix all the details. Later, Madhuri went to Govind's room and cried her heart out saying that she always thought Gobind was a sensitive and just man, but was now appalled by his hesitation to dismiss Dukhan. What should Gobind do now? (Can we apply the Laura Nash principles given in Chapter 2 to this case?)

(This is a modified version of the case of Subhir Ghosh 1994 used with the permission of the Lal Bahadur Shastri Academy of Administration, Mussoorie.)

Sexual Stereotyping in Advertisements

The women's movements in India have been concerned about stereotyping of women in advertisements. Women are depicted as sex objects or as domestic workhorses: they are silly and childish, definitely not serious individuals with need for self-fulfilment (see Chapter 10 for details). In the West too, advertisements are responsible for demeaning stereotyping of women. Mills (1995) reveals how the advertisements of British Airways systematically show that women can never hold positions of power, prestige or authority. Though the British Airways employ women pilots, the advertisements never mention them!

Harming through Products

The ethical process of product development was discussed in Chapter 10. The discussion did not highlight gender-related issues in product development. In this chapter, we will illustrate the implications of the cautions we discussed in Chapter 10 in its application to gender-related consequences. The discussion is a little subtle as it emanates from a not-so-obvious framework of the need to respect and support the primal mystery as the basic feature of gender ethics. This involves one's understanding that suppression of this primal mystery could take three extreme forms: one of exploitation of women by men, a second of women attempting to be manipulative due to the insecurity born out of this exploitation, and a third of an attempt to totally destroy the difference in a desperate quest for avoiding gender problems. This is a rebound. Being a rebound, it shares the pathological features of the original cause. In an effort to capture these psychological needs of women, the ethical requirements of clearing products for safety, discussed in Chapter 10, are thrown to the winds by unethical marketers.

Advertisements also put pressure on women in the choice of products; they work in their most vulnerable psychological chinks. An undue importance to live up to the sexual fantasies of men is one such pressure. Thus, there are more products in the market to make women 'alluring' than to make men more 'attractive'. This is a direct consequence of the insecurity of women in the face of exploitation.

A rebound would be to suppress the natural biological features of women to make them 'equal to men'. Typically, products to make women cope with the awkwardness of their monthly periods exploit the shame of their womanhood. A well-known case covered by this second feature was the one of tampons marketed by Procter and Gamble (Beuchamp 1983). These were released without adequate testing. Many woman using these had serious side-effects, even convulsions.

The third compulsion arises from the misery they have to undergo with large families. But the remedy for this is thrust on them, interfering with their bodily rhythms, whereas the men do nothing about it themselves. The several contraceptive pills released in India are not all free from side-effects.

A fourth awful pressure for some Indian women is to make sure that they give birth to only male progeny. The case at the end of this chapter on the portable ultrasonograph illustrates this.

A fifth type of situation is where the 'products' promise to deliver women from the unpleasant experiences of motherhood. The atrocious case of thalidomide comes under this category. It promised women to be 'free from trouble' during the periods of morning sickness. But its use resulted in millions of deformed children all over the world.

The reader will note that all these cases are, in a way, attempts to defy the primal mystery of womanhood.

Affirmative Action towards Women

It is considered possible to start the process of justice to females by compensating them with special protection for employment. Such protection available to other exploited classes is not yet legally available to women. Political space is available for women by reservation in *panchayats*. Reservation in education and financial concessions for female students are extensively available. Financial support for female entrepreneurship is also now available under different schemes. It is hoped that these would induce mindsets that will make for gender equality as much as gender balance.

Special Strategies to Help Women

Ethical business practices should opt for special strategies like flexitime for women (and also men) to enable them to look after their children. Many progressive organisations in India have this arrangement. The organisations do not harp on equality but aim to adapt methods that help and support the fulfilment of the primal mystery of womanhood. Admittedly, this flexibility can be used manipulatively as a subterfuge for maintaining an exploitative wage. The law has to ensure this does not happen. As of date, the law is not friendly to the flexitime concept, ostensibly to ensure that such a provision is not misused by unethical organisations. It can be accepted and implemented only in a freer atmosphere of cooperation than confrontation.

The Double Harassment of Poor Women

Gender issues in books on business ethics have tended to talk more about the travails of educated women who are trying to break the shackles of servitude. This is the preoccupation of Western career women as well as of those belonging to the newly emancipated Indian middle and upper classes. Little is written about the double misery of the women who are also poor. Gender literature other than on ethics is however full of them. It is typical of Indian thinking that they are quick to adopt the most current concerns of the West but are slow to react to the explosive ethical issues of the poor nearer their homes.

This comes from the alienation of the managerial classes from the working classes in India. We discussed this unfortunate trait in Chapter 7. Business ethics has to wake up now. Nandini Bedi's powerful poem invokes this thought.

Ladies Unreserved

W're moving around in straight lines . . .
Yesterday it was vegetables in Sion
Today another load . . .
We're moving now, on those tracks
And in that restless roving train breasts
flattened, sarees flung
Waist laid bare,
And arms and legs bare . . .
The Railway police . . .
Pants tight on bulging crotch
Young eyes that calmly watch
Lying figures in swollen sacks.
And along he comes and just stands there
In Ladies Unreserved

—Nandini Bedi in Manushi,
November–December 1993

SUMMARY

This chapter attempts to delineate the manner in which gender exploitation can and does take place. Two cases cited at the end of the chapter should sensitise the reader to the factor of gender discrimination. Discrimination can take place in the least suspected places. The poor are doubly discriminated. In order to deal with discrimination in India, we have to consider the ground realities. Finally it does seem that rather than resorting to confrontation, creating a mindset appreciative of the complementarity of the sexes and the unethical nature of exploitation of any kind should lead to a more lasting gender balance.

ISSUES TO PONDER OVER

- Reflect on the past one year of your life and see if gender ethics was involved in any of the incidents. Write a page on the issue.
- How far do you think would law be helpful in setting the desirable gender ethics?
- Reflect on the mindset of someone close to you and see if it makes for gender balance.

CASE 14.1   **The Portable Ultrasonograph**

'Never before has it happened in my life. We have failed in our public relations,' bemoaned Virji Suratwala, Chairman, Universal Electronics, as he watched the small group headed by Dr Arulnayagam (hereafter referred to as the doctor), fasting in front of his factory gates. Their banners proclaimed to the whole world that 'Universal Electronics are mercenary murderers of innocent babies'. As they caught a glimpse of his face, they roared lustily. The doctor was protesting against the latest Universal Electronics product, a much-vaunted revolutionary technology in ultrasonography brought into the country in collaboration with a world-famous American multinational. The product was a small-sized, portable, ultrascan sonographic recorder, small enough to be packed in a briefcase. The foetus tests would become much easier and could be carried out even at home. For a year the doctor had tried every other means to persuade Universal not to make it. Picketing was his last desperate step to stop them.

The doctor felt that in India the instrument could have only one effect. It would dramatically increase the number of female foeticides as it would be easier to determine the sex of the child; if it was a girl it would be aborted. For their complicity in this unethical outcome, he branded Universal Electronics as the most unethical company in India. Paradoxically, both Universal Electronics and the American multinational with whom they were collaborating prided themselves as being ultra-ethical. Both companies had won many international awards for ethical excellence. Ironically, the American company had also provided that the Indian company should distribute along with the machine a note by a known American doctor on the ethics of using the ultrascan machine. It said that the chances of a baby girl being mistaken for a baby boy were seven per cent in the first 20 weeks of pregnancy and therefore it would be unethical for parents with a history of haemophilia to abort a child identified as male just because the chances of males getting the disease were high. But the notes ignored that baby boys can never be mistaken for baby girls. It frivolously also added that one might as well wait for the baby to be born before deciding if the nursery walls should be coloured pink or blue!

Universal Electronics had been chosen after a long search for an ethically strong Indian company. Virji still recalled the demeaning ethical examination he was put to by the foreign multinational. 'As if all Indians are crooks and all Americans are angels,' he remarked. 'We have given up crores of rupees of profits because we refused to offer bribes. And everyone knows that in this industry, bribery is most rampant,' he added. He was speaking the absolute truth. He had ensured that the induction programmes for his new recruits drilled them on ethics. The slightest fall in standards would mean the sack. For him, unethicality meant only corruption. This perception of unethicality was also shared by the foreign collaborator.

Virji's legal advisors first disputed the doctor's statistics. But that was a fruitless approach. He was a well-respected public health statistician. He could back his statistics to the hilt. Then the PR line harped on the woman's right to abort 'abnormal foetuses'. The doctor then detailed case histories to show that in most of the decisions, the new portable instrument could be used secretively. The family seniors could overrule the mother. Social activists had little opportunity to intervene. Otherwise they could at least park themselves in front of the sonograph clinics. The abortion usually pushed the mothers to months of intense depression. Universal's next line of defence was that the instrument did nothing more than make the currently used technology more efficient and cost-effective. The machine could easily be moved into the labour rooms in hospitals and used concurrently with the delivery of the child. If sonographs were right, portable sonographs too were right. The doctor countered this by saying that the new portable technology was like giving the users a pistol with a silencer to kill a person and destroy evidence.

Lastly, Universal stated that the instrument was only a means of ascertaining the medical facts correctly and could have many other positive uses other than determining the sex of the child. It could detect foetal abnormalities. If used for criminal purposes, the perpetrators of the crime were either the mother and those who forced her, or her doctor, and not Universal. They quoted the provisions of the Prenatal Diagnostic Techniques Act 1994 under which communicating the sex of the foetus to the mother is an offence punishable with a three-year sentence, and the doctor concerned can be struck off the membership of the state medical council. The mother and other family members can also be punished. All users of such machines had to be registered under the Act. Universal thought they had clinched the legal angle. The doctor had no patience for legal or ethical analyses. He said that he was not doing a right or wrong analysis but a with or without analysis. With the instrument, babies were killed. Virji's world was crumbling. His company's ethical image was being mercilessly shaken up. He was convinced that Universal was not being unethical, but he doubted if others would look at it the same way. 'If only I had persuaded the doctor before his views had got hardened, everything would have been fine. It was a failure of my PR and not ethics,' he said and cursed his fate.

If he now went back on the project, Universal would lose at least Rs 20 crore.

(The case is not entirely but partly fictional. Voluntary agencies have been agitating exactly in the manner described here. It is also a fact that the company marketing and manufacturing the product, as also their foreign collaborators, have a strong ethical reputation. But their ethical culture is oriented towards anti-corruption rather than product responsibility.)

Analyses for the reader

1. Do you agree with Virji that the problem in the case arose because of the failure of public relations and that it was not an ethical failure?
2. What is your suggestion to Virji?

CASE 14.2 My Shame and Sorrow

Equality of men and women is seen in the modern world to also mean that men do not ever attempt to either dominate the thinking of women or suppress their individuality. Gandhi did not appear to follow such a principle. Admittedly, he made it possible for women to increasingly be a part of public life. But as a general style of ethical code, he had a compulsive desire 'to reform' those who sought his company. He tried to impose his norms of asceticism on them. This attitude could be questioned as unethical; it was a form of intolerance and tyranny. When the subject of such a tyranny was his own wife Kasturba, it raises even greater issues of the ethics of gender discrimination. B.R. Nanda (1990) reports two such instances:

'Unlike most ashrams, the Sabarmati Ashram attached little importance to the niceties of religious doctrine and ritual. Gandhi's emphasis was on the daily conduct of inmates—how far they were able to conform to the vows of truth, chastity and poverty they had taken. He had a way of dramatising the code of conduct for the inmates. Once there was a theft of a box belonging to Kasturba. Instead of reporting to the police, Gandhi made this theft the subject of his talk after evening prayers. It was apparent, he said, that the thieves believed that the ashram had things worth stealing, and that the ashramites had failed to imbue the people of the locality, including potential thieves, with the spirit of the ashram. As for Kasturba's box, he was, he said, surprised that she had possessed one! When she explained that it contained her grandchildren's clothes, he told her that it was for her children and grandchildren to mind their own clothes. On another occasion, it came to light that a sum of four rupees, given to Kasturba by some visitors to the ashram, had not been promptly deposited by her with the manager of the ashram. Gandhi expressed his dismay at this incident, since private possession of wealth was inconsistent with the principles of the ashram. Gandhi took the extraordinary step of recounting the incident in his weekly paper *Navajivan* in an article entitled "My Shame and Sorrow". It was a ruthless analysis of his wife's conduct:

> She has stood by me in the changes of my life … Although impelled by her sense of wifely devotion, she has renounced so far as the world knows earthly possessions, longing for them has persisted … The rule of the mandir (ashram) is that even such personal presents may not be kept for private use. Her action, therefore, amounted to theft.

'The sum involved was petty, and it was probably no more than a lapse of memory on Kasturba's part in not immediately passing on the four rupees to the manager. The fact is that Gandhi had been distressed by some other and more serious disclosures at this time. He discovered that his cousin Chhaganlal Gandhi who had been with him since his South African days, had committed a series of "petty larcenies" over a number of years. Chhaganlal repented, confessed his guilt and made over (at Gandhi's instance) all his savings to the ashram. Nevertheless, it was a humbling thought for Gandhi that even those living with him had not been able to shed their love of money and worldly goods. He was assailed by remorse. Could the back-slidings of his associates in the ashram be a reflection of his own imperfections?

'"Who knows", Gandhi wrote, "my aberrations in the realm of thought have reacted on the environment round me? The epithet of 'Mahatma' has always galled me. Now it almost sounds to me like a term of abuse.

'"But what am I to do? Should I flee or commit suicide or embark on an endless fast or immure myself alive in the mandir (ashram) or refuse to handle public finance or public duty?"'

(The incidents are reported in Nanda (1990). See Acknowledgement.)

Analyses for the reader

1. Was the incident a case of gender discrimination?
2. How do you think Gandhi should have handled the situation?

15

OM SHANTI SHANTI SHANTIH
A Summing Up

Going through the 14 chapters, you may have sometimes got an uneasy feeling of getting lost in a labyrinth of ideas, with no signposts or guidance provided by unifying principles. But this was because we did not set about seeking such a unifying set of maxims or laws or fundamental truths, as it were, in the first place; the choices were there for you to make. The situations and cases given in the book were intended to evoke responses from you, at both the intellectual and emotional levels, and to enable you to discover your own path to progress, as a pilgrim would. Nevertheless, in retrospect, a set of broad considerations do seem to have emerged. Without in anyway offering them as distilled wisdom, we will state, in as simple a manner as possible, 10 of the most important elements.

The first consideration is that ethical norms emerge from self-discovery by people who have several subtle ways to integrate social cohesion with self-realisation. The second is that in spite of vast differences in the context of different societies across the world and across time, there are remarkable similarities in these ethical norms. Some have greater applicability in some situations than in others. Indian traditions too can provide useful insights. And, while there is a great deal to be gained by learning from each other and from the past, there is also a need for re-examination at every point of time.

> At the close of his crowded course . . .
> Having studied the new and the antique . . . Yet underneath clearly see .
> . . The dear love of man for his comrade. . .
>
> —Walt Whitman (1958: 118)

The third element is that transactions involving exchange of goods and services, which may be described as 'business', are important in this process of integration of social and individual values. The instrumentalities of business are *ipso facto* meant to further the ethics of the greatest good for the greatest number, provided they are deftly complemented by other instruments of social will, such as the state and civil society. Therefore, business need not be defensive and apologetic about ethics—it constitutes ethics in itself even while it pursues profits. In India, business and the state have not had a mutually supportive relationship so far; some of it can even be traced to ancient Indian traditions. Alternatively the state either suppresses business or becomes its lackey. The satisfactory resolution of this conflict is an ethical imperative for India.

Having recognised business as *ipso facto* ethical, we must recognise that even while pursuing profits, it affects people all around in a variety of ways. Precisely because of this, it is of prime ethical importance that such consequences of its actions are fully understood by the managers. This is the fourth important element. The fifth aspect relates to business that adversely affects others. It will get what it deserves in due course, sooner or later. The wheels of ethical reprisal are always moving.

The sixth element is that the appeal to social cohesion can often be misused by the power structure to exploit the poor and underprivileged. One has to be particularly wary of this happening in India as the managerial classes are largely drawn from the privileged sections of society. Business situations constantly call upon managers to innovate technically and managerially to ensure that the outcome of their actions is for the good of all. Therefore, much of business ethics is merely being technically competent and resourceful. This is our seventh consideration.

The eighth element is that of hierarchical layers of ethical responsibility; the accountability of one level cannot substitute that of another. Thus, every individual has an ethical responsibility and accountability which he cannot shift to his superiors or subordinates, or to his organisation. Similarly, organisations cannot push their responsibility to individuals. The responsibility of political leadership is there for all to see, but making them a scapegoat is ethical escapism. This unfortunately is the present trend. On the other hand, ethical living requires every individual to cope with the given organisational environment and for every organisation to similarly cope with the given political environment. The environment has to be taken in one's stride as it is, so that the outcome is the best possible under the given circumstances. There is much to be gained in ethical living by a spontaneous bonhomie than by philosophical arguments. Ethics is a matter of action and not of theoretical hair-splitting. This is the ninth aspect that must be borne in mind.

The tenth element is the golden rule that there are no golden rules. This summary would be of no help to anyone who has not experienced and responded to the feelings and thoughts in the text and cases in the earlier chapters. The *summum bonum* of ethical education is experience and sensitisation, and not what is given in rule books. This tenth consideration is the most dominant message, as also the most demanding. It requires you to individually and personally apply yourself to every task on hand and find your own way, whether you are a young manager or an aspiring one, a middle-level manager, a chief executive or an administrator.

REFERENCES

Aguilar, Francis J. (1994), *Managing Corporate Ethics*, Oxford University Press, London.

Albert, Ethel, Theodore Denise and Shelby Peterfreund (1987), *Great Traditions in Ethics*, Eurasia Publishers, Delhi.

Ambedkar, B.R. (1949), Address to the Constituent Assembly, 25 November, in *Collected Works* (in Marathi), Maharashtra Rajya Sahitya Ani Sanskrit Mandal, Pune.

——————(1950), Address to the World Buddhist Bodhgaya Conference, 6 June, in *Raghuvanshi Ramesh Collection* (in Marathi), Raghuvanshi Prakashan, Pune.

Anthony, Peter (1995), 'A Response to Mills, Townley and Mangham', *Organisation*, 2(2).

Apte, V.S. (1965), *The Students' Sanskrit English Dictionary*, Motilal Banarasidass, Delhi.

Arendt, Hannah (1961), 'Truth in Politics in H. Arendt', *Between Past and Future*, Viking Press, New York.

Arya, Smita and Anupama Rao (1995), 'Ethics in Advertising', Unpublished Paper, T.A. Pai, Management Institute, Manipal.

Aurobindo, Sri (1985), *The Essays on the Gita*, Aurobindo Ashram, Pondicherry.

——————(1986), *The Yoga of Divine Works—Karma Yoga*, Aurobindo Ashram, Pondicherry.

——————(1992), *The Foundations of Indian Culture*, Aurobindo Ashram, Pondicherry.

——————(1994), *Essays Divine and Human*, Aurobindo Ashram, Pondicherry.

Bal, Arun (1993), 'Consumer Protection Act and Medical Profession', *Indian Journal of Social Sciences*, LIV (2).

Banerjee, Nirmala (1995), 'Women's Equality and All', *Administrator*, July–Steptember.

Banerjee, Tuhin, Ravichandra Aithal and Trivikram Soni (1995) 'The HLL-TOMCO Merger', unpublished paper, Birla Institute of Technology and Science, Pilani.

Bardhan, Pranab (1995), 'Rational Fools and Co-operation', in Kaushik Basu, K Patnaik and K Suzumara (eds), *Choice Welfare and Development*, Clarendon Press, Oxford.

——————(1996), 'Unseen Gains of Institutions', *The Economic Times*, 10 January.

Baron, James N. and Michael T. Hannan (1994), 'The Impact of Economics on Contemporary Sociology', *Journal of Economic Literature*, XXXII (3).

Barua, S.K. and J.R. Varma (1993), *The Great Indian Scam*, Vision Books, New Delhi.

Baumol, William J. (1982), *Economic Theory and Operations Analysis*, 4th edition, Prentice-Hall, New Delhi.

Beaty, J. and S.C. Gwynne (1993), *The Outlaw Bank: A Wild Ride into the Secret Heart of BCCI*, Random House, New York.

Becker, G.S. (1964), 'Crime and Punishment: An Economic Approach', *Journal of Political Economy*, March–April, 19(217).

——————(1976), *Economic Approach to Human Behavior*, Chicago University Press, Chicago.

Bedi, Nandini (1993), 'In Ladies Unreserved', *Manushi*, November–December.

Beteille, Andre (1996), 'Sociology and Common Sense', *Economic and Political Weekly*, Special Issue XXXI (35, 36, 37).

Beauchamp, T. (1983), *Case Studies in Business Ethics*, Prentice-Hall, New Jersey.

Bhagat, Achal (1997), 'Lack of Feedback', *Business World*, 16–30 April.

Bharati, Subramanya (1957), *Bharatyar Kavithaigal* (in Tamil), Palaniappa Brothers, Madras.

Bidwai, Praful (1984), 'Bhopal Gas Case', *The Times of India*, 12 December.

Bowie, Norman (1990), 'Morality, Money and Motor Cars' in M.H. Hoffman, R. Fredreichs and R.S. Penny (eds), *Business Ethics and Environment*, Qurom Books, New York.

Boyd, Julian (1950), *The Papers of Thomas Jefferson*, Princeton University, New Jersey.

Burton, B.K. and J.P. Near (1995), 'Estimating the Incidence of Wrong Doing', *Journal of Business Ethics*, (14).

Business India, 'Who Knew Who Profited', 18 November 1996.

Business Standard, 'Bajaj Resigns', 9 May 1997.

——————, 'Takeovers and Mergers', 15 May 1997.

Cadbury, Adrian (1983), 'Ethical Managers Make their Own Rules', *Harvard Business Review*, January–February.

Capra, Fritjof and Gunter Pauli (1996), *Steering Business Toward Sustainability*, Response Books, New Delhi.

Carr, A.Z. (1968), 'Is Business Bluffing Ethical?', *Harvard Business Review*, (46).

Chakraborty, S.K. (1986). 'The Will to Yoga', *Vikalpa*, IIM(A), III (2).

—————— (1991), *Management by Values*, Oxford University Press, New Delhi.

——————(1993a), *Managerial Transformation by Values: A Corporate Pilgrimage*, Sage, New Delhi.

——————(1993b), 'Value Driven Management: The Challenge and Response', Paper presented at the Barcelona Conference of Global Development.

——————(1995a), *Ethics in Management: Vedic Perspectives*, Oxford University Press, New Delhi.

——————(1995b), Lecture at workshop on Ethics, T.A. Pai Management Institute, Manipal, 14–15 December.

Chandra, Prasanna (1995), 'Corporate Governance', *ICFA Journal of Applied Finance*, 1(2).

Chattopadhyaya, D.P. (1989), *In Defence of Materialism in Ancient India*, People's Publishing House, New Delhi.

Chaturvedi, T.N. (1995), Editorial, *Journal of Indian Institute of Public Administration*, July–September.

Chawla, N. (1992), *Mother Teresa, A Biography*, Penguin, New Delhi.

Ching-Ning-Chu, J. (1995), *Thick Face and Black Heart*, Nicholas Bradley Publishing Co., London.

Chonko, Lawrence B. (1995), *Ethical Decision Making in Marketing*, Sage, New Delhi.

Chua, W.F. (1986), 'Radical Development in Accounting Thought', *Accounting Review*, 19 October.

Clutterbuck, D., D. Dearlove and D. Snow (1992), *Action Speaks Louder*, Kingfisher, London.

Coase, Ronald (1937), 'Nature of the Firm', reproduced in Williamson and Winter (1991).

Coleman, Julius L. (1992), *Risks and Wrongs*, Cambridge University Press, Cambridge.

Cyert, Richard and J. March (1962), *A Behavioural Theory of the Firm*, Prentice-Hall Inc., New Jersey.

Dadaji, Javaji (1908), *Brahad Storarathnakara* (in Sanskrit), Sreya Ankanalya, Pune.

Daly, H. (1996), 'Ecological Tax Reform', in Fritjof Capra and Gunter Pauli (eds), *Steering Business Toward Sustainability*, Response Books, New Delhi.

Dandekar, Natalie (1993), 'Can Whistle Blowing be Fully Legitimated', quoted in T.I. White (ed.), (1993), *Business Ethics*, Macmillan, New York.

Dantwala, M.L. (1996), *Dilemmas of Growth: The Indian Experience*, Sage, New Delhi.

Das Gupta, Gurudas (1993), *The Securities Scandals*, People's Publishing House, New Delhi.

Davies, Peter (1996), 'Ethical Issues in Strategic Management', in Alan Kitson and Robert Campbell (eds), *The Ethical Organisation*, Macmillan, London.

De Macro, L.D. and R.M. Fox (eds), (1986). *New Directions in Ethics*, Routledge and Kegan Paul, London.

Deming, W.E. (1980), *Out of the Crisis*, MIT Press, Massachussets.

Dewey, John. (1920), *Reconstruction of Philosophy*, Mentor Books, New York.
———— (1929), *The Quest for Uncertainty*, Milton Balch, New York.
Dobbler, D. W., L. Lee Jr and D.B. Burt (1984), *Purchase and Material Management*, Tata McGraw-Hill, New Delhi.
Dodd, E.M. (1932), 'For Whom are Corporate Managers Trustees', *Harvard Law Review*, 45.
Donaldson, Thomas (1996), 'When Different is Just Different and When it is Wrong, *Harvard Business Review*, September–October.
Donaldson, T. and L. Preston (1995), 'The Stake Holder Theory of the Corporation', *Academy of Management Review*, 20(2).
Doniger, Wendy and Brian K. Smith (1994), *The Laws of Manu*, Penguin Classics, New Delhi.
Donne, John (1987), *Devotion Upon Emergent Occasions*, Oxford University Press, New Delhi.
Dore, R. (1993), 'What Makes Japan Different', in Colin Crouch and David Marquand (eds), *Ethics in Markets, Cooperation and Competition within Capitalist Economies*, Blackwell, Oxford.
Douglas, Mary (1995), 'Convergence on Autonomy', in O.E. Williamson (ed.), *Organisational Theory from Chester Barnard to the Present and Beyond*, Oxford University Press, New York.
Drucker, Peter (1985), *The Changing World of Executives*, Random House, New York.
Dubey, Muchkund (1996), *An Unequal Treaty*, New Age International, New Delhi.
Durkheim, Emille (1957), *Professional Ethics and Civic Morals*, Routledge and Kegan Paul, London.
Duska, R. (1990), 'Whistle Blowing and Employee Loyalty', in T.I. White (ed.) (1993), *Business Ethics*, Macmillan, New York.
Dutta, Sudipt (1997), *Family Business in India*, Response Books, New Delhi.
Economist, The, 'The Barrings Debacle', 22–28 July 1995.
Eisenhardt, K. M. (1989), 'Agency Theory: An Assessment and Review', *Academy of Management Review*, 14(1).
Elliot, Robert (1993), 'Environmental Ethics', in Peter Singer (ed.), *Companion to Ethics*, Basic Blackwell, Oxford.
Engels, F. (1878) (reprinted 1975), *Anti–Duhring*, People's Publishing House, Moscow.
Epicurus (1926), *Epicurus, The Extant Remains*, Clarendon, Oxford.
Evan, W.M. and R.E. Freeman (1988), 'A Stakeholder Theory of Modern Corporation', in T. Beuchamp and N. Bowie (eds), *Ethical Theory in Business Ethics*, Englewood Cliff–Prentice-Hall, New Jersey.
Ferrel, O.C. and J. Freidrichs (1994), *Business Ethics*, Houghton Miffin, Boston.
Foong, A. L. F. and J.C. Oliga (1992), 'The Entrepreneural Economy', *Entrepreneurship Innovation and Change*, 1(4).
Freeman, R.E. (1984), *Strategic Management: A Stake Holder Approach*, Bantam Pitman, New York, quoted in Daniel T. Ostas (1995), 'Religion and Business 'Enterprises', *Journal of Human Values*, 1(1).
Friedman, Milton (1962), *Capitalism and Freedom*, University of Chicago, Chicago.
————(1970), 'The Social Responsibility of Business', *New York Times*, 13 September.
Fukuyama, Frances (1995), *Trust: The Social Virtues and Creation of Prosperity*, Hamish Hamilton and Free Press, London.
Gajendragadkar, P.B. (1993), 'Historical Background and Theoretical Basis of Hindu Law', *The Cultural Heritage of India*, Volume II, Ramakrishna Mission, Calcutta.
Garg, P.K. and I.J. Parikh. (1995), *Crossroads of Culture: A Study in the Culture of Transience*, Sage, New Delhi.
Gergen, Kenneth (1995), 'Global Organisation, Imperialism and Ethics', *Organisation*, 2(3/4).
Ghosh, Anjan (1996), 'The Problem', *Seminar*, October.
Ghosh, Subir K. (1994), Case published in *Administrator*, XXXIX.
Gilligan, C. (1982), *In a Different Voice: Psychological Theory and Women's Development*, Harvard University Press, Boston.
Giri, Anant K. (1994), 'Values & Business', Unpublished manuscript, Personal Communication.
Glazer, P.G. and M.P. Glazer (1989), *The Whistle Blowers*, Basic Books, New York.
Goodpaster, Kenneth (1983), 'Some Avenues for Ethical Analysis', *Harvard Business School Case 9–38–007*, Harvard Business School, Boston.
————(1995), 'Commentary on McIntyre and Mangham', *Organisation*, 2(2).

Gore, M.S. (1993), *The Social Context of an Ideology: Ambedkar's Political and Social Thought,* Sage, New Delhi.

Gorky, Maxim (1923), *Moi University,* Mir Publishing, Moscow.

Grant, Robert (1995), 'AMR Captures TQM', *Academy of Management Review,* January.

Gupta, Ranjan (1996), 'Is there a Place for the Sacred in Organisational Development', *Journal of Human Values,* 2(2).

Gustavsson, B. (1995), 'Consciousness and Experience for Organisation and Management', in S.K. Chakraborty (ed.) *Human Values in Managers,* Wheeler Publishing, New Delhi.

Habermas, Jurgen (1987), *Theory of Communicative Action,* Cambridge Polity Press, Cambridge.

————(1989), *The Structure of Transformation of the Public Sphere,* Cambridge Polity Press, Cambridge.

————(1990), 'What does Socialism Mean Today', *New Left Review,* 183.

Hardin, G. (1968), 'The Tragedy of the Commons', *Science,* 13 December.

Hare, R.M. (1986), 'Why Applied Ethics', in J.D. De Macro and R.M. Fox (eds), *New Directions in Ethics,* Routledge and Kegan Paul, London.

Harris, Nigel (1989), *Professional Codes of Conduct in UK,* Mansel, London.

Hass, Robert D. (1994), 'Ethics a Global Business Challenge, *Vital Speeches of the Day,* (60).

Hawken, Paul (1993), *Ecology of Commerce,* Harper Collins, New York.

Hawley, Jack (1993), *Reawakening the Spirit in Works: The Power of Dharmic Management,* Tata McGraw-Hill, New Delhi.

Haydok, Wes (1996), 'Ethical Issues in Human Resource Management', in Alan Kitson and Robert Campbell (eds), *The Ethical Organisation,* Macmillan, London.

Hemingway, Ernest (1948), *For Whom The Bell Tolls,* Charles Scribner, New York.

Henry, Sarojini (1995), *Reinhold Niebuhr's Critique of Gandhi,* Gandhi Marg, 17(3).

Herbig, Paul and J.E. Golden (1992), 'Killing the Golden Goose', *Entrepreneurship,* 1(4).

Hess, Linda and Sukhdev Singh (1985), *The Bijaks of Kabir,* Motilal Banarasidass, New Delhi.

Hesse, Herman (1971), *Sidhartha,* Bantam Books, New York.

Hider, Saraswati (1996), 'Misconceptualisation of National Policies for Women', *Mainstream,* XXXIV(29).

Hiraway, Indira (1992), Private discussion with the author.

Hirayanna, M. (1958), *Outline of Indian Philosophy,* George Allen and Unwin, London.

Hirsh, M. (1995), 'The Ministry of Fear', *Newsweek,* 23 October.

Hirschman, Albert G. (1982), 'Rival Interpretations of Market Society: Civilising, Destructive or Feeble', *Journal of Economic Literature,* XX.

Hixon, Lex (1995), 'Value Systems Workshop', in S.K. Chakraborty (ed.) *Human Values for Managers.* Wheeler Publishing, New Delhi.

Hoffman, Michael W. (1993), 'Business and Environmental Ethics', in T.I. White (ed.), *Business Ethics,* Macmillan, New York.

Hofstede, G. (1984), *Culture's Consequences: International Differences in Work-Related Values,* Sage, California.

————(1996), 'Organisational Culture', *International Encyclopaedia of Business and Management,* Volume IV, Routledge, London.

Horngren, C. T., G. Foster and S.M. Datar (1994), *Cost Accounting a Managerial Emphasis,* Prentice-Hall, New Delhi.

Hosmer, L.T. (1987), *Ethics in Management,* Richard Irwin–Universal Book Stall, New Delhi.

———— (1995), 'Trust the Connecting Link Between Organisational Theory and Philosophy of Ethics', *Academy of Management Review,* April.

Hudson, R., A.O. Olgeche and C.M. Kochunny (1995), 'Ethics and Transnational Corporations', *Journal of European Markeitng,* 2.

Hunt, Shelby D., and Scott J. Vittel (1993), 'A General Theory of Marketing Ethics', in N. Craig Smith and John A. Quelch (eds), *Ethics in Marketing,* Richard Irwin, New York.

Hunt, Shelby and Artuso Vasquez–Paraga (1993), 'Organisational Consequences of Marketing Ethics and Sales Supervision', *Journal of Marketing,* XXX.

Hymen, M., L. Tessey and J.W. Clerk (1994), 'Research in Advertisement Ethics', *Journal of Advertisement,* 23(3).

Ijiri, Yuri (1975), *Theory of Accounting Measurement*, American Accounting Association, Sarasota.

———— (1983), 'On the Accountability Based Concepts in Finance and Accounting', *Journal of Accounting and Public Policy*, 2(2).

India Today, 'Editorial', 15 October 1996.

Irvine, William (1993), 'Insider Trading in Ethical Appraisal', in T.I. White (ed.), *Business Ethics*, Macmillan, New York.

Iyengar, Sreenivasan R.R. (1994), *Asian Versions of the Ramayana*, Sahitya Akademi, New Delhi.

Jackal, Robert (1988), *Moral Mazes: The World of Corporate Managers*, Oxford University Press, New York.

Jain, R.B. (1995), 'Political and Bureaucratic Corruption', *Indian Journal of Public Administration*, September.

Jain, Sagar, L.F. Gooch and E.V. Grantham (1971), *Case Writings Do's and Don'ts*, University of North Carolina, Chappel Hill.

James, Gene G. (1993), '*Whistle Blowing Its Moral Justification*', in T.I. White (ed.), *Business Ethics*, Macmillian, New York.

Jayakar, Pupul (1982), *The Budha*, Vakils, Bombay.

Jensen, Michael C. (1993), 'Takeover Folk Lore and Science', in T.I. White (ed.), *Business Ethics*, Macmillan, New York.

Jesani, Amar (1993), 'Medical Ethics and Patient's Rights', *Indian Journal of Social Work*, IV(2).

Johnson, Deborah (1985), *Computer Ethics*, Englewood Cliff, New Jersey.

Johnson, Mark (1993), *Moral Imagination, Implications of Cognitive Science for Ethics*, University of Chicago Press, Chicago.

Jones, Thomas (1995), 'Instrumental Stake Hold Theory—A Synthesis of Ethics and Economics', *Academy of Management Review*, 20(2).

Kakkar, Sudhir (1996), *The Indian Psyche*, Penguin, New Delhi.

Kamath, M.V. (1991), *A Banking Odyssey*, Vikas, New Delhi.

Kanai, Toshihiro (1995), 'Seven Entrepreneurial Paradoxes and the Taxonomy of Networking', *Annals of the School of Business*, Kobe University, 39.

Kane, P.V. (1969), *The History of the Dharma Sastras*, Bhatkande Oriental Research Institute, Pune.

Kanitkar, Ajit (1995), *Green Revolution Entrepreneurship*, Wiley Eastern, New Delhi.

Kanitkar, Ajit and Nalini Contractor (1992), *In Search of Identity*, Entrepreneurship Development Institute, Ahmedabad.

Kant, I. (1985), *Foundations of Metaphysics of Morals*, Longmans, London.

Kao, Henry S.R., Durganand Sinha and Ng Sek-Hong (eds) (1994), *Effective Organizations and Social Values*, Sage, New Delhi.

Kaur, Parvinder (1994), 'Management of Values—An Investigation of Managerial Transition', in N.K. Gupta and Abad Ahmed (eds), *Managing Transition*, Wiley Eastern, New Delhi.

Kautsky, Karl (1906), *Ethics and Materialistic Concepts of History*, Charles H. Kerr and Co., Chicago.

Kennedy, Carol (1994), *The Management Gurus*, Business Books, London.

King Jr, Ralph T. (1995), 'Farmer's Almanac: Grace Patent on Pesticide Spurs Indian, Global Debate', *Asia Wall Street Journal*, 14 September.

Kitson, Alan and Robert Campbell (eds) (1996), *The Ethical Organisation*, Macmillan, London.

Kolstoe, John (1995), *Developing Genius*, George Reynold, Oxford.

Kohlbergh, L. (1981), *Essays in Moral Development*, Volume 1, Harper & Row, New York, quoted in Thomas (1993).

Koontz, H. and H. Weihrich (1988), *Essentials of Management*, McGraw-Hill, Singapore.

Kosambi, D.D. (1964), *The Culture and Civilisations of Ancient India*, Routledge and Kegan Paul, London.

Kothari, M. and L. Mehta (1988), 'Violence in Medicine', in Ashis Nandy (ed.), *Science Hegemony and Violence*, Oxford University Press, Bombay.

Krishnamurthi, J. (1971), *The Urgency of Challenge*, Victor Gollancz, London.

Krishnamurthy, V. (1994), *Ten Commandments of Hinduism*, Wiley Eastern, New Delhi.

Levi-Strauss, C. (1963), *Structural Anthropology*, Basic Books, New York.

Levinson, M. and M. Meyer (1995), 'Billion Dollar Bath', *Newsweek*, 9 October.

Littlefield, J.E. and A. Kirkpatrick (1970), *Advertising Mass Communication in Marketing*, Houghton Miffin, Boston.

Lovelock, J. (1996), Report in *Newsweek* ,15 April.

Lunati, Teresa (1996), 'Markets and Morality', in Alan Kitson and Robert Campbell (eds), *The Ethical Organisation*, Macmillan, London.

Lynch, John J. (1991), *Ethical Banking*, Macmillan, London.

Ma, H.K. (1997), 'The Affective and Cognitive Aspects of Moral Development', in H.S.R. Kao and D. Singh (eds), *Asian Perspectives On Psychology*, Sage, New Delhi.

Macaulay, T.B. (1898), *Complete Works*, Albion, London.

MacIntyre, Alasdair (1981), *After Virtue*, Duckworth, London.

Mahesh, V.S. (1993), *Thresholds of Motivation*, Tata McGraw-Hill, New Delhi.

Malloy, D. C. and L. Lang (1993), 'An Aristotelian Approach to Case Study', *Journal of Business Ethics*, 12.

Mangham, Ian L. (1995), 'MacIntyre and the Manager', *Organisation*, 2(3/4).

Maoro, Paul (1997), *Why Worry about Corruption*, International Monetary Fund, Washington.

Marx, Karl (1932), *Economics and Philosophy*, Marx-Engels Institute, Berlin.

Massey, James (1994), 'Role of Christianity among Dalits', *Religion and Society*, XLIC.

Mcdonald, Ross (1993), 'An Open Letter to North American Business Ethicists', *Journal of Business Ethics*, 12.

McDormitt, John (1986), 'Pragmatic Sensibility: The Morality of Experience', in J.D. De Macro and R.M. Fox (eds), *New Directions in Ethics*, Routledge and Kegan Paul, London.

Messick, D.M. and M.H. Bazerman (1996), 'Ethical Leadership and Psychology of Decision Making', *Sloane Management Review*, Winter Issue.

Michalos, Alex C. (1995), *A Pragmatic Approach to Business Ethics*, Sage, New Delhi.

Mill, J.S. (1897), *Utilitarianism*, Longman Green and Co, London.

Mills, Albert J. (1995), 'The Case of the British Airways', *Organisation*, 2(3/4).

Mintzbergh, H. (1996), 'The Need for Balance', *The Week*, 22 December.

Minz, Nirmal (1993), 'Cultural Identity of the Tribals', *Social Action*, 43(11).

Monappa, Arun (1987), *The Ethical Attitudes of Indian Managers*, All India Management Association, New Delhi.

Moore, Jenifer (1993), 'What is Really Unethical about Insider Trading', in T.I. White (ed.), *Business Ethics*, Macmillan, New York.

Morgan, C.T., R.A. King, J. Wang and J. Schopler (1994), *Introduction to Psychology*, Tata McGraw-Hill, New Delhi.

Murthy, K.S.R. (1996), 'Corporate Governance', *Management Review*, 8(3/4).

Murthy, Sachidananda K. (1965), *The Indian Spirit*, Andhra University, Waltair.

Nader, Ralph, P.J. Petkas and Kate Blackwell (eds) (1972), *Whistle Blowing: A Report on the Conference of Professional Responsibility*, Bantam Books, New York.

Nair, Prabhakaran (1996), 'Seed Genes and Future', *The Hindu*, 21 October.

Nanda, B.R. (1990), *In Gandhi's Footsteps*, Oxford University Press, New Delhi.

Nandy, Ashis (1994), *The Illegitimacy of Nationalism*, Oxford University Press, New Delhi.

————(1995), Public lecture at the Manipal Higher Academy of Education, Manipal.

Narayanam, D. (1992), 'The Right Stuff', *Purchasing and Supply Management*, October.

Narula, K.K., A. Kansel and Veena Joshi (1995), 'Managing the Environment—Some Issues', in Sunil Khanna and Krishna Mohan (eds), *Wealth from Waste*, Tata Energy Research Institute, New Delhi.

Nash, Laura (1989), 'Ethics Without Sermons', in Kenneth Arrow (ed.), *Ethics for Practising Managers in Modern Corporations*, Harvard Business School, Boston.

————(1995), 'Whose Character', *Organisation*, 2(3/4).

Nathan, Dev and Arvind Kelkar (1997), 'Collective Villages in China', *Economic and Political Weekly*, 3–9 May.

Near, J.P. and M. P. Micelli (1995), 'Effective Whistle Blowing', *Academy of Management Review*, 20(3).

Nehru, J.L. (1989), 'Pandit Nehru's Views of Scheduled Tribes', *Scheduled Tribes Research Bulletin*, 11(24).

Niebuhr, R. (1932), *Moral Man and Immoral Society*, Charles Scribner, New York.

Nietzsche, Fredrich (1924), *The Will to Power*, Macmillan, New York.

Newsweek 'Corruption', an article reporting the views of Professors Putnam, Vishy and Schleifer, 4 November 1994.

————, 'Bust', 10 March 1995.

Newton, Lisa H. (1993), 'The Hostile Takeover—An Opposition View', in T.I. White (ed.), *Business Ethics*, Macmillan, New York.

Noe, T.H. and M.J. Rebello (1994), 'The Dynamics of Business Ethics and Economic Activity', *The American Economic Review*, June.

Novak, M. (1982), *The Spirit of Democratic Capitalism*, Simon Scheleider, New York.

Nozick, R. (1974), *Anarchy, State and Utopia*, Basic Books, New York.

O' Toole, James (1995), *Leading Change*, Jessey-Bass, San Francisco.

Olson, Mancur (1965), *The Logic of Collective Action*, Harvard University Press, Boston.

Omvedt, Gail (1995), *Dalit Visions*, Orient Longman, New Delhi.

Orme-Johnson, D. Eva Zimmerman and Mark Hawkin (1997), 'Mahrishi's Vedic Psychology', in H.S. Kao and D. Sinha (eds), *Asian Perspectives in Pscyhology*, Sage, New Delhi.

Ostas, Daniel T. (1995), 'Religion and Business Enterprises', *Journal of Human Values*, 1(1).

Pai, V.S. (1995), 'The HLL–TOMCO Merger', *Business Line* 23–24 June.

Paine, Thomas (1792), *The Rights of Man*, E.P. Dutton, New York.

Pande, Govind Chandra (1991), 'Two Dimensions of Religion', in Elliot Deutch (ed.), *Culture and Modernity*, University of Hawai Press, Honolulu.

Pande, Vikas and Akhileswar Pathak (1996), 'Beyond Conventional Sociology of Organisations', *Economic and Political Weekly*, 25 February.

Pangare, Ganesh and Vasudha Pangare (1992), *From Poverty to Plenty: The Story of Ralegaon–Sidhi*, INTACH, New Delhi.

Parikh, Bhiku (1987), 'Gandhi and the Logic of Reformist Discourse', in B. Parekh and T. Pantham (eds), *Political Discourse: Explorations in Indian and Western Political Thought*, Sage, New Delhi.

Pavarala, Vinod (1996), *Interpreting Corruption: Elite Perspectives in India*, Sage, New Delhi.

Piper, T.R., M.C. Gentle and L.D. Parks (1993), *Can Ethics be Taught*, Harvard Business School, Boston.

Purohit, S.K. (1994), *Ancient Indian Legal Philosophy*, Deep and Deep, New Delhi.

Radhakrishnan, S. (1993), *Indian Philosophy*, Volumes I and II, Oxford University Press, New Delhi.

Raj, Matireyi Krishna (1996), 'Androgyny Alternative to Gender Policy', *Economic and Political Weekly*, XXXI.

Ramaseshan, Radhika (1984), 'The Bhopal Gas Tragedy', *Economic and Political Weekly*, 15 December.

Ramaswamy, E.A. (1984), *Power and Justice*, Oxford University Press, New Delhi.

Ramu, S. Shiva (1997), *International Licensing: Managing Intangible Resources*, Response Books, New Delhi.

Rand, Ayn (1968), *The New Left*, (including 'The Age of Envy'), Signet, New York.

Rangathananda, Swami (1968), *Politics and Administration in Total Human Development*, Indian Institute of Public Administration, New Delhi.

Rangarajan, L.N. (1987), *Kautilya's Arthasastra*, Penguin Classics, New Delhi.

Rao, G.P. (1996), *Human Values in Industrial Organisations: A Feminine Perspective*, Indian Institue of Management, Calcutta.

Rawls, J. (1971), *A Theory of Justice*, Harvard University Press, Boston.

Reddy, Pratap K. and R.C. Sekhar (1993), 'Civic Culture Ambience and Collective Controls', International seminar on Cooperatives, Institute of Rural Management, Anand.

Reed, Herbert, Michael Fordham and G. Addler (1954), *The Collected Works of Jung*, Volumes 7, 8, 9 and 17, Routledge, London.

Robertson, D. and E. Anderson (1993), 'Does Opportunity Make us a Thief', in Smith N. Craig and John A. Quelch (eds), *Ethics in Marketing*, Irwin, Boston.

Rorty, Amelie Oksenbergh (1992), 'The Advantages of Moral Diversity', *Social Philosophy and Policy*, 9(2): 38–62.

Ross, S.A. (1973), 'The Economic Theory of Agency', *American Economic Review*, 63.

Roy, Mira (1991), *Ayurveda, The Cultural Heritage of India*, Volume III, Ramakrishna Mission, Calcutta.

Russel Bertrand (1930), *The Conquest of Happiness*, Routledge, London.

—————(1949), *Authority and the Individual*, Unwin Paperbacks, London.

Ryan, L.V. and W.L. Scott (1995), 'Ethics and Organisational Reflections', *Academy of Management Review*, 20(2).

Saher, P.J. (1989), *Zen Yoga*, Motilal Banarasidass, New Delhi.

Samuelson, P.A. and W.D. Nordhaus (1992), *Economics*, McGraw-Hill, New York.

Schmidt, Rudolf (1997), International conference on Ethics and Development, Crenieo, Chennai.

Schumpeter, J.A. (1942), *Capitalism, Socialism and Democracy*, Harper, New York.

Schwarz, S.H. and W. Belinsky (1987), 'Towards a Universal Psychological Study of Human Values', *Journal of Personality and Social Psychology*, 53.

Sekhar, R.C. (1993), 'Sustainable Systems of Control for Sustainable Rural Development', Proceedings of the International Conference on Sustainable Rural Development, University of Colorado.

—————(1995), 'Ethics and the Indian Manager', *Economic and Political Weekly*, 23 November.

—————(1996a), 'Law Sans Ethics', *Chartered Financial Analyst*, New Year Issue.

—————(1996b), 'Corruption in Business', *Chartered Financial Analyst*, April.

—————(1997), 'Untruth a Fatal Weakness in the Polemics of Justice', International conference on Ethics and Development, Crenieo, Chennai.

Sen, Amartya K. (1990), *On Ethics and Economics*, Oxford University Press, New Delhi.

Seshan, T.N. (1995), *The Heart Full of Burden*, UBSPD, New Delhi.

Seth, Meera (1997), 'A Question of Ethics', *Business World*, 16–30 April.

Sethi, P., N. Namiki and C.L. Swanson (1984), *The False Promise of the Japanese Miracle*, Pitman, London.

Sharma, M.K. (1997), 'Collective Failure', *Business World*, 16–30 April.

Sharma, R.A. (1994), 'Strategic Choice of the Indian Firm', *Journal of Entrepreneurship*, 4(2).

Shaw, Bill (1993), 'Should Insider Trading be Outside the Law', in T.I. White (ed.), *Business Ethics*, Macmillan, New York.

Shefrin, H. and M. Statman (1993), 'Ethics Fairness and Efficiency in Financial Markets', *Financial Analysis Journal*, November–December.

Shroff, Shardul (1997), 'Breach of Fiduciary Duty', *Business World*, 16–30 April.

Sidgwick, H. (1925), *The Methods of Ethics*, Macmillan, London.

Simmonds, Nigel (1985), 'Rights, Socialism and Liberalism', *Legal Studies*, 5(1).

Simons, Robert (1995), 'Control in the Age of Empowerment', *Harvard Business Review*, March.

Sinclair, A. (1993), 'Approaches to Organisational Culture and Ethics', *Journal of Business Education*, 12.

Singh, Katar (1994), *Managing Common Pool Resources*, Oxford University Press, New Delhi.

Sinopoli, Richard (1995), 'Thick Skinned Liberalism', *American Political Science Review*, 89(3).

Smith, Adam (1952), *An Enquiry into the Nature and Causes of Wealth of Nations*, Benton, Chicago.

Sommers, C.H. (1994), 'Teaching the Virtues', *Span*, January.

Spinoza, Benedict (1898), 'Ethics Demonstrated in Geometric Order', in *Chief Works of Benedict Spinoza*, George Bell and Sons, London.

Srivastava, Paul (1994), *Strategic Management*, South Western, Ohio.

Starr, Martin Kenneth (1964), *Production Management Systems and Synthesis*, Prentice-Hall, New York.

Stevenson, C.L. (1947–48), *The Nature of Ethical Disagreement*, Volume 1–2, Sigma, Milan.

Stevenson, R.L. (1987), *Dr Jekyll and Mr Hyde*, Oxford University Press, London.

Stevenson, Sinclair (1984), *The Heart of Jainism*, Oxford University Press, New Delhi.

Subba Rao, Budhi Kota (1995), 'The DAE Beneath a Veil of Secrecy', *The Hindu*, 14 February.

Subramaniam, Kamala (1981), *The Ramayana*, Bharatiya Vidya Bhawan, Bombay.

—————(1993a), *The Mahabharata*, Bharatiya Vidya Bhawan, Bombay.

—————(1993b), *Srimad Bhagavatam*, Bharatiya Vidya Bhawan, Bombay.

Swaminathan, S. (1996), 'Olympic Grade for Corruption', *The Hindu*, 23 October.

Tagore, Rabindranath (1988), *Sadhana*, Macmillan, Madras.

Tawney, R.H. (1926), *Religion and The Rise of Capitalism*, Harcourt Brace World, New York.

Taylor, Peter (1996), 'Ethical Issues in Accounting', in Alan Kitson and Robert Campbell (eds), *The Ethical Organisation*, Macmillan, London.

Thakur, Sarojini Ganju (1995), 'Making Women Visible', *Administrator*, July–September.

Tharoor, Sashi (1989), *The Great Indian Novel*, Penguin, New Delhi.

Thingalayya, M.K. and Vijayanath Shenoy (1985), *The Saga of Sixty Years,* Diamond Jubilee Volume, Syndicate Bank, Manipal.

Thomas, Laurence (1993), 'Morality and Psychology', in Peter Singer (ed.), *Companion To Ethics*, Basic Blackwell, Oxford.

Thomson, E.P. (1961), 'The Long Revolution', *New Left Review*, May–June.

Thomson, J.D. (1967), *Organisations in Action*, McGraw-Hill, New York.

Time, 'The Barring's Case', 13 March 1995.

Tucker, A. W. (1955), 'Game Theory and Programming', Oklahoma State University, quoted and explained in William Baumal (1982), *Economic Theory and Operational Analysis*, Prentice-Hall, Stillwaters.

Tumanov, V.A. (1974), *Contemporary Bourgeois Law: A Marxist Evaluation*, Peace Publishers, Moscow.

Valesquez, Manuel G. (1982), *Business Ethics*, Prentice-Hall, New Jersey.

Vasquez-Paraga, Artuso and Ali Kara (1995), 'Ethical Decision Making Today in Sales Management', *Journal of Euro-Marketing*, 4(2).

Venkataswaran, C.S. (1962), *Ethics of the Puranas in Cultural Heritage of India*, Volume II, Ramakrishna Mission, Calcutta.

Verwoerd, Wilhelm (1997), 'Justice after Apartheid', International conference on Ethics and Development, Crenieo, Chennai.

Vivekananda, Swami (1962), *Complete Works*, Vol II, Ramakrishna Mission, Calcutta.

Weber, J. (1995), 'Influence of Organisation on Ethics', *Organisational Science*, 6(5).

Weber, Max (1947), *The Theory of Social and Economic Organisations*, Free Press, New York.

—————(1958), *The Protestant Ethics and the Spirit of Capitalism*, Charles Scribner, New York.

Werhane, Patricia (1993), 'Ethics of Insider Trading', in T.I. White (ed.), *Business Ethics*, Macmillan, New York.

Werner, Simcha B. (1983), 'New Direction in the Study of Administrative Corruption', *Public Administration Review*, March–April.

White, T.I. (ed.) (1993), *Business Ethics*, Macmillan, New York.

Whitman, Walt (1958), 'The Base of All Methaphysics', *Leaves of Grass*, Penguin, New York.

Williamson, O.E. (ed.) (1995), *Organisational Theory From Chester Barnard to the Present and Beyond*, Oxford University Press, New York.

Williamson, O.E. and S.H. Winter (eds) (1991), *The Nature of the Firm*, Oxford University Press, London.

Wood, J. (1992), *The Yoga System and Patanjali*, Motilal Banarasidass, Delhi.

Wood, Graham (1996), 'Ethics in Purchasing', in Alan Kitson and Robert Campbell (eds), *The Ethical Organisation*, Macmillan, London.

Wright, Richard (1995), 'The Evolution of Despair', *Time*, 28 August.

Xavier Labour Relations Institute (1994), 'Management and Labour Studies: The Caux Principles', 19(3).

SELECT READINGS

Chapters 1 and 2

Albert, Ethel, Theodore Denise and Shelby Peterfreund (1987), *Great Traditions in Ethics*, Eurasia Publishers, Delhi.
Balachandran, S. (1996), *Managing Ethics*, Sangeetha Associates, Bombay.
Das Bhagwan, (1990), *Essential Unity of all Religions*, Bharatiya Vidya Bhawan, Bombay.
Dewey, John (1920), *Reconstruction of Philosophy*, Mentor Books, New York.
Hick, John H. (1983), *Philosophy of Religion*, Prentice Hall, New Delhi.
Hirayana, M. (1958), *Outline of Indian Philosophy*, George Allen and Unwin, London.
Michalos, Alex C. (1995), *A Pragmatic Approach to Business Ethics*, Sage, New Delhi.
Midgely, Mary (1993), 'Origins of Ethics', in Peter Singer (ed.), *Companion to Ethics*, Basic Blackwell, Oxford.
Mohapatra, A.R. (1990), *Philosophy of Religion*, Sterling Publishers, New Delhi.
Williams, Bernard (1972), *Morality*, Cambridge University Press, Cambridge.

Chapters 3, 11 and 12

Lunati, Teresa (1996), Chapter 9 in Alan Kitson and Robert Campbell (eds), *Ethical Organisation*, Macmillan, London.
Samuelson, P.A. and W.D. Nordhaus (1992), Chapter 12, *Economics*, 14th edition, McGraw-Hill, New York.
Sen, Amartya (1990), *On Ethics and Economics*, Oxford University Press, New Delhi.
White, T.I. (1993), Chapter 16, *Business Ethics*, Macmillan, New York.

Chapter 4

Freeman, M. D. A. (1994), Chapter 7, *Introduction to Jurisprudence*, Maxwell, London.
Hunt, Allen (1978), *The Sociological Movement in Law*, Macmillan, London.

Chapter 5

Chakraborty, S.K. (1993), *Managerial Transformation by Values: A Corporate Pilgrimage*, Sage, New Delhi.
————(1995), *Ethics in Management: Vedic Perspectives*, Oxford University Press, New Delhi.
Chandiramani, Sheila (1991), *The Panchatantra*, Rupa, New Delhi.
Chandrasekhar, Saraswati Swami (Sankaracharya) (1995), *The Hindu Dharma*, Bharatiya Vidya Bhawan, Bombay.
Doniger, Wendy and Brian K. Smith (1964), *The Laws of Manu*, Penguin Classics, New Delhi.
Gandhi, M.K. (1985), *Bhagavad Gita*, Orient Paperbacks, New Delhi.

Garg, Pulin and Indira J. Parikh (1995), *Crossroads of Culture: A Study in the Culture of Transience*, Sage, New Delhi.

Iyengar, B.K.S (1993), *Light on Yoga*, George Allen and Unwin–Harper Collins, New Delhi.

Kosambi, D.D. (1964), *The Culture and Civilisation of India*, Vikas, New Delhi.

Krishnamurthy, V. (1994), *The Ten Commandments of Hinduism*, Wiley Eastern, New Delhi.

Kulandaiswamy, V.C. (1995), *The Immortal Kural*, Sahitya Akademi, New Delhi.

Radhakrishnan, S. (1983), *The Bhagavad Gita*, George Allen and Unwin, London.

Rangarajan, L.N. (1987), *Kautilya's Arthasastra*, Penguin Classics, New Delhi.

Rangathananda, Swami (1990), *The Message of the Upanishads*, Bharatiya Vidya Bhawan, Bombay.

Reddy, Dwarka Nath (1994), *Can God Improve My Balance Sheet*, Affiliated Press Ltd, New Delhi.

Subramaniam, Kamala (1981), *The Ramayana*, Bharatiya Vidya Bhawan, Bombay.

———(1993a), *The Mahabharata*, Bharatiya Vidya Bhawan, Bombay.

———(1993b), *Srimad Bhagavatham*, Bharatiya Vidya Bhawan, Bombay.

Thomas, Lawrence (1993), 'Morality and Psychology', in Peter Singer (ed.), *Companion To Ethics*, Basic Blackwell, Oxford.

Chapter 6

Fukuyama, Frances (1995), *Trust*, Hamish Hamilton, London.

Chapter 7

Williamson, O.E. (ed.) (1995), *Organisational Theory from Chester Barnard to the Present and Beyond*, Oxford University Press, New York.

Chapter 8

Hosmer, L.T. (1987), Chapter 6, *Ethics in Management*, Universal Book Stall, New Delhi.

Mahesh, V.S. (1993), *Thresholds of Motivation*, Tata McGraw-Hill, New Delhi.

Ramaswamy, E.A. (1984), *Power and Justice*, Oxford University Press, New Delhi.

Chapter 9

White, T.I. (1993), Chapter 12, *Business Ethics*, Macmillan, New York.

Chapter 10

Chonko, Lawrence B. (1995), *Ethical Decision Making in Marketing*, Sage, New Delhi.

Chapter 13

Capra, Fritjof and Gunter Pauli (1996), *Steering Business Toward Sustainability*, Response Books, New Delhi.

Elliot, Robert (1993), 'Environmental Ethics', in Peter Singer (ed.), *Companion to Ethics*, Basic Blackwell, Oxford.

Chapter 14

White, T.I. (1993), Chapters 14 and 15, *Business Ethics*, Macmillan, New York.

INDEX

INDEX

Garg, Pulin and Indira J. Parikh (1995), *Crossroads of Culture: A Study in the Culture of Transience*, Sage, New Delhi.

Iyengar, B.K.S (1993), *Light on Yoga*, George Allen and Unwin–Harper Collins, New Delhi.

Kosambi, D.D. (1964), *The Culture and Civilisation of India*, Vikas, New Delhi.

Krishnamurthy, V. (1994), *The Ten Commandments of Hinduism*, Wiley Eastern, New Delhi.

Kulandaiswamy, V.C. (1995), *The Immortal Kural*, Sahitya Akademi, New Delhi.

Radhakrishnan, S. (1983), *The Bhagavad Gita*, George Allen and Unwin, London.

Rangarajan, L.N. (1987), *Kautilya's Arthasastra*, Penguin Classics, New Delhi.

Rangathananda, Swami (1990), *The Message of the Upanishads*, Bharatiya Vidya Bhawan, Bombay.

Reddy, Dwarka Nath (1994), *Can God Improve My Balance Sheet*, Affiliated Press Ltd, New Delhi.

Subramaniam, Kamala (1981), *The Ramayana*, Bharatiya Vidya Bhawan, Bombay.

————(1993a), *The Mahabharata*, Bharatiya Vidya Bhawan, Bombay.

————(1993b), *Srimad Bhagavatham*, Bharatiya Vidya Bhawan, Bombay.

Thomas, Lawrence (1993), 'Morality and Psychology', in Peter Singer (ed.), *Companion To Ethics*, Basic Blackwell, Oxford.

Chapter 6

Fukuyama, Frances (1995), *Trust*, Hamish Hamilton, London.

Chapter 7

Williamson, O.E. (ed.) (1995), *Organisational Theory from Chester Barnard to the Present and Beyond*, Oxford University Press, New York.

Chapter 8

Hosmer, L.T. (1987), Chapter 6, *Ethics in Management*, Universal Book Stall, New Delhi.

Mahesh, V.S. (1993), *Thresholds of Motivation*, Tata McGraw-Hill, New Delhi.

Ramaswamy, E.A. (1984), *Power and Justice*, Oxford University Press, New Delhi.

Chapter 9

White, T.I. (1993), Chapter 12, *Business Ethics*, Macmillan, New York.

Chapter 10

Chonko, Lawrence B. (1995), *Ethical Decision Making in Marketing*, Sage, New Delhi.

Chapter 13

Capra, Fritjof and Gunter Pauli (1996), *Steering Business Toward Sustainability*, Response Books, New Delhi.

Elliot, Robert (1993), 'Environmental Ethics', in Peter Singer (ed.), *Companion to Ethics*, Basic Blackwell, Oxford.

Chapter 14

White, T.I. (1993), Chapters 14 and 15, *Business Ethics*, Macmillan, New York.